Rogue Male

GEOFFREY GORDON-CREED, DSO, MC
AND
ROGER FIELD

Rogue Male

Roger Field

14.4.11

CORONET

First published in Great Britain in 2011 by Coronet
An imprint of Hodder & Stoughton
An Hachette UK company

1

A CIP catalogue record for this title is available from the British Library

Hardback ISBN 978 1 444 70633 8
Trade Paperback ISBN 978 1 444 70603 5

Typeset in Plantin Light by Hewer Text UK Ltd, Edinburgh

Printed and bound by Clays Ltd, St Ives plc

Hodder & Stoughton policy is to use papers that are natural, renewable
and recyclable products and made from wood grown in sustainable forests.
The logging and manufacturing processes are expected to conform
to the environmental regulations of the country of origin.

Hodder & Stoughton Ltd
338 Euston Road
London NW1 3BH

www.hodder.co.uk

To British soldiers everywhere – whether in uniform and in the open, or behind the lines and in the shadows: may they continue to fight their wars with compassion and humour, as 'Mister Major Geoff' always tried to fight his …

FOREWORD AND ACKNOWLEDGEMENTS

I have a number of thanks to those who helped make this book happen. First to Geoffrey Gordon-Creed's sons, Nick and Geoffrey, who not only let me loose with their father's treasured memoir but helped me at every turn. Geoff wanted his story to be published, and they have stayed true to that wish: thank you.

To Mark Booth, my publisher, for having the courage to take a gamble on a first-time author, and then encouraging me every step of the way.

To Alice, my wife, for giving me the space to keep writing and for being my best and foremost critic. I always try my ideas on her first and she is unerringly accurate with her opinions. To Arabella, my daughter, who has never had the slightest doubt that her dad was bound to be published and who, from quite an early age, would have gone round and sorted out any publisher who was short-sighted enough to turn me down. Her belief in me and my abilities has defied the laws of gravity. To my son, Sandy, for showing a patience way beyond that which most sons would pay their fathers as I tell him yet another of my stories.

And finally, to my parents, sadly now dead. Dad, one of that non-demonstrative war generation, would, I know, have been hugely proud to see me published. Mum would have wondered what all the fuss was about: of course her son was a genius. Although, as I headed for my first book-signing, I could just hear her telling me to make sure I had first brushed my hair.

★   ★   ★

In any non-fiction tale that involves its fair share of decidedly 'unofficial' and adulterous bedroom romps – ignoring, of course, the many explosions and more than occasional slit throat – the author has to be mindful of not upsetting anyone unnecessarily. Geoffrey Gordon-Creed, whose memoir this is, died in 2002. He can no longer bear witness to his adventures with these supposedly demure and blushing maidens who, as described in these pages, could turn into sexual wildcats when the occasion offered. As I have no wish to find myself facing a furious 90-year-old Greek matriarch claiming that her family now believe that she was one of Geoff's many conquests, I have completely changed the names and circumstances of all Geoff's 'girls', to ensure they cannot be identified. So if, in the course of reading this book, you get to wondering whether it is your mother, grandmother or even great-grandmother that Geoff is describing: forget it. It isn't!

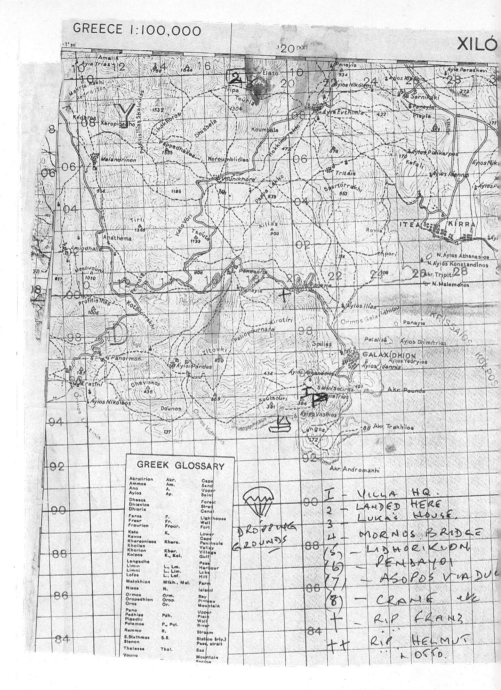

I – VILLA HQ.
2 – LANDED HERE
3 – LUKAS HOUSE
4 – MORNOS BRIDGE
(5) – LIDHORIKION
(6) – PENDAYOI
(7) – ASOPOS VIADUC
(8) – CRANE etc
† – RIP FRANZ
†† RIP HELMUT
& OSSO.

DROPPING GROUNDS

Map of main area of operations in Greece, 1943–4. Found among Geoff's papers, it appears to be a copy of the map he used at the time as it is very large scale and shows all the contour lines. A soldier in Afghanistan today would recognise this as perfect guerilla territory: deep valleys, high mountains and very few roads, making it near impossible – these were, of course, the days before helicopters – to catch Geoff's men unawares. Geoff, as can be seen, started to mark up the sites of various 'events' but was unable to do so with all of them as some took place 'off' the map, mainly to the North.

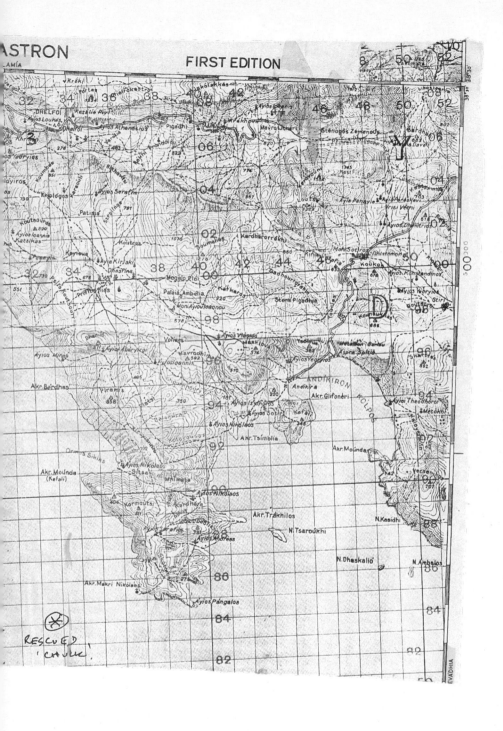

INTRODUCTION

I first came across the story of 'Mister Major Geoff' sitting over lunch with a friend in the garden of an English country pub one warm and sunny September afternoon. That friend was Nick Gordon-Creed, Geoff's eldest son and an ex-soldier like me. After a few beers we began to exchange war stories. Then he told me something of his late father. Geoff had led the team of saboteurs who had famously dropped the Asopos Viaduct, north of Athens – so critical to the Allies' strategic war plans that Churchill singled out the raid for particular mention in his *History of the Second World War*. Before joining the Special Operations Executive (SOE) and going behind the lines Geoff had fought in tanks in the Western Desert, as well as with the SAS. He had ended the war leading the round-ups of some of the top Nazis in northern Germany. Quite some war and quite some father.

Nick suggested I might read Geoff's memoirs. He could guarantee me some laughs because, while his father had been one of the most ferocious of soldiers, he had also been one of the most wicked, engaging and naughty of men. What was more, and in stark contrast to most of his generation, Geoff had been more than happy to write about what he had got up to, and in quite some detail. Nick assured me I would not be wasting my time – after all, I too had been a soldier once.

In 2007, the twenty-fifth anniversary of the Falklands War, the Ministry of Defence kindly sent me back there as one of a group of veterans available for interview by the media. The islanders and the British forces could not do enough for us. Asked if there was anything I particularly wanted to do I requested a range day, as I wanted to try out the newfangled guns that had come along since I had left. Four of us 'vets' went along for a morning of converting taxpayers' hard-earned money into thousands of spent rounds. We were looked after beautifully by a platoon of young soldiers recently back from a vicious tour in Iraq. They were training up to do the same in Afghanistan. They seemed to be genuinely in awe of what we had done twenty-five years earlier. I was in awe of what they had just done and were about to do again, and again and again.

But, and for all that, I am only too aware that in the last war those men constantly in the front line experienced a more pro-longed intensity of conflict, against an often better armed and certainly highly trained enemy, than anything I ever experienced. Extreme though the intensity of current war fighting is, six-month tours should end after six months. Men like Geoff found themselves, if not actually fighting, then certainly in harm's way for years on end.

My front-line service – short but intense – meant that I too have known fear, have known the sense of anger and helplessness that comes when another's incompetence looks to get you killed. I too have exulted in the rush of adrenalin that comes from surviving, from winning, and the cold slough of depression that follows so soon after. In contrast, Major Geoff survived years of sustained warfare in which he saw nearly everyone close to him killed.

I read the memoir and found myself enthralled by a man who took the war to the enemy, first in tanks and then behind the lines, even hand to hand.

In places it was a dark tale of slitting prisoners' throats, of torture and assassination, of what a Special Forces soldier needed to do to survive under extraordinary circumstances. Critically, though, I found myself reading the authentic, unvarnished, unhomogenised side of the Second World War that might well have been hinted at in other memoirs, but which we never get to read about in any contemporary detail, except of course in works of fiction. The likes of Alistair MacLean and Ian Fleming made fortunes by telling what were, in essence, 'real' war stories. To an older generation that sort of behaviour was perhaps acceptable – even admirable – as fiction, but not as non-fiction.

What is more, while I knew Geoff's story to be history, his voice sounds utterly modern. Soldiers in Afghanistan today would recognise him and claim him for their own, would want him leading them into battle or into a bar. Aggressive, dangerous, always up for devilment and a laugh, he was clearly a man I would have been privileged to fight alongside; a man I would have been honoured for him to call me his friend; a man I would have dreaded as my enemy.

His is not a voice we have heard before from the last war. Perhaps the accepted version we grew up with, of John Mills and Kenneth More, of *Ice Cold in Alex* and *The Dam Busters*, of stiff upper lips and a chaste kiss for the wife as the hero heads off to battle, was a necessary myth for those who chose to write their memoirs. But the reality has to have been very different. Enjoying sex was not an invention of the 1960s. Why were none of that war generation more candid? Perhaps they feared to rock the boat, or needed to maintain the facade of a noble British world for their own sanity, needed to maintain the vision of a civilisation for which they had risked their all. Perhaps they simply felt it was vulgar to tell stories that did not necessarily paint their fellows in a flattering light.

So, while the histories from World War II ring true about one side of the British soldiers – their grit, their humour, their sheer doggedness and essential decency – to me, there is usually a critical element missing. The young men I soldiered alongside were almost invariably wicked. They had an evil sense of humour: gallows humour when it went SNAFU – 'situation normal, all fucked up' – as of course it almost invariably did. Girls were always on our minds and, given an opportunity, most soldiers I knew would risk heaven and hell and any orders from higher command to the contrary to get at them. We were pragmatic about life and death. Certainly no saints. That other, older, generation cannot have been that different.

For me, the stories written by my parents' generation about 'their' wars are of people I recognise only dimly in these respects. That is, until I read Geoff's memoirs.

In August 1941, a couple of days before his regiment shipped out to Egypt and the Desert War, he married his first wife, Ursula – the first of four. Not that he was to let that inconvenient detail curtail his amorous activities. He was not to see her again for another three years. As he was setting out on his adventures as a soldier, it was clear what his priorities would be:

Whether I am right or wrong I cannot be sure, but I believe that over the years I have come to recognise certain characteristics in faces that denote extreme sexuality. Slightly buck teeth for example, a certain shade of slatey blue eyes and a longish, slightly pinched nose. There are others. Written down like this it doesn't sound too attractive but, nevertheless, and ignoring the more obvious 'chemistry' that one encounters from time to time, I have found that a girl with one or more of the above traits will usually prove to be a most enthusiastic bedfellow.

And Geoff, ever on the lookout to test that theory, made the most of such opportunities as he found. From the beginning and in the years to follow, his attraction to women, and their attraction to him, is another constant theme in his story: a source of sometimes hilarious stories but also of personal complications.

In his womanising he probably had a lot more opportunity

than many soldiers who, stuck in their regular formations, only rarely got to go behind the lines and meet 'normal' women. Wartime England, for a man such as the then Second Lieutenant Geoffrey Gordon-Creed, would have been full of young women for whom the alpha male of the moment would have been someone in a glamorous uniform. Egypt would turn out to be similar, Cairo in particular having a wild social life for those with the right contacts. And then came Greece. The Greeks loathed the Germans and, in his area of operations, he was the one leading the fight against them. Certain girls would have wanted him. In fact, and as he relates, the problem was the reverse to the normal one. So many wanted him that, if he was seen to have one particular girlfriend, it might easily put her, and thus him, in danger of betrayal by a spurned rival.

Geoff did have one great advantage over me and my contemporaries. Back in the 1970s and 1980s I reckoned there was rarely much advantage to letting on to a girl too quickly that you were in the army: 'boring' was the likely answer. Of course, and thankfully, there were others who had a clear and sometimes obvious predilection for soldiers (doubtless sailors and airmen also had their fan clubs) and there were still yet other girls, somewhat bizarrely, who seemed devoted to certain corps, or even regiments. But on the whole, I reckon soldiers of my day tended to be thought of as being somewhat 'straight', coupled with being saddled with the reputation for being 'here today and gone tomorrow', which we were.

Geoff encountered no such problems. Handsome, charming, dangerous, he would have been as desirable to a glamorous 1940s woman as a successful singer, fashion photographer or celebrity restaurateur to one of today's 'celeb' girls.[1]

---

1   Even as I was writing this I came across the obituary in the Daily Telegraph of Rear-Admiral Derick Lawson, who once described such a scenario: Lawson's light cruiser was torpedoed and badly damaged on a Malta convoy in June 1942. Towed back to Gibraltar after heroic efforts to save the ship, Lawson wrote that 'the

That said, I reckon you could have put Geoff anywhere, any time, and he'd have charmed the birds from the trees. He was just one of those guys. I've long believed that 10 per cent of the guys probably get 90 per cent of the girls. He was in the top 1 per cent of that 10 per cent, still causing mayhem with female hearts late into his sixties.

Not that he got much time for playing the lover early on. He was pitched straight into the massed tank actions of the Western Desert, which could be on a par with the battles of the First War for percentage loss of life and low survival rates. On his very first day in action Geoff (then a junior second lieutenant) won a Military Cross. When the guns finally fell silent his regiment had been all but annihilated, but he had narrowly avoided death and had sent a number of the enemy to Hades in his stead.

He was that rare thing: a natural warrior, with almost superhuman instincts, instincts which improved the more he experienced. He once actually saw – 'sensed' is perhaps a better word – a shell coming at him and started to jump just before it struck, blowing the turret off his tank and him out with it, his boots on fire. To anyone who has fought in an armoured vehicle that story alone puts him in a different league. To have the sharpness of eyesight to spot an incoming shell is extraordinary enough. To then get your body to react in the split second between awareness and sphincter-releasing, muscle-freezing terror and detonation defies description.

We were taught – in my case in the now obsolete 55-ton Chieftain tanks and, later, lightweight Scimitars – that our defences were a mixture of some or all of our superior firepower (killing the enemy before he got close enough to kill you), camouflage (staying hidden or presenting as small target

---

Gibraltar people – especially the Wren officers – were disposed to lionise us. We didn't deter them . . .'

a target as possible) and speed (it isn't the easiest skill to master, hitting a moving vehicle at long range with a single-shot gun). In Chieftains we also had immensely thick armour, albeit few illusions about the state of our bodies if we took a direct hit from a modern main battle tank. The general wisdom was that while the tank might still be serviceable, they would be scraping us out with a spoon.

In the Western Desert in 1941 and 1942 the Allied armoured regiments had none of these advantages. Rarely anywhere to hide in the desert, comprehensively out-armoured and totally outgunned, all they had was their bravery and their numbers. As Geoff recollects, they often went into battle with a three to one advantage, an advantage they needed as the Germans invariably knocked out three Allied tanks for every one of theirs. Not the best thought to wake up to just before dawn, freezing cold and hungry, and in the distance the grumble of approaching German Panzers . . .

The horror and intensity of sustained warfare will tend to accentuate a person's characteristics, for good or bad. When, like Geoff, a man has witnessed the death of so many of his friends, that experience will either break him or harden him. In his case it made Geoff even more determined to survive, yet more callous and contemptuous of death. For, as he tells us:

I have been involved directly and indirectly in the deaths of scores of men. How do or should I feel about this? My answer must be nothing. Duty bound, one is prepared to kill the enemy. But if the enemy is misguided enough to try to kill one such as me, unprovoked, then let him beware.

I am a peace-loving and timid man, but once frightened or severely angered I act on a ferocious impulse which is alarming. The adrenalin flows and I can actually feel the hairs on the back of my legs rising up like a dog's.

Like any successful warrior, Geoff was exceptionally lucky. His regiment was destroyed twice but he narrowly survived – including being captured and escaping – until he decided he needed a change.

For my part, having regard to my experiences during the past fifteen months, my confidence in my commanders had waned somewhat. I determined that, from here on in, if I were to be killed it would be through my own fault or misjudgement and not through that of a superior.

His introduction to the world of Special Forces was, as ever with Geoff, somewhat unorthodox. He bumped into an SAS pal at a brothel not far from the pyramids.

Mary's House was much patronised, not so much for the charms of 'les girls' but because after every other place of entertainment in Cairo had closed, they still served drinks at reasonable prices as well as the most excellent early morning breakfast of bacon and eggs.

Keen to try a different way of taking the fight to the enemy he signed up for the abortive SAS raid on the port of Benghazi. Relieved and lucky to survive yet again – the enemy were expecting them and harried the survivors mercilessly as they fled back across the desert – he decided that even the SAS was too structured for him, and joined SOE, the Special Operations Executive, set up in 1940, only two years previously. They were the secret agents and saboteurs[2] of World War II.

At this point, the tone of Geoff's memoir changes. Up to his joining SOE and becoming almost solely responsible for his own survival, I had the feeling that he was something of a victim of war. Others told him what to do and he tried to carry out those orders to the best of his ability. As his son Nick told me, he was no respecter of rank, but once he gave you his loyalty he would do anything for you and would follow you regardless of the consequences.

---

2 SOE operatives did not consider or refer to themselves as 'spies' as such, although – typically and perversely – Geoff does so on occasion.

The death in battle of his first squadron leader had hit him hard and I sense that he was, thereafter, leery of those who commanded him. Nevertheless, and being Geoff, he tried to have as much fun as he could along the way, never really believing he would survive or had any right to expect to survive. As the war progresses, this need to extract some fun out of the horror of existence brings an extraordinary element to the memoirs. The attitude of many of his contemporaries, I suspect.

A fellow SAS officer on the September 1942 Benghazi raid, who travelled with Geoff for much of it, devotes fifty-five densely typed pages of his memoir to the attack and the retreat. Geoff gives the mission ten very sparse pages, of which two recount a fairly bizarre near-death experience in a plane taking him to the rendezvous – busy shagging his then girlfriend, he had managed to volunteer to jump a lift rather than spend two weeks crossing the desert to get to the SAS form-up point – and a further two pages to the scene of debauchery when he got back to her flat in Cairo. Two very brave men, the same action-packed raid, two entirely different accounts, but then that is part of what makes Geoff's stories so compelling.

It is when he gets to Greece that his memoirs also develop a vivid visceral quality. As one who once believed that the ineffectualness of his commanders stood as much chance of getting him killed as the enemy, I fully understand Geoff's relief at breaking free. On the other hand, I can have no idea of the stress of being alone and without support for so long, facing certain brutal interrogation and death if captured. The Germans did not make long-term prisoners of SOE men they caught, especially in Greece. However, for him, the risks seemed to be worth it. He was now in charge of his own destiny, almost free of the constraints and idiocies of high command, fighting his war and in his own way. He had become the hunter, only rarely the hunted.

Churchill had ordered SOE to 'set Europe ablaze', and in his memoirs he praises one operation in particular for helping convince Hitler that the Allies, now victorious in North Africa, were next to invade Greece. It was Geoff who in June 1943 led the team that destroyed the Asopos Viaduct, earning himself an 'immediate' DSO, as near to a VC as you can get. The result of this high-profile 'spectacular', and all the subsequent guerrilla activity, was that two German divisions were sent to Greece to defend against an invasion that never arrived, thus helping set off a crucial chain of events that was to result in Italy being knocked out of the war.

When not 'blowing bridges and killing Germans', Geoff was beginning to show equal ruthlessness when it came to seducing the local women. He was discovering the advantages of being a guerrilla leader, especially when the locals detested their oppressors and needed his protection. The large store of gold sovereigns he had at his disposal did nothing to discourage his admirers, either . . .

Each man, while trained to react in the same way under fire, will think differently when the bullets begin to fly. Some might pray, others think of their families, yet others fantasise about their women. But they will usually have one thing in common: their focus narrows down to survival, survival at almost any cost. And survival means not only of the individual, but of the group. When it is kill or be killed, men will do things – and even be applauded for it by their comrades – that would be morally repugnant at any other time. It is not that they become amoral, it is that what is moral and acceptable – even laudable – changes at that precise moment.

Put bluntly, it is clear from these pages that Geoff did not expect anything but torture and death were he to be captured. He did not like it, but he had no choice but to accept it. By the same token, since the enemy had dictated these were the rules of war in Greece and on the basis of 'do as you would be done by', any German or Italian captured by Geoff and his band of cut-throats could expect to be treated in the same brutal manner.

More broadly than this, most people's sense of morality will tend to shift in wartime, whether they be man or woman, soldier or civilian. When we know we might be killed at any moment, many of us will tend to grab at whatever fleeting pleasures life has to offer. After all, this was not a six-month tour, awful though such a tour most certainly is. This was a pit-bull fight to the death, a war that had already been going for over three years and obviously had plenty of bloodletting left in it.

In the context of modern peacetime morality I can quite understand why some might ask whether these women had any real choice, whether there was an element of coercion in what Geoff got up to. My own view is there was no coercion and these women gave themselves to him enthusiastically, as anxious as he to have some fun in a world gone mad. In fact, and as already said, his problem was often the reverse: he was a devilishly attractive man and these women were squabbling over him.

Geoff spent nearly every moment of his fifteen months in Greece in fear for his life. With a large price on his head – the wanted poster called for the death or capture of 'Mister Major Geoff' – he lived in constant danger of betrayal. Inevitably, his reserve of resolve – he says his 'reserves of courage', but I somehow doubt that – began to run dry and he decided that enough was enough. As ever, he took matters into his own hands and wrote a deeply offensive official message about the behaviour of certain of his Greek compatriots which he knew would set off alarm bells back at HQ SOE, Cairo. Sure enough, there were calls for disciplinary action and the inevitable recall. There were to be no repercussions, although I wonder if he would have cared that much had there been. An astute staff officer guessed what he was up to and, in any event, higher command had no intention of pressing charges against a genuine war hero on the say-so of some Cairo desk jockey.

And shortly thereafter his memoir ends, with him on a flying boat back to England worrying that some bright spark might send him off behind the lines again, this time to fight the Japanese: a fate that befell some of his compatriots from Greece, a fate he was anxious to avoid.

Fortunately for posterity, a friend read his memoirs and told him that he could not leave the reader hanging in mid-air, so to speak, especially as there was so much more trouble that he was yet to cause to friend and foe alike, both in the field and in the bedroom. Geoff relented and wrote a booklet of 'letters', and I have used these as the main source for his adventures post-Greece.

Geoff managed to stay in Europe where he ended up in charge of rounding up the top Nazis in north-east Germany. High-profile captures included Admiral Doenitz, the Reich's leader after the death of Hitler, and Albert Speer, Minister of Armaments and War Production.

Thereafter he was promoted to lieutenant colonel and took up a military position in Beirut, where he continued working in the shadowy world of military intelligence. He retired from the army in 1948 only to discover, like so many other warriors before and since, that the attributes that had made him so feared in war were not necessarily what people look for in peace.

He tried, unsuccessfully, to make money in various ventures in Africa. This included fish farming – he lost the fish when hippos broke down the dykes between the farm and the sea – and crocodile-hunting: highly profitable, but foul smelling, occasionally dangerous and mainly boring. Greek detractors wrote of rumours that he had even worked as a mercenary.

Although his letters show brief and amusing glimpses of

things he got up to, much remains shadowy, as befits a man whose life had depended for so long on keeping secrets and leaving no tracks. Not least are the 'mysterious' two years in the mid-1950s in which Geoff once again became First Lieutenant and then Captain Geoff. During these two years family legend has it that he was kept on stand-by as a 'shooter' in case someone with his skills was needed by the government to dispose of one particularly troublesome future Commonwealth head of state. When the operation was compromised Geoff did a runner with his family to Jamaica, resigning from the army at the same time.

Nor did it stop him enjoying himself: one of the more salacious letters tells of a passionate interlude with the actress Ava Gardner – the film star many at the time considered the most beautiful woman in the world – while she was taking a break from filming *Mogambo* in Kenya with Clark Gable and Grace Kelly. She offered herself to him for seven days. He ended up getting eight . . .

Even when he did finally settle down to a 'proper' job, running a division of Firestone Tires in South Africa, he did it in style. He married Christy Firestone, wife number three and his future boss's daughter – and, it just so happened, a very wealthy heiress. A cunningly orchestrated stunt had the international press photographing the happy couple – but the wrong happy couple. Meanwhile the real bride, seven months pregnant, remained hidden in Chelsea Register Office, to the fury of the press when they realised they had been duped. War heroes were just not expected to behave like that. A 'celeb' today, desperate to outwit the paparazzi, could do worse than study Geoff.

Perhaps this ruthlessness, this amorality, this total disregard for convention, were some of the characteristics that were to draw Ian Fleming to Geoff when they befriended each other in Jamaica in the 1950s. Drinking late into the night, Geoff would tell Fleming his stories and Fleming, who had himself worked in intelligence during the war, would listen. In later life Geoff would enthral female admirers by hinting that he was one of the models for James Bond. Reading these accounts of necessary killing and sex and looking at his handsome dark face, I for one would love to believe him.

Determined to see Major Geoff's story in print, I showed the memoir to Mark Booth. A publisher of many great military stories, he loved it, instantly latching on to the fact that he had never read anything like this from the war. But, and as so often in publishing, there was a problem. In his preface, Major Geoff described his memoir as 'a few vignettes and stories mostly relating to myself during World War II'. With little background or context to his various campaigns and, as often as not, a humorous and self-deprecating anecdote to shroud the true horror of something better forgotten, this was a pretty accurate summary of his memoir. The letters are even more problematic: a bright but random patchwork of often hilarious incidents frequently detached from any sense of time or place. Mark wanted someone to pull the disconnected parts into a coherent story and that someone – he had heard snippets of my rackety military past – was me.

We decided that the key was to keep Major Geoff's words where possible. He wrote: 'Someone once observed that, whatever its subject, a story is a good story or a bad story only by the style in which it is told.' Were I to tamper with his unique style I would risk degrading his story.

Our solution has been to use Major Geoff's words with a different font to mine so it is easy to see who has written what. I have used various other sources to try and fill in the gaps: military histories, third-party accounts of his actions and conversations with his sons.

Because his memoir starts with the moment he joins the army, there is no mention of family or background. We need to know more about this if we are to begin to understand this complex and secretive man, so there will, by necessity, be more of 'me' early on. He wrote short accounts of his early training, followed by the tank war in the desert – accounts that are often far too brief – followed by the disastrous SAS raid and induction into SOE. Once he parachutes into Greece, Geoff can be left to do most of the talking: why tamper with near-genius? Post-Greece I am fairly reliant on the letters and family recollections, so there is ever more of 'me' again as I try to give context to his post-war wanderings and get to tell some outrageous stories that are crying out to be heard.

I suspect most writers itch to analyse their subjects, try to understand and explain their motivations. I will try not to, but I know I will inevitably give it a go. When I left the army – just like him, aged 28 – I agonised over what to do next. Like Geoff, I had spent my military years investing every penny I earned into having fun. Like him, I badly needed money. I looked at my military contemporaries, with their often parallel lives and interests. 'If my great friend X can go into banking/stockbroking/insurance/whatever and be happy and obviously successful, why can't I?' I reasoned. It took me many years to fully understand that I should revel in being different and that, as humans, we can tick many of the same boxes and yet be so very different. Thus, while Geoff and I might have shared many similar experiences, that does not mean that I will necessarily ever come to understand him. He was clearly made from a somewhat alternative mould.

So, should he and I meet in Valhalla, and should I have got some things wrong in this, his book, I hope he treats me kindly. It is a foolish man who gets on the wrong side of Mister Major Geoff.

Anyway, here goes . . .

I

Playing the game

Happy families it was not to be. Geoffrey Anthony Harrison was born in Cape Town, South Africa, on 29 January 1920. His mother, Molly, a highly talented concert pianist, had scandalised her parents by eloping with and marrying one William Harrison.

But within a year or so of Geoff's birth, William had 'gone off' with a young man from Portsmouth – 'ran off with a bloody docker' is how the family put it today. The scandal was instant and devastating. Molly immediately got a divorce: a social stigma back in the 1920s. While William gets a name check in the family tree, he was otherwise expunged from the family record. Who he was and where he came from, and what happened to him thereafter, the rest of the family no longer know.

Then Molly's life changed completely, and for the good. In a Cape Town auditorium one evening she played a concert. In the audience was a captain from the glamorous 17th Lancers: the 'Death or Glory' boys with their famous skull and crossbones cap badge which commemorates their heroic part in the Charge of the Light Brigade. This captain fell in love with Molly and, shortly after, they were married. And he must have been besotted to accept the social death that came with marrying a divorcee.

Soon after the remarriage young Geoffrey was given his second surname, that of his stepfather. But his new name was itself to become an issue in time. Because, while her dashing captain of cavalry had fought bravely in the trenches on the Western Front in the First War, Molly's husband had a very unfortunate name for an Englishman: Herman Eckstein.

Even the Royal Family had changed their surname from Saxe-Coburg-Gotha to Windsor, not unreasonable when you were in the middle of a death brawl with Germany. I cannot but wonder – in fact it takes no imagination at all – how Herman's soldiers and fellow officers played with his name in the trenches. The British soldier then would have been like his compatriot today: merciless and unerringly accurate. It would have been a never-ending and very effective piss-take. Geoff would not make the same mistake.

However, I wonder whether there may be more to it than that. Geoff made the change by deed poll to Gordon-Creed in late 1938, well before the actual start of hostilities. Neville Chamberlain, the prime minister, had returned from Munich on 29 September of that year famously declaring 'peace for our time'. Churchill and a small group of malcontents were the only ones who were convinced that conflict was inevitable. Perhaps Geoff agreed with Churchill.

He had left school in July 1938, aged 18, and we know that he travelled that summer to Germany as there are some photographs he took of Nuremberg, complete with Nazis in all their military regalia. Maybe, having seen the Fatherland for himself, he was realist enough to be in no doubt where this was all heading.

Whatever the case, Geoff left school in summer 1938 with a divorced mother, a disgraced biological father he never mentioned and, shortly thereafter, a third change of name. When he made the third and final change he took his mother's maiden name, Creed, and aggrandised it with another associated family name to make up the smart-sounding Gordon-Creed. With that one act alone, the name 'improvement', the young Geoff was already showing signs of calculation, a trait he would need to develop as one of nature's adaptors and concealers. Listed on the first page of a CV for a prospective agent and saboteur, it could hardly be bettered.

By this time in his life he had learned other invaluable soldiering skills as well. In 1928, Herman Eckstein had taken Molly, stepchildren Betty (the eldest) and Geoff, and their three other children to their new home: a run-down 1000-acre farm called Maryland, 6500 feet up in the Kenya Highlands, surrounded by wild forest. This was no luxury farming. The house was a small bungalow, three miles from the nearest neighbours. There were locust infestations, and drought would periodically ravage the crops. The cattle had to be dipped every four days lest they died of East Coast Fever. When the bush had been cleared, the family planted coffee and maize.

The young Geoff learned to walk and ride the forests, up this high the haunt of leopard and buffalo and myriad poisonous snakes. Herman had, in his time in the army, been in charge of remount riders – breaking in and training cavalry horses – a tough discipline where you either do things 'right' or they go very wrong. Herman taught Geoff how to do things 'right' and thus how to be reasonably safe, even when surrounded by danger. He taught him to shoot straight and how to be trusted with a weapon – although his half-sister Mary recalls Geoff not being averse to 'winging' his sisters with his airgun. She also says that gun was confiscated for a whole year when Herman caught him waving it around dangerously. When the airgun was replaced by a rifle, Geoff learned to hunt. He was, says his half-sister, 'a real outdoor boy': in fact, the sort of person who makes an ideal Special Forces soldier.

I spent a year training young recruits at what was then known as the Junior Leaders Regiment – 16- to 18-year-olds, many of whom would go on to become senior NCOs. I know what it is like to start by teaching someone how to tie his boots properly and move on from there in incremental stages before finally turning him into the finished article. A recruit who is already a marksman, who is absolutely safe with a rifle in his hands, who knows how to move silently and look after himself in all weathers, who is fit and strong from years spent in the outdoors: chances are he will make the best soldier of all. Not always, but usually.

Interestingly, the initial nucleus of the Long Range Desert Group (LRDG) – who fought so effectively behind the lines in North Africa in the Second World War – consisted mainly of New Zealanders. Asked why he had chosen them, Major (soon to be Colonel) Ralph Bagnold, founder of the LRDG, said these men just happened to be at a 'loose end' as they had arrived in Egypt without their heavy weapons, which had been lost at sea: 'I chose them because I wanted responsible volunteers who knew how to look after things and maintain things.' And these men were tough farmers, used to driving vehicles – still a rare skill at that time when cars were usually owned only by the rich. Also, the fact that they can handle weapons and shoot straight tends to be a given with most farmers. Captain David Lloyd Owen, commander of LRDG's Yeomanry Patrol, concurred, saying of his yeomen – also trained on tanks and armoured cars – 'they were mostly countrymen, they were not scared of being alone in the dark like some town men . . . [Out there] you are completely on your own. You will get no help from anyone else.'[1] In fact the sort of man they were looking for was someone like Geoff, someone who had learned to hunt and look after himself in the mountains of Kenya.

On my first 'real' exercise in Chieftain tanks, I and the squadron second-in-command, a countryman born and bred, were watching a troop of three Chieftains moving forward in line abreast to a start line: three 55-ton lumps of slow-moving steel grinding their way over and around some muddy, track-torn hillocks.

1   Both quotes from *The Imperial War Museum Book of War Behind Enemy Lines* by Julian Thompson.

Ted pointed to the Alpha call sign. 'Watch him carefully.'

The other two tanks were powering up and over anything in their way. The commander of Alpha was snaking his way round the bottom of the hillocks, even though the actual test phase had not started, instinctively making himself as small a target as possible.

'He's a natural,' said Ted. 'His father was a bloody poacher. Always hiding. Wish all my tank commanders were gamekeepers or poachers.'

I believe it was the great West Indian batsman Viv Richards who said, on being asked what was behind his 'luck', that he found that the more he practised the luckier he got. 'Train hard, fight easy,' is one of the sayings of the SAS. Put the SAS in a line and send them marching over the top, as the troops were sent over on the first day of the Battle of the Somme, and they would probably have been gunned down as effectively and completely as any company of soldiers. Left to themselves, their training, their ability to move fast and present as small a target as possible, their ability to shoot straight and quickly kill those shooting at them, mean they dramatically increase their chances of survival.

That is what men like Geoff do. Fully confident within themselves, they focus their thought processes on thinking and planning and surviving, not on wondering whether their rifle is loaded and the safety catch is on or off, or even whether they have enough puff in their lungs to make the next move. Certainly, you learn fast in your first battle, but before you can call yourself a veteran you have to survive it. Chances are that the first men to do the dying are the ones who are moving in a straight line, who have not camouflaged themselves properly, who lack fitness and therefore move more slowly and jink about less often. The stray bullet or ricochet will take out the best soldier as effectively as the dullard, but the aimed bullet is more likely to be directed at the dozy bugger rather than the one who is moving low and fast.

Even the willingness to shoot and kill – fundamental to success and survival – is less prevalent than has been assumed. While it is acknowledged that there is considerable controversy over figures that imply that as few as 15 per cent of American soldiers in World War II even fired their weapons at the enemy,[2] such a figure, even if overstated, demonstrates that not all men are natural fighters, even in the heat of battle. For some, perhaps for many, the natural human reluctance to kill can overpower their need to survive.

The converse is that well-trained, motivated soldiers are more likely to do the killing than their poorly trained counterparts. Men like Geoff, who hunted and shot from youth, are much more likely to fire, and without hesitation. And when they fire they are very much more likely to hit their target. The news footage we see on our television screens from so many Third World 'wars' tells the story: poorly trained soldiers pouring unaimed fire in the general direction of the enemy. When that is countered by trained soldiers taking carefully aimed shots, it becomes the gulf between victory and defeat.

On being asked whether anyone was surprised at what Geoff went on to achieve, his half-sister Mary said no, the family had always assumed that he would be very brave and highly competent. She followed that up with the somewhat startling fact that, of the five boys in their mountain district who went off to the war, every single one of them came back with some sort of gallantry medal. Geoff came back with two. This is a fairly stunning statistic. Unlike a number of other armies, the British have never handed out gallantry medals with the rations: quite the opposite. Even 'putty medals' or 'turning up medals', as I like to call them, have to

2 S.L.A. Marshall, *Men Against Fire, The Problem of Battlefield Command* (William Morrow, 1947).

be earned the hard way. So those five young men must have all had something about them that was very special indeed.

Put in context, it is perhaps no surprise that so many men from tough outdoor places like New Zealand, Australia and Southern Africa naturally gravitated to the SAS, the Long Range Desert Group and SOE. Tough, resourceful and brave, these were naturally dangerous men who needed the bare minimum of conventional training to turn them into superb fighting soldiers.

With no proper education to be had up on their mountain, Geoff was sent to board at Pembroke House, a prep school in Kenya. He did well there, ending up as head boy and noted for being particularly good at games. But, come age 13, it was time to leave and Herman took a deep breath and decided to do the right thing by his stepson by sending him to Downside, a Catholic school run by monks deep in rural Somerset. Why the pause for thought? And why Downside?

Not long after Geoff had started at school, things turned sour for farmers in Africa. This was the time of the Great Depression and exports collapsed, taking with them farm rents and income. Herman found himself strapped for cash and wondering how he was going to pay the 60 guineas a term. His letters make it clear that he was always deeply mindful that a 'government' school back in Kenya would cost only 10 guineas a term.

And Downside because, although Herman was a Protestant himself, and a very devout one at that, Molly was an equally fervent Catholic and she was determined that Geoff should be brought up in her faith.

Although initially Geoff was, as he later put it, 'terrified at being cast adrift among a mob of noisy apes', by the time he was 16 he had carved a place for himself at school. German surname or not, he had become a popular boy who excelled at sports and was keeping up with his studies.

But when Herman travelled to London in the summer of 1936 and spent a few weeks with 'the boy', he was clearly deeply unimpressed by what he found. That August he wrote in a fury to the headmaster: 'I am very upset at his bad manners. His language, his selfishness, also his general slackness – his table manners are bad too. I believe the cinema has a lot to do with it and I think he imagines he is copying some screen hero.' Herman then rails about the fact that Geoff 'will not attend mass on Sundays unless forced to . . .' and goes on to paint a picture of a headstrong teenager happily going off the rails.

By that September Herman had had enough and decided that as 'the boy has got hold of the most amazing ideas, I think the sooner he leaves England the better'. He gave the headmaster a term's notice.

Shortly after this pronouncement, there was another meeting between Herman and Geoff. Herman subsequently wrote to the headmaster, reversing his decision:

'I spent yesterday afternoon with Geoffrey and got closer to him than I have ever succeeded in getting before. He really opened up and assured me that he had realised from what I had said to him that he had been thoughtless and selfish and that he realised that his manners had got to be changed. He convinced me yesterday of his sincerity.'

Life continued much as before for the next two years: Herman fretting and Geoff getting up to God knows what, but now playing enough within the rules to ensure he stayed in England and at Downside. He finished up a school prefect and continued to excel at games, as did so many of the pre-eminent soldiers of his generation. By July 1938, aged 18, he had passed his exams, left school and been interviewed and accepted by Jesus College, Cambridge. Writing to Downside to offer him a place starting in October 1939, the Admissions Tutor wrote that Geoff 'will make a very useful and interesting member of the College'. And well he might have, had Adolf Hitler not intervened.

2

Under the table at Rosa's

'Can you hear?'

'Can you see?'

'You appear to be breathing. Drop your pants . . . now cough. Splendid. You are passed A1 fit. Move along.'

The Lord knows how we young men had tried throughout the year to get into a Territorial Army unit, any unit, knowing that war was inevitable after the shameful Munich business in 1938. I must have applied to a dozen regiments, but the answer was always: 'Sorry, but our establishment is full.' Now war had been declared. The floodgates were open and countless thousands of young men like myself rushed to join the colours. Our main fear was that the enemy might somehow be defeated before we had the chance to show our mettle.

I had an advantage in that my father had once been a cavalry officer in the regular army and that I had, perforce, spent four years playing the fool in my school Officer Training Corps. I trotted along to the recruiting depot with an asterisk against my name that alerted my future commanders to consider me as 'Potential Officer Material'.

I knew very well, however, that I would have to earn my commission, and that meant starting off at the bottom and going through the ranks. But now fate now took a hand and provided me with an entertaining interlude.

This being that period now known as 'the Phoney War', with the pre-war 'professional' armies of France, Britain and Germany facing off against each other along the Franco-German border but next to no fighting actually taking place, there seemed no urgency on the part of our masters to get us new recruits trained and into uniform. And so, and as instructed, I had returned home to await my orders. 'Home', in my case, was a large house on the outskirts of Maidenhead belonging to a step-aunt. I detested her but was greatly attached to her two sons who, incidentally, had taken the King's shilling at the same time as myself. We all killed time while awaiting further orders, doing volunteer work on farms, firefighting and so on, and, it being a particularly severe winter, amused ourselves on weekends skiing down a fairly steep slope near Bourne End. We were thus engaged one crisp Saturday morning when we were accosted by a civilian of military aspect who had stopped his car to watch us. 'Good morning,' he said.

'Good morning, Sir,' I replied.

'You all seem to be pretty good at that. Been at it long?'

'We're a bit out of practice but, yes, we've all done quite a lot of skiing.'

'What are you doing now? I mean, have you joined up yet?'

I explained that indeed we had.

'Would you be interested in joining a special, rather hush-hush unit which is being formed and which involves skiing?'

Would we!

'My name is Colonel Martineau. Ask for me at Hobart House. Do you know where that is? Buckingham Palace Road.' He nodded and smiled.

We were there on Monday.

It could only happen in the British army, an army where eccentrics and private armies have never been discouraged. Some bright spark had sold the War Office on the idea of raising a ski battalion to fight in Scandinavia. Who we were meant to be helping, Finns or Norwegians, was never made clear.

In those days not many skied and most of those who did tended to be better off. It followed that those who skied were usually deemed 'officer material'. Volunteers with skiing ability were called for throughout the army to serve in the 5th (Ski Regiment) Battalion, Scots Guards. And, be you a major, a captain, a lieutenant or a nobody like me, you agreed to drop your rank temporarily and serve as a guardsman – the most junior rank in the army.

The response was, of course, enormous and hundreds were turned away disappointed. We three got in through the good offices of Colonel Martineau and because we were early birds.

In the various histories of the Second World War I have looked in vain for any mention of us gallant volunteers, and found none. This surprises me not at all as the whole affair was one short but hilarious balls-up.

We mustered at a depressing place near Aldershot called Bordon. We ate at local pubs whenever we could. We were issued with splendid Arctic survival equipment and skis and eventually arrived in Chamonix for joint training with the French specialist mountain troops, the Chasseurs Alpins: *les diables bleus* ('the Blue Devils').

This was a hoot. The little resort suddenly rebounded from its wartime slump and the whores and the hustlers arrived in their droves to entertain and comfort *les braves Écossais*. Alas, it became quickly apparent that 50 per cent of our number had lied themselves blue in the face and did not know one end of a ski from another. We three, when not too busy whooping it up, became instructors.

The idyll lasted three short weeks before we were rushed back to England, rushed in huge discomfort up to Scotland, rushed aboard a troopship, rushed off again and rushed back down again to Bordon . . . where we were disbanded. The Germans or the Russians, I never knew which, had unsportingly done something during the interim which had destroyed our *raison d'être*.

★　　★　　★

There is in fact a very full description of the comedy of errors that was the 5th (Ski Regiment) Battalion, Scots Guards, to be found in *When the Grass Stops Growing*, written by another of those intrepid ski-volunteers, Carol Mather – who was later to fight alongside Geoff in the SAS raid on Benghazi in 1942. The volunteers, described in the regimental diary as 'men from all parts of the British Empire . . . Regulars, Territorials, veterans of the Spanish war, soldiers of fortune, undergraduates and all varying in age between twenty and forty', assembled at Aldershot on 5 February 1940.

There were famous polar explorers and mountaineers. The colonel was a noted expert on the Cresta Run, the infamous one-man, face-down ice run in St Moritz. There were a number of characters who were later to achieve fame in Special Forces, including a sergeant called David Stirling, later Colonel Stirling, legendary founder of the SAS. In fact, this was one of the first of many 'private' armies in the making and the young and very newly renamed Private Gordon-Creed had instinctively gravitated towards it.

However, and as Mather recalls, there were certain other 'issues' that first had to be overcome before the regiment would be capable of fighting anybody: being given only three weeks to form, train and organise before they shipped out was ludicrous; they had no radio sets; and it was only when they were finally issued with weapons that it was discovered that a number of the regiment had never even fired an army-issue Lee Enfield rifle. While many of them might have acquitted themselves in style in a skiing gala, the Ski Regiment was nowhere near ready to take on the Russians in the hostile and snowy wastelands of Finland.

A company of regular Scots Guards was then attached to the regiment, as a 'stiffener'. The only flaw with this cunning plan to introduce some professionalism was that it soon became all too apparent that, while these redoubtable warriors might be second to none when it came to soldiering, they had no idea how to ski.

Having finally made it to Chamonix, the Chasseurs Alpins threw a grand 'welcoming' reception for the Ski Battalion. It was not an unmitigated success. The regular jocks got heroically pissed and hijacked the microphone on the stage, singing 'Roll out the Barrel' and 'Kiss Me Goodnight, Sergeant Major'. Their hosts could not get their heads around the fact that some of their guests spoke French and drank wine, while others spoke no French, drank beer and got roaring drunk.

Geoff and his friends finally established that the *raison d'être* of the Ski Battalion was to fight alongside the Finns. But, and all too soon, it was what we used to call 'berets on, berets off', and back they came to Britain. Neutral Sweden had refused permission for the British to fly over her airspace – and thus risk being pulled into the war against the Russians – just as the Finns were also overwhelmed in what is now known as 'the Winter War'. The Ski Battalion was disbanded.

Disappointed and fed up we were given a week's leave and told to report to our various units – mine being 57th Heavy Training Regiment, Royal Armoured Corps, based at Warminster in Wiltshire, where we were to learn the rudiments of soldiering.

It was a nasty jar indeed being taken out from such a congenial outfit and being thrown back to the bottom of the military heap. Luckily, I soon discovered that my fellow soldiers were an honest, cheerful and friendly bunch of youngsters and all were volunteers like myself. As I was destined to live and train with them for two or three months before progressing to my Officer Cadet Training Unit – if I ever did – I decided I had better muck in and become one of the boys.

I did, and to my surprise I enjoyed the experience, even the endless drill. Our squad was soon transformed by our sergeant from a gaggle of buffoons into disciplined automatons who were able to perform their drill movements with great snap and precision.

I was only once in minor disgrace. In any squad there will always be one unfortunate whose reactions and reflexes are a little slow, ruining the whole, larger effect. Our poor bugger always tried his heart out but somehow was always that fraction of a second behind the rest of us. With our passing-out parade coming up fast, Sergeant O'Malley was becoming almost hysterical. For the tenth time that morning, poor Trooper Williams had failed to achieve perfection in some particular movement. Sergeant O'Malley, his face purple, his mouth working and his eyes popping, approached to within inches of the quivering Williams:

'Yew horrible hobject!' he screamed. 'I'm gonna piss in yore ear.'

That's when I laughed, with inevitable and horrible consequences . . .

Eventually, with my friend Mike Muir, another potential officer who had been on the same course, I received orders to report to an Officer Training Regiment, the Westminster Dragoons. More drill and bullshit, and tremendous pressure was laid upon all thirty of the cadets in our troop to excel. It was common knowledge that around 25 per cent of us would be rejected for one reason or another and so we worked our backsides off to pass our various tests: in military law, map-reading, administration, physical training and so on.

The course included four weeks at Bovington in Dorset learning driving and maintenance of tanks, and a further four weeks of tank gunnery at Lulworth, a few miles away. The summer of 1940 was one of the better ones weather-wise. France had fallen and air battles raged constantly above our heads. I felt fiercely envious of the RAF fighter pilots being able to do their thing while I was stuck in a classroom trying to fathom the mysteries of an epicyclic gearbox or the insides of some bloody tank carburettor.

However, the eight weeks turned out to be fun as well as hard work. Vast numbers of civilians had been evacuated from this south coast 'invasion' zone, and at the same time, typically, hundreds of typists and secretaries had been evacuated from bombed London and sent . . . guess where? Bournemouth, Dorset's principal resort town, where huge empty hotels were delighted to let their luxury suites to 'gentlemen cadets' for a very nominal sum.

I seem to recall an invasion false alarm late at night on 15 September. I was not so drunk that I did not register that all the church bells suddenly began to clang like mad and that there were loudspeakers bawling in the streets. But I also realised that I and my friends were in no condition to attempt the 25-mile drive back to where we ought to be. We would have been arrested at the first roadblock. We therefore did the only sensible thing and gave all our attention to activities of more immediate importance.

Came the dawn and the hangover, and all was calm and quiet. No Germans. How embarrassing it might have been, though – killed or captured 'in action', as it were.

The final eight weeks back in dreary Blackdown were the worst. Wireless exercises in trucks, simulated tank manoeuvres carried out in Bren carriers as there were no tanks. Night compass marches on which most of us got lost. Tests and more tests and the constant threat hanging over our heads: of being kicked out as unsuitable officer material. As predicted, over 25 per cent of our number were, in fact, RTU'd – returned to their units.

About ten days before the end of our nightmare and the passing-out parade, Mike and I had had enough. At noon on a Saturday, after the last parade, we sneaked out of barracks and drove up to London. We knew exactly where to go: the old Cavendish Hotel in Jermyn Street in London's West End where that famous character Rosa Lewis continued to defy the Blitz with a running champagne party in her parlour.

Enough has been written and televised about this unique and remarkable woman and I will only say that, having known me very, very slightly and my father rather well, she made us enormously welcome – as did the assembled company of brigadiers, colonels, lords and ladies, actresses and expensive tarts who came and went through the night.

Rosa was said to be the model for 'the Duchess', the cook-to-hotel-owner lead character in the 1970s TV series *The Duchess of Duke Street*. For a generation who will not have heard of her, she was clearly an 'eccentric's eccentric'. Born in 1867 – she must have been 73 when Geoff's visit took place – Rosa had long been famous for her cooking and had caught the eye of the future King Edward VII: one story has it that they had been lovers in the 1890s and that the newly enthroned King 'paid her off' by buying her the Cavendish Hotel in 1902. Richard Hillary wrote in *The Last Enemy*, his famous 1942 book about his experiences in the Battle of Britain, about visiting Rosa to commiserate after she had suffered a stroke:

'When we arrived, there she was, seventy-six years old, shrieking with laughter and waving a glass of champagne, apparently none the worse. She grabbed me by the arm and peered into my face. 'God, aren't you dead yet either, young Hillary? Come here and I'll tell you something. Don't you ever die. In the last two weeks I've been right up to the gates of 'eaven and 'ell and they're both bloody!' A few weeks later a heavy bomb landed right on the Cavendish, but Rosa emerged triumphant, pulling bits of glass out of her hair and trumpeting with rage. "Whatever else may go in this war, we shall still have Rosa Lewis and the Albert Memorial at the end."'

Back at the Cavendish Hotel . . .

⋆   ⋆   ⋆

Mike and I chummed up with two young officers from the 2ⁿᵈ Royal Gloucestershire Hussars who confided that they were, at that very moment, meant to be out in their vehicles on a detailed reconnaissance of the Isle of Sheppey.

The next day, after a night of debauchery during the course of which a largish bomb demolished a few unoccupied bedrooms of our hotel, we all got back together around a magnum or two of champagne. With the assistance of Rosa we helped the two young officers to compose what we agreed was an exceptional report calculated to satisfy the most pernickety of colonels.

Three days later, to our surprise and alarm, the Tannoy squawked: 'Cadets Gordon-Creed and Muir to report to the orderly room immediately.'

In great trepidation we reported and stood rigidly to attention.

'Ah . . . Good morning, Geoffrey. I've been looking forward to seeing you again. I am delighted that you'll be joining my regiment.'

I should explain that the previous year I had driven down to Colchester, where an uncle of mine was the general officer in charge of Eastern Command. I had ended up lunching in the officers' mess with the colonel of the 17/21ˢᵗ Lancers – my father's old regiment – and several of the officers, all of whom had been friendly and encouraging to a nervous and very shy youth. Of course I would be welcome, and they would keep in touch.

I gaped at the enormous man who greeted me and who I now recognised as having been the second-in-command of the 17/21ˢᵗ when I had visited them. He was wearing the same badges as those two pisscats I had last seen under the table at Rosa's. He had evidently been promoted and given a regiment of his own.

'Thank you, Sir,' I stammered, 'but I'm supposed to be joining the 17/21st.'

'Oh no you're not,' he rejoined. 'I was at the War Office this morning and it's all fixed up for you and your friend Muir to join my regiment in about two weeks' time. My two officers gave me excellent reports about you both.'

It later turned out that those silly bastards, to assuage their colonel's wrath at their pitiful recce report, had babbled something about having discovered 'valuable officer material'.

Kismet! Had this not happened I would have been stuck kicking my heels in England. Instead, I was whisked out to the Western Desert in October 1941 to take part in the desert campaign.

3

A pub lunch and a marriage

Mike and I reported to the 2nd Royal Gloucestershire Hussars in December 1940; 2 RGH – which I shall call them from here on in – was a yeomanry regiment.

Made up of 'weekend soldiers' during peacetime, yeomen fight as full-time soldiers during war, a tradition that started in the late 1700s when the threat of French invasion, coupled with typical crippling Treasury underfunding, meant there was a desperate need for emergency volunteers. The regiment had been in existence ever since, in the thick of the fighting in both the Boer War and the First War.

Some of the men were, of course, every bit as good as their regular counterparts: bright, multi-skilled free thinkers and each one of them every bit as brave. But, for all their keenness and skill, men who train on occasional weekday evenings, some weekends and once a year at a summer camp are going to be at a serious disadvantage against regular soldiers in battle, at least without a lot of extra training.

Soon after the war Stuart Pitman wrote an excellent regimental history, *Second Royal Gloucestershire Hussars, Libya–Egypt 1941–1942*. Pitman fought through the desert campaign with Geoff, and here he describes the effect on Lieutenant Colonel Charles Birley, late of the 17/21st Lancers, on taking command of 2 RGH in May 1940.

He found us unequipped and, therefore, only trained in the simplest military matters. He found it most difficult, if not impossible, to fathom, or indeed to cope with, the Yeomanry spirit and their light-hearted and friendly way of doing things. Their idea of military life and discipline was quite unlike any-thing in his experience of a regular cavalry regiment. He was haunted by a fear that something must be wrong, and that there would be a breakdown when the strain of fighting was put upon the structure. He wanted perfection, and he got it, but he did not realise it till he saw the Regiment in battle, for he failed to change the Yeoman outlook.

On the other hand, Geoff, with his instinctive dislike of authority, was perfectly suited to this informal style of lead-ership and soldiering, with its 'pleases' and 'thank yous' and 'would you be so kind as to go and do such and such' instead of direct orders.

The regular army has an annual training cycle. Low-level individual and troop training starts at the beginning of the year as you first get your troop of tanks to work as an effective unit. This leads up to squadron and then regimental exercises. With the regiment working well as a unit, the autumn sees brigade or divisional manoeuvres: an opportunity for all arms – cavalry, infantry, artillery, engineers, etc. – to train together and prac-tise and perfect their combined tactics. Every exercise tests the individual soldiers, NCOs and junior officers. The larger the exercise, the more senior the officers it tests. Just because an officer is senior does not mean that he and his staff are not just as badly in need of training and practice as the most junior driver.

Yeomanry regiments trained in their separate troops and squadrons throughout the year and only gathered together for regimental manoeuvres at their annual summer camp. They would not have practised fighting in brigade and division formations.

So none of those who had gathered for the RGH summer camp in July 1939 could have had any idea of the disparity in training and equipment there would be between them and the battle-hardened veterans of Rommel's Panzer battalions. With war so obviously imminent, and men desperate not to miss out on the chance of giving the old enemy another good kicking, over a thousand yeomen from the county of Gloucestershire and its surrounds reported for duty: this was in marked contrast to the three hundred or so that would normally turn up. The result of this abundance of manpower was that two regiments of RGH were formed. By being posted to 2 RGH, Second Lieutenant Geoff again pulled the right card: 1 RGH spent the war as a training and home defence regiment, although a stream of men were soon on their way to their sister regiment as casualty replacements.

There were three 'teeth' squadrons in 2 RGH and an HQ (headquarters) squadron, the latter responsible for such matters as supplying the forward troops with water, rations, fuel, ammunition and battlefield recovery and repair. Each squadron had four forward troops, each consisting of three tanks and commanded by a junior officer or senior NCO – in the army all soldiers understudy their immediate senior so that they can immediately take over that job if required – and a headquarters troop commanded by the squadron leader, a major.

Geoff was posted to 'H' squadron, 2 RGH.

After the frenetic atmosphere of Blackdown we found life very quiet. All we had to play with was a few old light tanks, some armoured cars, scout cars and a cruiser tank or two: hardly the intense preparation we should have been engaged in given what was ahead of us. The winter of 1940–1 was bitter but we were comfortably billeted by squadrons in the small village of Cranleigh in Surrey. I was soon bored stiff and gave serious thought to applying for transfer to the RAF or the Fleet Air Arm.

And there was the rub of it because, and as Geoff says, they should have been training hard for what was to come. But how could they? In summer 1940 the British Expeditionary Force had left much of its heavy equipment in France after its defeat and subsequent rout by the Germans. While Dunkirk was a miracle in terms of soldiers saved to fight another day, it was a catastrophe in terms of equipment and munitions lost. Not that, when it came to tanks, there were that many worth repatriating. Because, while the British in the First War had been every bit the equal of the Germans when it came to technology – and often their masters, for that matter – come 1939–40 the British were trying to play serious catch-up, and failing, especially when it came to tanks and anti-tank weapons.

In Afghanistan today individual skill and bravery, allied to infinitely superior space-age weapons systems, is much of what is holding the Taliban at bay. In 1940, the situation was reversed. It was the Germans who had the better weapons systems and tactics. At this stage of the war, whenever the British took on the Germans they got beaten, their heavy weapons systems invariably letting them down, and their piss-poor tactics only made a bad situation worse. When the British took on the Italians, they defeated them because the Italian tanks were as poor as their own, so it was a battle of courage and training: one the British usually won.

Not that Geoff and his men had any inkling of this. The British boffins had rushed into production a tank that was designated the Cruiser Mark VI: the Crusader, as it was called, although not by Geoff who for some reason always referred to it as a Cruiser.[1] The army genuinely believed it would be a

---

1 'Cruiser' was the designation given to all British fast 'medium' tanks from the mid-1930s right through till after the end of the war, as opposed to 'heavy' tanks designed to fight in support of the infantry or 'light' tanks that had more of a reconnaissance role. The Cruiser Mark VI – known as a Crusader – was but one in a longish line of Cruisers. This is why it is somewhat puzzling that Geoff refers to it as a Cruiser rather than a Crusader. But who am I to argue? He was the one who fought in them, not me.

match for the German Panzer Mark IIIs and IVs. Certainly, it looked the part: sleek and fast, although the tiny little 2-pounder gun should have been the giveaway as to how ineffectual it was to prove in battle. The German tanks, with their 75 mm guns and heavier armour, were a couple of levels better and, to make things even worse, in the German 88 mm anti-aircraft gun – which some bright spark had discovered was even more devastating when pointed horizontally against vehicles as opposed to vertically against aircraft – they had a battle-winning weapon that could destroy any Allied tank it was put up against right until the end of the war.

England in the winter of 1940–1 was the real world of *Dad's Army*. The Home Guard were watching the beaches and likely parachute drop points, and 2 RGH was on semi-permanent anti-invasion duties with little equipment and no time for proper tank training.

The general situation was summed up when Geoff was sent to umpire a Home Guard exercise. The scenario was that enemy parachutists had landed on a nearby hill. The participants were all ex-First War veterans. They were as keen as mustard, but instead of rifles they had been issued with pitchforks. It was only when those with the stamina to make it up the hill came to their final charge on to the objective that Geoff discovered that they were further improvising with bricks as hand grenades, with the inevitable bloody consequences for a badly concussed defender. It was amateur hour gone mad, and while funny on one level, desperately dispiriting on another.

Men like Geoff might well have been as fit as a butcher's dog but they did not have the weapons they needed to take their training the necessary stage further. When you train up a young man and then leave him idle, you are asking for trouble. There must have been many tens of thousands of Geoffs, kicking their heels and wondering what their masters thought they were up to. And all the while there was the grinding tedium of everyday army life in camp: 'blanco and bullshit', as soldiers say. 'If it moves salute it. If it doesn't move, paint it.'

Newly arrived and very junior officers are expected to behave themselves and treat their superiors with exaggerated respect, hardly Geoff's way of doing things. Failure to abide by the rules resulted in punishments: extra duties and tedious tasks designed to make you see the error of your ways and mould you into shape. Inevitably, Geoff soon got up to mischief.

New Year's Day 1941 was one of those rare days in England with sparkling frost and bright sunshine. A brother officer and I collected a driver, Trooper Morgan, and set off in the squadron's only Cruiser tank[2] to have lunch at the Hog's Back Hotel: quite a famous hostelry about twenty miles down the road. That particular tank was a prototype of those in which we eventually went to battle; it had an excellent turn of speed of around 40 mph – the official road speed was 27 mph but, by overriding the engine governor, a good driver could get 40 mph.

The three of us had a pub lunch washed down with several pints and then, feeling on top of the world, set off back for home.

'Give her the gun, Morgan,' I said. 'Let's see what she can do.'

He did. We roared through Guildford with sparks flying from the cobblestones. Mark and I, up in the turret with eyes and noses running, were ecstatic. On a long slow curve just out of town Morgan was driving superbly, his left track not quite nudging the curb and getting every ounce from his engine and gearbox.

---

2   The fact that the squadron had only one Cruiser – it should have had fifteen – demonstrates not only what a desperate situation British forces would have been in as regards equipment had the Germans invaded, but also how little training they were able to undertake in preparation for what was to hit them in North Africa.

I am almost sure that Morgan would have missed the motorcyclist – just – but the juggernaut roaring up behind him quite unnerved the poor fellow. His machine jumped the curb and ran down a steep slope into an oak tree. His front wheel buckled, his bowler-hatted head whacked into the tree and he bounced back on to the crossbar, landing on his balls. The poor sod, bent over in agony, had just enough strength to shake his fist as we roared on our way shouting: 'Happy New Year.'

'Morgan,' I said, 'I think you had better slow down a bit. I don't think I could stand any more excitement today.'

'I didn't hurt him, Sir, did I?' asked Morgan, a kindly soul.

'No, no, not at all, though he may have hurt himself just a little . . . but there you are, we live in dangerous times.'

There being nothing much to do as the regiment had practically no equipment, the young officers were routinely sent off on courses to get them out of the way.

I did not get along with the adjutant – an ex-regular officer and in charge of discipline within the regiment – but for that matter neither did most people. He sent me off on an anti-gas course somewhere in the wilds of Yorkshire. It was a dreary affair conducted in maximum discomfort by sadists. On being required to remove my gas mask in a room filled with some noxious substance that simulated phosgene, just for the pleasure of experiencing a roaring headache, I politely declined.

'I believe you,' I said, 'when you tell me that the stuff smells like geraniums. But I don't need another headache . . . I already have one from last night.'

I failed the gas course. With ignominy.

Colonel Charles was not best pleased and promptly had me sent off on a messing officers' course. This was held at the Army Catering School, just outside London, and was supposed to last ten days. I was fed up. I had not volunteered to join the army to count prunes and peer into murky cooking pots and so, having signed in, I promptly left for the fleshpots of the Big City. When I returned to the Catering School it was exactly as I had hoped and expected: no one had appeared to have missed me! To my dismay, however, I learned that on the morrow I was expected to take a practical test and prepare a meal for a company of soldiers.

The hell with it. I took the prunes, the disgusting liver, the potatoes and the powdered eggs and stuffed the lot into a large pot to stew with the powdered milk and water.

I failed that course also.

Colonel Charles was very miffed once again and the blasted adjutant was positively savage. There were dire threats of sending me on a physical training course – considered just half a step better than being gaoled.

In the nick of time, however, just as the army and I were about to fall out, things suddenly started to happen, and happen fast. First, at the end of May, we were moved to Warminster and shiny new Cruiser tanks and transports arrived. There we were ordered to form a brigade with two other regiments, the 3rd and 4th County of London Yeomanry, and carried out exercises of enormous futility and confusion – inevitable when the regiments had not been able to train together at low level, let alone at brigade level. The brigadier and his colonels were only now, and on their way to a war, trying to work out how to operate together. Meanwhile, the crewmen were trying to get the hang of the workings and idiosyncrasies of their brand new tanks.

Very suddenly again, because things were going badly for us in the North African desert, we were given a week's embarkation leave.

To the dismay of Colonel Charles, who found himself standing *in loco parentis*, I got married at eleven o'clock on the morning of my last day of leave and left my new wife two hours later, not to see her again for almost three years. If any son of mine at the age of 21 were to do such a thing, I would feel like shooting the idiot or at least have him committed.

4

The Gods of the desert

'Driver . . . halt.'

'Gunner . . . traverse left.' Wait for the gunner to find the target. 'ON!'

'Enemy tank, range 800, 2-pounder. FIRE!' Carefully observe fall of shot.

'Miss.' Work out necessary correction to land the next shell on target.

'Up 50 . . . FIRE!' Observe target.

'HIT! FIRE!' Give the enemy tank a second shell to finish it off. 'Enemy destroyed. Driver advance.'

The above drivel was more or less the correct sequence of a tank commander's fire orders to his gunner as taught at the Gunnery School at Lulworth, on the Dorset coast, in 1940. I would dearly love to have seen some of those gunnery instructors exposed to the realities of tank warfare in North Africa in 1941 and 1942.

I am sure that it is all very different nowadays but, at the time about which I am writing, a tank commander in the desert, sitting in one of our tanks, had more than a few problems vis-à-vis his German counterpart. True, we often outnumbered our enemy by three to one, but our losses were always three to one against. And that was because we never had a gun mounted on our tanks worth a damn. Our 37 and 40 mm guns were up against the Germans and their 50, 75 and 88 mm calibre weapons. Popguns versus real cannons. And our 35 to 45 mm thickness of defensive armour plate was no match compared to their 45 to 65 mm. Our tank guns could penetrate the side plates, but only the side plates, of a German Mark III 'medium' tank at a maximum range of about 800 yards – 500 yards was more like it. But they could not penetrate their front armour.

Their guns could punch holes in our tanks, front or side. They could do just the same at 800 yards and to 1000 yards plus from their Mark III and IV Panzers. Once their 88 mm anti-tank guns got involved it got a whole load worse: they could smash through 150 mm of armour at 2000 yards and could fire fifteen to twenty rounds a minute. The German 88 mm was a tank-killer. In short, we were hopelessly outgunned and out-armoured.

Fortunately or unfortunately, we were in blissful ignorance of these facts when we arrived in Egypt on 1 October 1941. We were the first brigade to be entirely equipped with the brand new Cruiser Mark VI tank. We had high hopes of what we, and they, would achieve.

We had enjoyed an astonishing trip out east in our fast convoy of ex-luxury liners, cargo ships and escorts. With the Mediterranean now sometimes little better than an Axis Powers lake, the only reasonably safe way of getting to Egypt – barring an unfortunate meeting with German U-boats – was the long way: 12,000 miles south-west, deep into the North Atlantic, before heading south-east and all the way round Africa, up to the Red Sea and, finally, the Suez Canal. It was a voyage that normally took ten to twelve weeks. We did it in eight.

We had travelled 'de luxe' on HM Troopship *Strathmore* – two travellers to a four-berth cabin – and had dined formally wearing mess kit in an air-conditioned saloon, on an only slightly amended pre-war first class menu. We had swilled the finest champagnes, and even Rhine wines, and had caroused far into the night with vulgar singsongs, poker and bridge games.

We had had a three-day stopover in Cape Town – three days that will remain in every man's memory for as long as he lives. The simple kindness, the hospitality, the warmth and enthusiasm of those South Africans was astonishing and heart-warming.

Came the dawn, and a thoroughly soggy regiment found itself disembarked at Port Tewfik at the southernmost end of the Suez Canal. A bombed and sunken troopship lying in the roads reminded us that there was indeed a war and an enemy not too far away. Apart from the wreck there were only a few scruffy buildings, billions of flies, hundreds of scrofulous Egyptian stevedores and, as far as one could see, just miles and miles of sweet FA.

It dawned on me then, for the first time, the need for trained staff officers who would know what to do next, how to organise the shambles. In no time at all, and miraculously to an innocent like me, the entire brigade, together with its transport and supporting services, was trundling northwards by road and rail a hundred miles or more to a desert campsite at El Amiriya, just to the south-west of Alexandria, on the Mediterranean coast. No man missed a meal. Three days were permitted to set up our tents and organise ourselves. Then desert training began in earnest.

The regiment, at full strength, comprised fifty-two Mark VI Cruiser tanks organised into three fighting squadrons: prefixed F, G and H, each with fifteen tanks. The Headquarters Squadron (HQ Squadron) had seven tanks and loads of lorries.

Each fighting squadron comprised four tank troops and a headquarters troop. Each troop consisted of three tanks. I was the 3 Troop commander of 'H' Squadron, and very proud I was of my small command. Each 'H' Squadron tank was named: Hotspur, Hengist, Hannibal and so on, after ancient heroes. But not mine. My personal tank I had painted with the name 'l'Hirondelle': the Swallow. The Cruiser Mark VI was, after all, swift and graceful to look at.

Our tanks had to be fitted with special air-filters and had to be camouflaged – painted in desert yellow and browns. We had to learn the art of navigation by sun compass and to learn how to exist with minimal food and water. We also learned how to cope with sandstorms, to recognise this and ignore that, and to accept the endless crap and discomfort with good grace because it was all pointing to the one single fact: we had been rushed out to Egypt to be in time to take part in a great offensive that would finally clear the enemy from North Africa.

Egypt had long been a British zone of control; Libya, to the west, was Italian. Mussolini had attacked Egypt from Libya in September 1940. The British first held the Italians and then counter-attacked in December 1940. By 5 February 1941 the British had cleared the Italians from much of North Africa, captured the key port of Tobruk and taken upwards of 140,000 Italian prisoners. It looked as if the war in North Africa was all but over.

But Hitler had other ideas. On 12 February 1941, Rommel arrived to take command of the Afrika Korps. On 31 March he attacked, and the British were soon in full retreat. By April we were back where we started, on the Egypt–Libya border. But Rommel had not taken Tobruk, which continued to hold out well to his rear and which threatened his long supply line: it was 1400 miles from Tripoli – the great Axis supply port, far to the west – to Alexandria, the main British port in Egypt. He had to retake Tobruk before he could turn his attentions to Egypt and, from there, move on to seize the vital oilfields of the Middle East.

Conversely, the British understood the danger, and were determined that Rommel should not have that great port city.

Come summer 1941, while Geoff and 2 RGH were kicking their heels in England on anti-invasion duties, there was fierce but inconclusive fighting in the Western Desert. With Rommel's supply lines about nine hundred miles long and Tobruk holding out, he could not muster enough men and fuel to attack the British in any meaningful way. The fuel trucks themselves used up an inordinate amount of the supplies they were carrying.

However, two major British counter-attacks in May and June 1941 ended in defeat, broken on the anvil of the Germans' superior tactics and weaponry. The stalemate was too much for Churchill, who sacked his commander and replaced him with General Claude Auchinleck, the 'Auk', who was told to create a new army: the Eighth Army.

The Auk started a build-up of men and equipment in preparation for his great offensive to relieve Tobruk. Come November 1941, Operation Crusader was finally ready to roll and 2 RGH was part of it.

Considering the short time we had available we achieved a certain competence in the basics. I, for one, could hardly wait for action: Second Lieutenant Gordon-Creed, proudly in command of his three tanks, stood poised and ready to wreak havoc upon his contemptible foes.

Second Lieutenant Gordon-Creed got his wish when, after just over a month of desert training, 22nd Armoured Brigade joined 7th Armoured Division: the Desert Rats. Starting at the frontier wire between Egypt and Libya, we were to advance into Libya as the left-hook element in a general offensive by the Eighth Army against well-dug-in Germans and Italians. The plan was for us to advance west and then north-west in a semi-circle towards Tobruk, which had by then been under siege for seven long months. At the same time the garrison was to break out and join us.

I would not bore you with the tedious details of our approach march, but on a certain chilly evening in November – 18

November to be precise – we learned that, on the morrow, we were committed in brigade strength to attack the Italian Ariete Armoured Division, twice our strength in numbers, which was dug in around Bir el Gubi. We were given a briefing by the brigade intelligence officer, who told us that the only tank that might worry us was the German Mark IV. But not to worry, there were only twenty of them in North Africa. The German Mark IIs and IIIs and the Italian M13s would present no problem.

Was I nervous and apprehensive that night? Of course I was. How would I behave under fire? Would I be killed – or worse, maimed? I lay awake and worried.

As I recall it was not until about nine the following morning, after we had been deployed in line of battle, three squadrons up and one held back in reserve, that dear old Charles Birley, the ex-17/21st Lancer and our colonel – remember the man who had 'volunteered' me into 2 RGH in the first place? – forgetting everything that he was supposed to have learned about modern war tactics, came up on the air. 'Royal Gloucestershire Hussars,' he trumpeted, 'the enemy are in front of you. You will attack and destroy them . . . Charge!' His voice rose to a scream. 'CHARGE!'

No mention, you might notice, of what we were supposed to be charging. Tanks? Dug-in anti-tank guns? Minefields? How far to go and when to stop? Just minor details, albeit of considerable interest to us. So . . . charge we did, and a very brave sight it must have been.

However, in those days a tank commander could see very little out of his periscope and I, like everyone else, was charging along with my head stuck well above the turret in order to see where I was going.

I became shortly aware of machine-gun tracer bullets approaching me from all angles and ducked down inside the turret, but not before I had been nicked through the very top of my scalp. Still, exhorted by my colonel I pressed on, and suddenly there were enemy tanks milling around – dozens of them, it seemed, and at short range.

'Driver . . . halt.' I remembered that much. Then: 'Gunner, can you see the buggers?'

'Yes, Sir.'

'Then shoot the sods!'

He destroyed two in short order, set another smoking and was about to administer the *coup de grâce* when there came a bang and my tank gave a violent swerve to the left.

I called my driver over the intercom. 'What the hell's up?'

'I think the left track 'as gorn, Sir.'

'Shit! Try to keep her moving or we're gorn.'

Scarcely had I spoken when a 50 mm shell pierced the turret with a hell of a bang. It smashed through my gunner's shoulder, ricocheted off the firing mechanism of our 2-pounder gun and ripped up the back of my loader/wireless operator, who was twisted around reaching for another shell. A three-inch steel splinter went deep into my thigh, although I was unaware of this until hours later when I tried to drop my pants.

Instant and total chaos – and no intercom working inside the tank.

The turret happened to be traversed to the seven o'clock position, back over the engine decks, when we were hit, which was fortunate as there was just a sufficient gap between the turret and the driver's compartment for me to yell at him to stop floundering around and bail out. While I was down another shell came through the turret higher up. I grabbed a hand grenade and the first aid box and hurled myself up and out of the tank and on to the sand. My first intent was to escape a death trap and then, somehow, to extricate my two desperately wounded men.

Outside, hugging Mother Earth, the noise, dust and

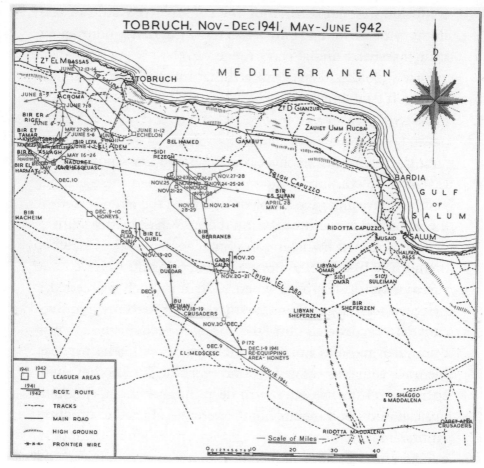

As the eleven day battle progressed the route of 2 RGH on this battle map looks like that of an increasingly demented spider. Stuart Pitman who fought with Geoff and who drew this map, on explaining why it looked so confusing said of his maps: 'They are not, however, anything like the muddle experienced at the time.'

confusion were horrendous. A limping Italian M13 tank drove slowly past me about thirty yards away and its commander, seeing me lying there, reached down and lobbed a grenade at me. He should not have done that. It went off with a flash and a bang. It frightened me witless and enraged me to the extent that I took pleasure, when his tank stalled a few yards further on, in sprinting across the sand, hopping aboard and dropping my grenade down his turret . . . blowing them all to hell! Live and let live, say I.

My driver, Trooper Parker, and I had a hard time getting the wounded loader and gunner out. We managed by dint of giving them near-lethal injections of morphine and I patched them up as best I could until our medical officer arrived and carted them off. Surprisingly, they both survived.

I got a corporal in the Rifle Brigade to hitch up his Bren carrier to my broken track, which I had located about a hundred yards from where we had finished up, and had him tow the track to within a few yards of l'Hirondelle. Murrow and I spent the entire night manhandling the swine, link by link, until we had got it repaired and reassembled on the sprockets. At first light we limped eastwards for about ten miles and, by good fortune, fell in with our brigade.

Our foolhardy charge had cost us eighteen tanks, four officers killed and six wounded, twenty-six of the men killed or missing and sixteen wounded.

So Geoff won an 'immediate' Military Cross on his first day in action, and a 'good' one at that. His citation read:

On 19/11/41 at El Gubi this Officer led his troop into action with great dash against Italian tanks. After having his tank hit and a track broken he continued to move around in circles on one track and knocked out two Italian tanks at point-blank range [note the different sequence of events to his later recollection]. His own tank was hit again through the turret and his gunner and wireless operator were both wounded … this Officer and his driver stayed out and repaired the tank although under artillery fire. They worked all night and brought in the tank at first light. Since then, in further action this Officer has shown great keenness and devotion to duty.

Stuart Pitman's regimental history has a more colloquial account of the incident:

Second-Lieutenant Gordon-Creed lost a track early on. It was clean broke by a shell and in his [Geoff's] own words: 'We roared round in a circle with two Wops chasing us. It was frightful, because my turret was traversing so fast I did not know which way I was facing, and everyone was shooting at me, too damn close to hit each other.' However Second-Lieutenant Gordon-Creed cannot have been as confused as he makes out. Both the enemy tanks perished with all their crews before he stopped his gyrations. His driver was wounded and had his leg shattered. Trooper Lee was hit in the head by a machine-gun bullet when getting out. Second-Lieutenant Gordon-Creed dealt with the leg himself and did it so effectively that the medical men complimented his skill.

Pitman also reports that 2 RGH had apparently destroyed seventy Italian tanks and the colonel had won a DSO. With his tank out of action, Colonel Birley had climbed on to the back of the second-in-command's vehicle so as to continue to command the action. Under constant fire he had been wounded, his arm badly broken, but had stayed on until the battle was over.

But 2 RGH now knew their tanks for what they were. As Pitman reports, early on in the action: 'Corporal Harmer came up and displayed four holes in his tank. This distressed us as we had not realised that our beautiful tanks could be penetrated so easily.' And, of course, these were only the Italian M13s they were up against. The German Panzers were to prove to be very much more dangerous.

By the end of that first day the remnants of 2 RGH regrouped near to where they had started. They had lost thirty tanks and were now down to squadron strength. However, and this was to be one of the features of the Desert War, they immediately began to reconstitute themselves. That night alone they managed to recover ten damaged vehicles from the battlefield. As long as a tank had not been burnt out or captured – and the Germans and Italians, themselves desperate for equipment and supplies, readily reused captured tanks, trucks and munitions – it could usually be repaired. Where possible, all abandoned vehicles were towed back, either for repair or, if too badly damaged to be put back into action, to be cannibalised for parts. Remnants of one crew were paired with survivors of others. A stream of replacement crews and vehicles arrived at the front. Troops and squadrons were re-formed overnight and the regiment would prepare itself for another day of battle and further losses.

This was to be day one of the horrendous eleven-day battle of Bir el Gubi. From this moment Geoff's memoir ceases to mention dates or places, and a look at Pitman's contemporary battle maps in the 2 RGH history shows why: it is as if the route of the regiment has been drawn by an increasingly demented spider (see map). As the Germans attacked from the flanks and from behind – from everywhere – 2 RGH moved forwards, backwards and then round in circles, initially over large distances of some hundreds of miles and then into a confused mass of positions and counter-positions. Pitman in his book says the routes shown on the map of the attack on Tobruk are 'muddling' and adds: 'They are not, however, anything like the muddle experienced at the time.'

The Germans, it later turned out, were as confused as the British. Outnumbered, they too often thought they were about to be overwhelmed. On one famous occasion, fighting done for the day, the German main headquarters[1] of the Afrika Korps

---

1 While each army had its main HQ way to the rear – the British in Cairo – their fighting headquarters were mobile and were often to be found just behind the front lines. Obviously they had radios in 1941, but the technology was still relatively

settled down for the night in the middle of nowhere. A New Zealand infantry brigade on a night march got lost and, finding the camp, it too settled down for a badly needed night's sleep. It was only after breakfast, when everyone was getting ready for another day of fighting, that the New Zealanders to their delight and the Germans to their horror discovered that the Korps headquarters was in the middle of their position. The Afrika Korps lost all their wireless vehicles and cipher staff.

By the end of that battle, however, 2 RGH had learned what they were in for. The Germans attacked as co-ordinated units: armoured recce and infantry tasked with finding the Allied positions and destroying their anti-tank guns.

While German tanks fired solid shot for use against tanks, they also fired high explosive shells for use against artillery, trucks and infantry. The British tanks were only issued with solid shot, so even when they did manage to spot a dug-in anti-tank gun and get close enough to fire at it they could not blow it up. Machine-gunning the crew or physically running over the gun was the only solution, otherwise the crews hid in their trenches till the British tanks had swept past and, often as not, took them out from behind. It is an old army maxim: 'Tanks can take ground, only infantry can hold ground' and our tank regiments at this time were unsupported by infantry. It was rotten tactics, no more, no less.

Much as King William the Conqueror's Norman knights had done to such devastating effect at the Battle of Hastings, when the British tank regiments did attack, the German tanks would turn and flee, leaving the British with little option but to chase after them and, all too often, straight into pre-prepared positions of German anti-tank guns, which then knocked out the British

---

basic and commanders needed to be able to see for themselves just what was going on. 'Good' generals have, throughout history, needed to see for themselves what is really happening and dislike relying too much on what their subordinates tell them. That is why good generals can and do get themselves killed or captured.

tanks at long range. It was only later, when the British were in retreat and moved into armoured 'boxes' – combinations of dug-in infantry, artillery and tanks – that the German losses began to pile up. Certainly, they continued to eradicate the British armour, but they began to take ever heavier casualties themselves. These casualties could only be replaced by convoys sent across the Mediterranean – bombed by the RAF from Malta and attacked by British submarines – to Tripoli. From there it was 900 long miles to the front. It was the length of that frail German logistics line that was keeping the British in the war.

The tanks fanned out from the *laager*[2] well before first light. The beginning of another day in the desert was always a pretty hateful procedure, at least for me. At the worst, one had fought an engagement on the previous day; had buried one's dead if there had remained anything left of them to bury; had taken up a defensive *laager* formation at last light. The Germans liked to attack out of the setting sun and when the sun was in our eyes. One had refuelled and replenished ammunition; had eaten a meal of bully and biscuit; had gratefully swallowed a mug of hot sweet tea; had attended the CO's Orders; and had set watches and posted sentries. One had seen one's men safely bedded down, had collapsed into one's own blankets around midnight and had probably received a few anti-personnel bombs from a German night fighter.

A few hours later, with gritty eyes and gritty teeth, you climbed into your tank and took your troop or squadron, as the case may be, a thousand yards or so out into the desert, there to remain at full alert to await developments.

---

2   *Laager*: a square formation affording all-round defence and used by armoured regiments at night. The lorries and soft-skinned vehicles were parked in the centre, the armour on the perimeter. The word is Dutch – like the word 'commando', for irregular guerrilla fighters – and was used during the Boer War to describe the Boers' square defensive formations: they used wagons instead of tanks, of course.

Meanwhile your 'eyes', the armoured car regiment attached to your brigade, had debouched farther afield and their reports of enemy presence or otherwise would start coming in over the air as soon as there was light enough to see. This was the worst time, the time of waiting to know if one was expected to fight another bloody battle, unshaven and on an empty stomach. I have never pretended to bravery, but with a fresh shave and something hot in my belly, I am as good as some, I daresay.

On a lucky day the sun came up and the armoured cars had nothing of immediate interest to report. Over the air, from the colonel would come the blessed signal: 'Brew up.'

We would tumble out of our tanks and set about our business. On a water ration of one gallon per man per day, for all purposes, one had learned to be more than parsimonious. Each tank, with a four-man crew, would make a fire in a can filled with sand soaked in petrol and proceed to boil up precisely four pints of water. At the right time in would go a palmful of tea leaves, followed by half a can of evaporated milk and a palmful of sugar. While this was being gratefully drunk, another pot containing about a pint of water, two cans of bully and four mashed-up ship's biscuits was being heated into a mush known as 'biscuit burgoo'. After this gourmet meal, a further two pints of water were heated up for shaving and ablutions.

Finally, before we felt ready to take on the Afrika Korps again, there remained one of the few untaxed pleasures left in life – the all-important good crap!

With us it was a natural and uninhibited function. One strolled off into the desert for a few yards with a couple of feet of paper and a shovel – it was known as 'going on a shovel recce' – dug a little hole, squatted down and made one's offering to the gods of the desert.

Nobody gave it a thought excepting Colonel Charles, an enormously tall man, stupidly brave and painfully shy. This was not for him. With the sun well up and having reassured himself that no action was pending, he would stealthily hop into his staff car and drive himself off a safe distance, about a mile from his regiment. He would dismount, look cautiously around and then proceed to do what the rest of us had done.

Bless him – he had forgotten all about the mirage effect.

While the entire regiment hugged itself with glee, its colonel daily performed his office while appearing about forty feet high and *upside down*! As my squadron leader said, with tears of pure joy running down his cheeks: 'Dear old Charles . . . He was ever a shy shitter.'

5

Honeys, boxes and cruisers

The next few days were spent in confused movement as the Germans smashed the neighbouring 4th and 7th Brigades. After a week they had almost been wiped out. Pretty much the only armour still fighting was 22 Brigade, of which the remnants of 2 RGH were part. The Germans, meanwhile, at times had over a hundred tanks concentrated together and they destroyed anything they came across. Not only were the British outgunned and outclassed, now they were also outnumbered. Losses of men and tanks continued to mount. Come 1 December, the remnants of 2 RGH were withdrawn and the regiment was re-formed: they were 170 miles farther east – towards their own lines – than when they had started eleven long and bloody days earlier.

Over the next few months we fought numerous engagements, some small, others large. In some we acquitted ourselves quite well and in others we got trounced.

Thank God we no longer essayed any more charges in the Light Brigade tradition, yet steadily our losses mounted: two colonels, including dear old Charles; two second-in-commands; two adjutants; three squadron leaders; eleven troop leaders and God knows how many tanks and men. I was shot out of three tanks, and on one occasion was the only survivor.

In a tank battle there is seldom such a thing as a slight wound, owing to the weight of metal being thrown at you. There was also, of course, the hazard of fire – relatively slow

if only the fuel tanks went up, but if a shell set off your ammunition you were usually toast. It happened to me once. It was
an 88 mm gun that did it. I was actually aware of the shell
coming and had started to jump as it hit. My tank simply
detonated and I was blown clear. I flew about twenty feet and
landed on my shoulders. I lay in the sand and watched the
entire turret sail into the air and then come crashing down
towards me. It pitched about six feet from me, teetered – and
fell the other way. The rubber soles of my boots were afire. I
was dithering and in no condition to resist when I was shortly
afterwards made prisoner by a sergeant of the German 90th
Light Division.

I was the guest of my captors for a day and was then handed
over to the Italians. I joined a group of about seventy other
British prisoners, odds and sods for the most part. Unlike the
Germans in the desert, the Italians were usually perfectly
bloody towards prisoners of war. We got nothing to eat and
very little to drink. We were screamed at and abused by little
runts for whom we had nothing but contempt.

The third night was dark, cold, wet and miserable. We prisoners huddled together for warmth while our guards, fewer
than a dozen, positioned themselves in a rough circle around
us.

At around 9 p.m. I staggered out a few yards towards one
of the sentries, clutching my belly and groaning. He raised
his rifle and shouted something but I ignored him, dropped
my pants and made realistic dysentery noises through my
mouth. Twenty minutes later and thereafter for two hours, I
repeated the charade, finally appearing to become so weak
that I crawled out on all fours. 'Gippy tummy', as we called
it, was a terrible affliction and I suspected that my Italian
had been a sufferer in his time. In any event, after my sev-
enth and eighth trips out I could sense that he was much less
vigilant.

Around midnight, groaning piteously, I crawled out, got set and ran like hell out into the night, dodging like a rabbit.

There were loud shouts and bang . . . bang-bang, and I ran. Lord, how I ran! I ran until my heart was bursting and until I crashed into a slit trench and knocked the remaining wind out of myself.

So I escaped by using a ploy which I thereafter dubbed 'the tactical shit'.

I lay and froze all night, and at dawn watched the enemy column move off westwards. I collected myself and started to walk east and, six hours later, fell in with one of our armoured car patrols.

I had already been reported 'Missing, believed killed in action' and consequently went without pay for two months until the bureaucrats managed to untie themselves. It irritated the hell out of me.

On 1 December, we were re-formed: after eleven days' fighting we needed sixteen officers and seventy other ranks to make up our losses. While by no means all the casualties were from the front-line tanks – our echelon trucks were bombed and shot up with monotonous regularity – the vast majority were. Given that there were only ever at best fifty-two tanks in a regiment, each with a four-man crew, that meant there was only ever a maximum of 208 men at the sharp end. We had lost near on 50 per cent of our 'front-line' men in those first eleven days. Not that it was to get much better in the weeks and months to follow.

But this time instead of getting our familiar Cruisers as replacements the regiment was re-equipped with fifty-two American M3 Stuart light tanks, popularly known as 'Honeys'. God knows why, as it was more of the same. They mounted only a tiny 37 mm gun and carried light armour, although I later gathered that some were impressed by its turn of speed and reliability. That last was at least an improvement on our

Cruisers, which used to overheat and break down with monotonous regularity. The Honeys' best feature was their pair of belt-fed .30 Browning machine-guns, which, although dating from the First World War, were highly accurate and usually reliable. In addition they had a third Browning mounted on top of the turret in an anti-aircraft role.

We received them on 5 December, moved up into a reserve position on the 9th and were in action by the 12th. Any regiment changing their tanks might reasonably expect to spend at least a month or more 'conversion' training as crewmen learned first how to use and then how to get the best out of their new machines and adapt their tactics accordingly. It is a testament to the ingenuity and good humour of the yeomen that they did this in a matter of days.

We had never seen these machines close up and were not enchanted to discover that there was no intercom system in them and that only one wireless transmitter was available per squadron. But worst and most criminal of all, there were no telescopic sights for the gun. Because of some logistical balls-up, these had been left behind somewhere. Where the all-important gunsight was supposed to be, there was just a small round hole through the armour plating. Within a few days we would be expected to take these tanks into battle against a better armed, better armoured enemy.

My squadron leader, Douglas Reinhold, was one of those exceptional men: brave, gentle and considerate. I loved and admired him and would have followed him anywhere.

'What the hell are we supposed to do, Duggie?' I asked him glumly. 'Just bang away in the general direction, I suppose, using the machine-gun tracers for sighting? Perhaps the Krauts will get so horrified by the noise that they'll just bugger off!'

He laughed. 'Well, perhaps the bloody sights will catch up

with us before anything too ghastly happens. We can always *CHARGE!* Don't forget.'

'Christ!' I said. 'Don't mention that word.'

Three days later, H Squadron, 2nd Royal Gloucestershire Hussars, found itself detached from the rest of the regiment and sent off – as part of a mixed column of guns and motorised infantry – on a long left-hook march westwards across the desert. We were ordered to cut off enemy formations, reputedly in retreat. Our destination was a spot on the map south of Benghazi, far to the west, named Anterlat. From there, an escarpment fell steeply away down to the coastal plain with its road, running north and south.

The march provided me with a moment of enormous satisfaction.

Bumming along one morning with one other tank, and far ahead of the column, I suddenly became aware of two German ME 109Fs – the latest clipped-wing jobs – flying around. I was sitting perched on top of my turret in an effort to avoid the dust and was supporting myself by clinging on to the .30 Browning on top of the turret. As they flew close I waved to them cheerfully and, much to my surprise, saw one of the pilots slide back his canopy, tip his wings and wave back. I hopped on the back of my tank and, standing behind the Browning, loaded and cocked it.

The fighter circled and approached me from head on at nought feet – buzzing. I admit to rather a funny feeling in my water when I looked straight down his guns as he roared up, but managed a few waves with my left hand while my right hand held steady on the trigger. As he screamed up I squirted off and he flew right through my tracers. His plane wobbled violently and emitted clouds of a white vapour. His engine cut out and he belly-landed in a cloud of dust about a mile away. I jumped back inside my turret just in time to avoid a salvo of 20 mm cannon fire from the other chap. When he had gone, we motored up to the wreck and pulled the pilot clear. He was literally weeping with rage.

He was the Luftwaffe equivalent of a group captain. He was an ace: a *Ritterkreutztrag* (Knight's Cross holder)[1] with twenty-seven victories to his credit. It was his first day in the desert with his new command, and he had assumed we were retreating Italians.

It was all so damned unfair! He could not believe it! He sat and sulked on the back of my tank for three days while we hooted.

Duggie called together all his tank commanders to discuss the best tactics should we find ourselves committed to an engagement with no way of aiming our guns. The regiment had already lost nine tanks that day to anti-tank guns and he himself had had a near-miraculous escape. Driving to the rescue of the crew of a knocked-out and burning tank whose crew had bailed out and stood to be captured or machine-gunned, he took a hit to the driver's compartment and his driver was killed. However, his vehicle continued to motor on, straight at the enemy guns. Trooper Rich, the driver of the burning vehicle, somehow managed to jump on to Duggie's still moving tank, scramble his way into the driver's seat and turn the vehicle around. Having then gone back to rescue his own stranded crew, Trooper Rich drove everyone to safety: he very deservedly won the MM [Military Medal].

'Seems to me,' Duggie said, 'that our best bet would be to stay closer to each other than usual and all fire at the nearest targets – if we get enough lead in the air we should score a good many hits. As you know I have the only

1   *Ritterkreutztrag*: the full title was Knight's Cross of the Iron Cross, an award for extreme battlefield bravery or outstanding leadership. While almost six million Iron Crosses were awarded during World War II, only 7,313 Knight's Crosses were awarded.

wireless transmitter set. I'll be flying a red pennant and it'll be up to you to keep an eye on it and conform to my movements. Broadly speaking our role will always be to attack from the flanks while the rest of the column, the guns and so on, bang away at the centre of anything we find ourselves tackling.'

I glanced across at him with a question and froze with horror. As plainly as I see the words I am now writing, I saw death in Duggie's face. It is hard to describe. The features in some subtle way appear to be more finely drawn and there is an aura of remoteness and melancholy. He caught me staring at him and I hurriedly dropped my eyes. 'You have a question, Geoff?'

'No, Duggie,' I muttered. 'No, it's OK.'

God, I felt awful. And afraid. You see, on two previous occasions I had experienced the same thing with close friends, both of whom had lost their lives within twenty-four hours.

At last light we got orders to move down the escarpment about five miles to a point from which our armoured recce cars had been watching a column of German tanks and transport. We were guided down in pitch darkness by a Rifle Brigade officer in a Jeep and told that, come first light, we could expect to see the enemy within 1000 yards.

That was a miserable bloody night. Cold as hell with nothing hot to eat or drink and no lights, of course. Just waiting out the long hours, alone with one's morbid thoughts. About 5 a.m., and it was still too dark to see, I heard the ominous rumble of heavy diesels starting up. They sounded unpleasantly close. I strained my eyes through my binoculars and gradually, as the dawn sky lightened, began to make out shapes of tanks and trucks at a range of only about 400 yards. I looked across to Duggie's tank, about forty yards away to my right, to signal by gesture that I was going to open up. He beat me to it with a bang from his 37 mm.

I told my gunner to begin by concentrating with the Browning on the trucks while we had the chance and before their tanks got into the act. There ensued a notable fusillade from our twelve Honeys, which caused a good deal of damage and dismay to our surprised enemy in the shape of several of his large trucks taking fire from our tracers. He was ready with his tanks, however, and in no time the fire from his Mk IIIs was making things hot for us. I was aware of one of our Honeys going up almost immediately, but was too busy concentrating with my gunner, trying to direct his fire on to the nearest Mk III, to pay more than passing attention. We certainly hit him a few times and I saw our shells ricochet off him.

I lost all sense of time and I was still blazing away when I noticed that I seemed to be receiving more than my fair share of attention. I risked a quick peek out of the turret to see where Duggie was and was alarmed to see him motoring rapidly away – red flag flying. I had been left behind with one other tank, my sergeant's, and so naturally we were attracting all the fire. High time to hop it, I decided.

At that instant, my sergeant's tank went up in flames, about thirty yards to my left. Sergeant Pearson and his driver, a large ginger-headed fellow whose name I have forgotten, bailed out and came pelting across the sand towards me. I waited for them, almost wetting myself with fear. Pearson hurled himself aboard and lay flat, but the driver, with about two yards to go, was neatly decapitated by a shell and crashed into the side of my tank, throwing fountains of blood a yard high.

'Hang on,' I yelled to Pearson, and then down to my driver, 'Spin her around right and go like hell.'

I must say that Honey could shift, especially with all the shit whistling around her tail. I took a parting shell through the top of the turret but by this time was prudently squatting behind my driver, directing him where to steer.

As I overtook Duggie's tank I could see that something was amiss. There was no sign of Duggie, but I could see a gash made by a glancing shell on the side of his cupola where his head would normally be visible. I pulled in front of his tank, halted and rushed back. He had taken a splinter through his left temple and another hit had killed his gunner. His demoralised driver was just trying to get the hell out and had unwittingly taken the survivors of the squadron with him.

Duggie was still breathing faintly. As we lifted him as gently as we could from his tank, he gave a little sigh and died in my arms. Do you know, I swear that I actually saw his spirit leave his body.

The command of H Squadron then devolved on me – and wouldn't you know it? Those bloody sights arrived that night with the rations.

It was Duggie's death that did it for me, in so far as fighting in tanks was concerned. What a fatuous, idiotic, goddamned waste, I thought.

After the tragedy of Duggie and a few other rather nasty sharp engagements, the regiment, much depleted, finally withdrew from the line on the first day of the new year, 1942, and was sent back to the Nile delta for leave and re-equipping.

Despite the horrors and the appalling losses, Operation Crusader succeeded in driving the Germans almost five hundred miles to the west. Little did they know it at the time, but it was only the difficulties of resupply that had given Rommel no alternative but to retreat from the borders with Egypt all the way back across Libya. Losses in 2 RGH were testament to that imbalance in equipment and tactics: included in the dead, wounded and lost as PoWs in those hellish six weeks were twenty-two officers and 147 other ranks.

Nor, as they headed back for some badly needed rest and

recuperation, did they realise that the tide of war was swinging back in Rommel's favour. They had fought their last battles of the old year at Agedabia, 900 miles to the west of the British supply depots of Alexandria. That meant that they were now the ones with the supply problems – the Honey did just seventy-four miles on a full tank of petrol – while Rommel only had to drive his trucks 300 miles from Tripoli.

It was about to be all change in the desert, but 2 RGH weren't to know that as they headed off for a bit of well-deserved leave.

After six months in the desert a soldier would get a week's leave to enjoy the fleshpots of Egypt. His priorities were, more or less, to wallow in countless baths, get something better to eat than bully and biscuits, get a bellyful of booze and, more often than not, to try and 'get his end away', as the saying went.

The general officer commanding in the delta in Egypt was an amiable old fraud, cursed with a wife who was the inter-fering bossy witch from hell.

Prior to the advent of Mrs General Dogooder, a bloke could shuffle off to an official and inspected brothel to assuage his needs with little risk of VD or danger to his marriage. The Germans and Italians, in this respect, were pragmatic and usually had caravans of whores travelling along with their armies.[2] Mrs General managed to get the Cairo and Alexandria

---

2   The Germans were more than 'pragmatic': 'Teutonic' in their thoroughness, more like. The Wehrmacht had about 500 brothels in all, staffed more by sex slaves – women from the captured territories forced into prostitution at gunpoint or the threat of starvation – than sex workers. The girls were checked constantly by doctors anxious to limit the risk of disease. German soldiers were issued chits that had to be signed off so that, if they caught an infection, the source could be tracked down. To further minimise the risks, condoms were compulsory, and soldiers had to go through a laid-down cleansing process both before and after sex and have their chit signed off by the prostitute to prove they had done so.
   As Geoff says, the Italians had travelling brothels – the British captured one when they took Tobruk – but they were privately run. The British, as hypocritical as ever, closed a Nelsonic eye while accepting that they were a necessary evil and that it was much better to have them properly run than driven underground.

brothels closed, and VD rates rocketed 180 per cent within six months. This was quite some achievement, as the treatment back then required each infected man to spend four to five weeks in hospital. She was more dangerous to our war effort than a regiment of German Mark IIIs. She deserved a medal from the enemy for her good intentions.

The troops had it hard enough and it wasn't all that much better for officers. There was only a week before returning to the desert for another long period of discomfort and deprivation. If you did not choose to blow a week's pay in one of the rip-off nightclubs, you sometimes still had the urge for some fun – or maybe 'mischief' is a better word.

Cairo, and to a lesser extent Alexandria, was *the* honeypot for us soldiers.

Britain had long had a major army headquarters in Cairo: General HQ Middle East Command. It was here that the legendary Lawrence of Arabia had been officially stationed in the First War. It still had something of a pre-war feel to it in that it could be an 'accompanied' posting for senior officers: that is to say, they were allowed to bring wives and even daughters with them. Soldiers did make girlfriends of those daughters and some even went on to marry them, doubtless under the watchful eyes of their parents: courting the daughter of a senior officer could be a career-threatening, or career-enhancing, undertaking.

Then there were those headquarter staffs. With the war they had ballooned, and there were any number of enthusiastic and often accommodating British and Commonwealth women in the ATS, WAAF and WRNS (the army, air force and navy women's arms), not forgetting, of course, nurses, both military and Red Cross.

Finally, to give Cairo real underworld seedy glamour, there was a liberal sprinkling of more exotic types: White Russians (escapees from the USSR) and sundry Middle European refugees as well as assorted spies, Mata Haris and Walter Mittys. If they were fleeing the Nazis, one of the obvious places to head for was Cairo. With its horse-racing track at Geziret, sailing clubs, well-stocked restaurants, nightclubs and bars, it was a much more entertaining place to sit out the war than dreary, bombed and rationed Britain.

There were the likes of Countess Zofia Tarnowksa – a beautiful Polish refugee – who held court in a villa called Tara on an island outside Cairo. Here such dashing characters as Patrick Leigh Fermor, Billy Maclean, Xan Fielding and David Smiley – SOE agents all – lived and partied hard in between assignments behind enemy lines: much more fun and a lot cheaper than booking into a hotel as most men on leave had to do.

Not that Geoff had yet moved into that exotic league. He was still but a junior yeomanry lieutenant. But that was soon to change. With the catastrophic loss of life in the desert, promotion came quickly to those who survived.

On one occasion, bored and on mischief bent, I took a cab with a couple of mates out to a nightclub on the Nile: a houseboat named the *Deck Club*.

The place was jumping, packed with rich locals, staff officers and their bimbos. We cast off the upstream mooring, put our shoulders to the gangplank and shoved. As the current caught her, the houseboat swung off the land. The electricity cables snapped, the lights went out and total chaos ensued. What a damn fool thing to have done. There could and should have been a horrible tragedy.

As it happened she swung around on her downstream mooring and fetched up in the mud about eight feet off the bank. The first off was a screaming matron with about fifty thousand quid's worth of diamonds around her quivering neck. She made a great and valiant leap which took her about four feet into thick black mud. By the time about a hundred people had used her as a stepping stone to safety, she was sunk up to her tits and screaming blue murder.

We savoured the tableau and fled back to Shepheard's.[3]

The MPs and other snoopers were thick as flies for days and at least five chaps buttonholed me in the bar to say, 'God, Geoff, you should have been there. Old so-and-so and I set the *Deck Club* adrift.'

If people only learned to keep their mouths shut, no one would ever be caught.

While my friends continued to taste the delights of Alexandria and Cairo, I hitchhiked a lift with the South African air force down to Kenya to visit my family. I got there easily enough, but getting back proved difficult. I sent a signal to this effect to my colonel, whose reply was succinct: 'Walk . . . or come by Nile steamer, but get back here pronto.'

I was lucky to bum a ride in a repaired medium bomber flown by a moustachioed maniac masquerading as an RAF squadron leader. I learned some time later that a few days after he had landed me back in Cairo, he took six of his intoxicated fellow pilots up in a plane to celebrate the award of a DFC (Distinguished Flying Cross – one below the VC for the RAF) to one of them, buzzed the mess a bit too close, crashed and killed all aboard. Quite a contribution to the war effort, I thought.

After a few weeks camped outside Alexandria, the regiment, sleek, hung-over and re-equipped with two squadrons of Cruiser tanks and one squadron of American Honeys, was once again in the desert facing the Germans on a line, north to south roughly, about sixty miles west of Tobruk. While we had been away, the Eighth Army had been pushed back a good couple of hundred miles and was now trying to hold what came to be called the Gazala Line.

3   Shepheard's Hotel: the best hotel in Cairo, where many officers stayed when on leave. With nothing to spend their pay on in the desert, they could afford to live the high life on their brief returns to civilisation.

In the process of reaching our battle positions we were involved in an elaborate 'exercise', a strategic advance behind a screen of armoured cars reporting make-believe enemy forces for us to deal with.

So, one midday, hotter than hell, I was dozing in my tank. Bored stiff, I was vastly uninterested in what was supposed to be going on. By pure luck I happened to glance behind me and saw, rapidly approaching, what looked like a couple of scout cars and a staff car flying a pennon. I grabbed the mike and woke up the other tanks in my troop. 'Look alive, chaps,' I radioed. 'There's trouble coming.'

So I was earnestly searching an empty horizon through my field glasses when the staff car drew up beside the tank. I recognised our divisional commander, General Herbert Lumsden.[4] A magnificent soldier in every respect, he also had few equals as a martinet . . .

'What are you doing?' he barked.

'Sir. I command No. 3 Troop, 'H' Squadron, Royal Gloucestershire Hussars. I am the leading troop behind the armoured cars and I am awaiting orders to advance and engage the enemy.'

'Very good,' he said. 'I'm glad that some people take this bloody war seriously. What is your name?' I told him and his ADC made a note. Phew!

Unfortunately about fifty yards away was a Bren carrier belonging to our supporting rifle regiment. No sign of life there, just the feet of some rifleman sticking up. On the side of the carrier, alas, some artistic wag had painted a caricature of

---

4 Lieutenant General Herbert Lumsden, CB, DSO, MC: he was indeed well known for being extremely prickly and extremely brave – he argued with his superiors as much as he terrorised his subordinates. He won his MC in 1918, his first DSO as a colonel in the retreat to Dunkirk and a bar to that DSO in 1942. His demise was fairly bizarre for a British lieutenant general: on 6 January 1945, as Churchill's representative to General MacArthur, Commander in Chief of American forces in the Pacific, he was on the bridge of the USS *New Mexico* when it was hit by a kamikaze plane: he was killed instantly.

a monocled officer in boots and breeches and had captioned it 'General Balls Up'.

Oh dear. Herbert Lumsden spotted this.

'Show me your weapon, Rifleman,' he hissed to the first unfortunate who woke up. 'Ha. Just as I thought . . . filthy. It's not General Balls Up who is going to lose this bloody war, but Corporal Balls Up and Rifleman Balls Up! Your platoon officer will report to me personally by sundown.'

Poor bugger, I thought, what lousy luck.

A couple of days later we arrived at our appointed battle stations and settled in to wait for as long as it took to make something happen. The powers that be, in their wisdom, had devised the strategy already alluded to of strongly defended 'boxes' manned by infantry and gunners. This was an attempt to emulate the Germans' devastating use of co-ordinated all-arms groups that had caused us such trouble during Operation Crusader. Our armour was disposed between and behind these defended localities. The idea was that the enemy would attack the 'boxes' and get bogged down by minefields and guns, whereupon the armour would sweep in with lethal effect from the flanks.

Rabbie Burns would have enjoyed these best-laid plans going 'agly'.

It was 26 May 1942 and our brigade, the 22nd, was several miles to the south of the 'Knightsbridge Box', manned by the Guards and other doughty warriors. To our south was another armoured brigade, the 4th, and beyond them another 'box' at Bir Hachiem, manned by the Free French.

We knew that an attack was imminent, but were not too worried as we could expect ample warning through air reconnaissance or whatever. I suggested to Willie White, my new squadron leader, that I take a truck and whatever money we could raise between us and motor off to a NAAFI[5] depot

5   NAAFI: Navy, Army, Air Force Institute – a shop for the armed forces.

which we heard had set up shop in the desert somewhere about thirty miles away to the rear, and buy ourselves some 'goodies' in the form of Scotch, canned fruit, jam and so on.

I eventually found the place and got back to the squadron to loud cheers, with fifteen bottles of Johnnie Walker and a case or two of canned goods. We proceeded to celebrate a little in our mess tent.

Around midnight I wobbled outside to relieve myself and noticed on the horizon, to my south, the distinctive yellow long-burning flares of German Verey lights.

'Party's over, dammit,' I observed to Willie, who had joined me. 'Looks like the buggers are coming in from the south.'

'Not to worry,' said Willie. 'There's plenty in between us and them. We had better turn in and stand to.' 'Stand to' involved being in our tanks at 0500 hours, engines running and ready for battle, in case of a dawn attack. 'I'd better check with the Colonel to see if he knows what the form is.'

The form was, of course, that the Germans, rather unsportingly, had elected not to conform to our battle strategy. They had bypassed the defended localities and had hammered in from the rear, causing total chaos among our undefended supply transport. It was especially galling to realise that they were probably already stuffing themselves with goodies from the NAAFI which had just taken a large wad of our money.

We manned our tanks at 5 a.m. with about thirty minutes to spare before 15th Panzer Division was upon us in full force. It appeared that the 4th Armoured Brigade had literally been caught napping.

A squadron of tanks in an armoured regiment had a major commanding, a captain as second-in-command and another captain (me – I'd been promoted) as third-in-command. The second-in-command was always left out of battle at the onset of an engagement in order that, should the squadron leader be knocked out, there would be a fresh and experienced officer to take over.

This time the arrangement didn't work, as things moved too fast. Willie's tank was disabled very early in the day so I found myself in command. We were continuously in action on that first day of confusion for eleven hours, and I replenished my ammunition three times. We slowly fell back to the Knightsbridge Box and hung in there during the next seven days of heavy fighting. I honestly do not think I had more than three hours' sleep a night during all that time, and had it not been for that case of Scotch, diminishing inside my turret, I don't think I could have lasted.

Geoff's battles were part of an enormous engagement that came to be known as 'the Cauldron': aptly named. The Eighth Army had greater numbers of men and tanks, increasingly better anti-tank guns which could at last kill German tanks, just as the 88 mms had been killing ours, and vital signals-intercept information which told them of Rommel's plans. But the British generals continued to fail to react in time to the German thrusts and feints. Rommel comprehensively out-generalled them. Time and again the British armoured brigades found themselves launching attacks or defending positions in penny packets, unsupported by anti-tank guns and infantry.

According to the American military attaché in Cairo, when the Germans attacked the Gazala Line on 27 May the Eighth Army had 742 tanks (with a further 372 replacements, totaling 1142 tanks committed to battle). The Panzerarmee had 561, of which 228 were Italian and of much lesser quality. Unlike the 'muddled' going around in circles of the earlier battles, when the Allies had been on the attack, they were immediately on the retreat as Rommel's men smashed up and overran the various defensive 'boxes' – all but Knightsbridge.

So while a percentage of the tank crews survived being hit,

they had no opportunity to recover and repair their knocked-out and broken-down tanks, which had to be left behind on the battlefield. Come 10 June, that same attaché reported that there were only 133 tanks left in the whole of the Middle East. The 2 RGH history reports that by 13 June the Eighth Army was down to its last fifty Cruisers and twenty Honeys. The armoured regiments had been almost annihilated, and 2 RGH along with them. Not only had 2 RGH lost huge numbers of men and tanks but also, within a few days of each other, their beloved colonel, the second-in-command – who had just taken over as commanding officer – and the adjutant.

By 13 June, and the end of the battle, the remnants of the Eighth Army were in full retreat towards the Egyptian border. They only finally stopped, turned and dug in when they reached El Alamein on 26 June, fifty miles west of Alexandria and 250 miles east of where 2 RGH had started in November 1941. No wonder that back in Cairo they were burning the files in the various headquarters. One last push from Rommel and it would all be over for the British in the Middle East.[6]

On the eighth day, extremely groggy, I was relieved by the second-in-command and sent off to have a few days' rest at the rear. As I recall, I slept and twitched for forty-eight hours and then some character arrived asking for me. 'My name's Hitchcock,' he announced. 'The General wants you to command his advanced HQ.'

'Why me?'

'My dear fellow . . . how the hell would I know? The last bloke caught a Stuka bomb yesterday and you appear to be on

---

6 It was an unmitigated disaster, although with two upsides, albeit difficult to see at the time. Rommel's forces had taken very heavy casualties: the Eighth Army had sold their lives, tanks and guns dearly. And, once again, Rommel was the one at the far end of a long supply line, although – and disastrously – this time he was to retake Tobruk. Once he got the port working his supply line would be halved.

his list. You had better collect your bits and pieces and I'll take you to where he is.'

Another quirk of fate. My regiment took such a beating during the ensuing ten days' fighting that they were never re-formed during the desert campaigns.

In fact, with their colonel, his replacement and the adjutant all dead, it was the end of 2 RGH as a fighting unit, although its men continued to fight throughout the war with other regiments.

The 'Butcher's Bill', to use Royal Navy parlance, was horrific, especially given that there were only ever upwards of 200 men in the front line: seventy-two dead, ninety-five wounded and eighty-five prisoners of war, of whom a further four died and one was shot having been recaptured after escape. Those numbers alone are a testament to the valour and sacrifice of 2 RGH. Colonel Birley, who was killed on 6 June and who had harboured serious doubts about the regiment and their 'yeomanry' way of going about things when he first took over, said, after first seeing them in action at Bir el Gubi back in November 1941: 'After that I understand a lot of things that were strange to me. No regiment can touch them.'[7]

As of 11 June I found myself in command of a motley collection of six tanks, four armoured cars, three ACVs (armoured command vehicles) and about sixty assorted vans and trucks, which comprised the Advanced HQ of 1st Armoured Division. I took over just as the retreat to Alamein was beginning, and it would be my responsibility to navigate, mostly by night, the

---

7   Thereafter the men of 2 RGH continued to fight throughout the war as RGH squadrons, but split up and attached to other regiments. One general, on taking a squadron under command, found the calibre of the NCOs to be so high that he had a number of them commissioned. Their approach was different, though: while delighted to be made officers they would have much preferred to remain yeoman NCOs, fighting with their beloved 2 RGH. Colonel Charles Birley would have been proud.

whole shemozzle back to safety and also to protect it from attack.

The retreat, as I recall, took about a week. But we got there safely and fairly well ahead of our enemies, with time enough to dig in, recoup and prepare a counter-stroke.

We had been near Alamein about three weeks, I suppose, and I was getting fidgety. General Lumsden had expressed himself well satisfied with my performance during the retreat and I had heard on the grapevine that there was a plot afoot to have me attached to his staff as a G3. I admired the man with all my heart, but to be a paper-pusher on the staff was not my idea of fighting a war.

One morning, in a mood of ennui, I collected my soldier servant, Trooper Bransgrove, a Bren gun[8] and a Jeep and headed west through our lines and minefields just to have a look-see, as the RAF had been reporting sporadic enemy activity.

We drove with increasing caution into a no-man's-land and then, peering over a rise, I saw three 3-ton trucks standing abandoned in a small wadi or valley only about 300 yards away.

'What do you think, Bransgrove?' I said. 'They're ours, all right. I wonder what the hell they're doing. Look, you cover me with the Bren and I'll nip down and take a look. We may be able to rescue one.'

I scanned the surrounding hills through my glasses for a while and then, sensing nothing threatening, set off down the hill towards the trucks. I had noticed slit trenches around them, as I would have expected.

I had got to within twenty feet of the first truck when

---

8   Bren: a British .303 light machine-gun fed by a thirty-round magazine. It was an excellent weapon. Its major weakness, bizarrely, was that it was too accurate, which meant that the bullets did not 'spray around' enough, something one tends to look for in a machine-gun.

machine-gun bullets from God knows where started clipping the air around me. With a desperate plunge I made the shelter of a shallow slit trench. I landed belly-to-belly and face-to-face on to a German soldier who had lain there ripening long enough to have generated a ton of gas in his bloated belly and to have attracted tens of thousands of filthy blue-arsed flies.

One can puke just so much; after that it's the dry heaves which hurt. Flies from his dead nose and gaping mouth flew into mine, along with foul eructations of gas.

I had to endure an hour of this before blessed sunset permitted me to stagger weakly back up the hill to where Bransgrove had been bravely popping away with his Bren gun to discourage any attempt to capture me.

As he scented me, he threw up.

We drove back some way and I took off my clothes and burned them. Wrapped up in a camouflage net I got back to Advanced HQ where, thank God, I found the mess was just still open for the drink for which I would have given my soul.

'You look a bit green, old chap,' said Lieutenant Colonel Somebody, the G1 staff officer. 'Glad I caught you. I was chatting with the General during dinner and we agreed that it might be a good idea if you were to shove off from time to time and see if there's anything interesting going on up front. Stop you getting bored and that sort of thing.'

Since you ask, and some have . . . yes, I have had the occasional bad dreams.

6

The Fleshpots

For my part, I had become a little leery of tank warfare. My confidence in the weaponry at my disposal and in my commanders, with a few notable exceptions, had waned somewhat. I determined that, from here on in, if I were to be killed it would be through my own fault or misjudgement and not through that of a superior. In August 1942 chance led me to a reunion one night with a chum and erstwhile sparring partner of mine, Brian Dillon, at Mary's House. This establishment, not far from the pyramids, was a most decorous officers' brothel. It was much patronised, not so much for the charms of 'les girls' but because after every other place of entertainment in Cairo had closed, they still served drinks at reasonable prices as well as the most excellent early morning breakfast of bacon and eggs.

Learning of my desire for a change of scenery, Brian introduced me a few days later to one Sandy Scratchley, who had been on a few operations with the now legendary David Stirling. Between the wars Sandy had been one of the best amateur steeplechase jockeys in Britain and was a most likeable and intrepid fellow.

'You've heard of David?' he asked.

Who hadn't?

By mid-August 1942, when this conversation took place, David Stirling was already becoming a legend. Forgetting the fact that he had, infamously, knocked out a cab-horse in a Cairo street – by way of objecting to being overcharged by the cab driver – he had been busy taking the war to the enemy.

He had been sent to the Middle East in February 1941 as part of Layforce – four battalions of commandos commanded by Colonel Robert Laycock. The commando battalions had by July 1941 suffered such severe losses in men killed or captured during the failed defence of Greece and its islands that they were all but disbanded. Many of the survivors were only too happy to return to their parent regiments, some fed up with constant cancellations of operations while their 'regular' brethren were fighting the Germans for real. One bit of graffiti found on a Royal Navy landing ship summed up the mood of many of those who had had enough of the promises of their starry-eyed commanders: 'Never in the whole history of human endeavour, have so few been buggered about by so many.'[1]

All commandos were, at this time, 'on attachment', but a few kept the faith and stayed on to form what came to be called Middle East Commando. This included L Detachment, Special Air Service Brigade, under Stirling, which was to morph into the SAS, and the Special Boat Section – the future Special Boat Squadron (SBS).

On the night of 17–18 November 1941 – while Geoff was fighting his first battle – Middle East Commando had gone on its first SAS mission: to cause confusion behind enemy lines. In an effort to kill him, 3 Troop attacked what was said to be Rommel's headquarters. Only two of the thirty or so men who launched the eventual attack on the house – it had, it

---

1   A clever and bitter play on Winston Churchill's famous post-Battle of Britain speech: 'Never in the field of human conflict was so much owed by so many to so few.' These commandos – often the toughest and brightest soldiers – had volunteered for special ops in the dark days after Dunkirk, when raiding seemed the only way of taking the fight to the enemy. However, come 1941, many had hardly fired a shot in anger while the regular army had been fighting hard, at least in the Middle East. Hence their disillusionment. Graffiti quoted in Charles Messenger, *The Commandos 1940–46* (William Kimber, 1985).

transpired, never been used by the Feldmarshall – made it back: the rest were killed or captured. L Detachment, under Stirling, carried out a confused and failed parachute attack on an airfield. The only thing that worked was that the survivors – approximately twenty-two out of sixty-five – were successfully extracted and transported home by the Long Range Desert Group (aka 'Libyan Taxis Limited'), thus starting a long and usually, but not always, fruitful relationship between the two outfits. For a time LRDG became the SAS's cross-desert taxi drivers, albeit taxi drivers with ferocious talons and teeth.

Since those failed missions the SAS had given up the idea of parachuting and, instead, had been specialising in driving to their target and doing 'beat-ups' – their term for it – of airfields and supply depots, sometimes far behind the front lines. Not only did this damage Rommel's means of fighting the war, but the very effectiveness of these attacks meant that the Germans had to station large numbers of men on guard duty instead of using them where they were most needed: on the front line, fighting the Eighth Army. This was a foretaste of the type of war that Geoff was later to fight in Greece: tiny groups of men tying up disproportionate numbers of the enemy. So frustrated did Hitler become by commando raiding that he issued his infamous *Kommandobefehl* – 'Commando Order' – that was later, in Greece, to account for the lives of several of Geoff's men:

The Führer
SECRET

1 For a long time now our opponents have been employing in their conduct of the war methods which contravene the International Convention of Geneva. The members of the so-called Commandos behave in a particularly brutal and underhand manner; and it has been established that those units recruit criminals not only from their own country but even former convicts set free in enemy territories.

From captured orders it emerges that they are instructed not only to tie up prisoners, but also to kill out-of-hand unarmed captives who they think might prove an encumbrance to them, or hinder them in successfully carrying out their aims. Orders have indeed been found in which the killing of prisoners has positively been demanded of them.

2 In this connection it has already been notified in an Appendix to Army Orders of 7.10.1942 that in future Germany will adopt the same methods against these sabotage units of the British and their Allies; i.e. that, whenever they appear, they shall be ruthlessly destroyed by the German troops.

3 I order, therefore:

From now on all men operating against German troops in so-called Commando raids in Europe or in Africa, are to be annihilated to the last man. This is to be carried out whether they be soldiers in uniform, or saboteurs, with or without arms; and whether fighting or seeking to escape; and it is equally immaterial whether they come into action from ships and aircraft, or whether they land by parachute. Even if these individuals on discovery make obvious their intention of giving themselves up as prisoners, no pardon is on any account to be given. On this matter a report is to be made on each case to Headquarters for the information of Higher Command.

4 Should individual members of these Commandos, such as agents, saboteurs, etc., fall into the hands of the Armed Forces through any means – as, for example, through the Police in one of the Occupied Territories – they are to be instantly handed over to the S.D. [the Gestapo].

To hold them in military custody – for example in PoW camps, etc. – even if only as a temporary measure, is strictly forbidden.

5 This order does not apply to the treatment of those enemy soldiers who are taken prisoner or give themselves up in open battle, in the course of normal operations, large-scale attacks or in major assault landings or airborne operations. Neither does it apply to those who fall into our hands after a sea fight, nor to those enemy soldiers who, after air battle, seek to save their lives by parachute.

6 I will hold all Commanders and Officers responsible under Military Law for any omission to carry out this order, whether by failure in their duty to instruct their units accordingly, or if they themselves act contrary to it [and we all know what that meant in that fun-filled dictatorship – death].

(Sgd) A Hitler

In a nutshell, this meant that if you were Special Forces and you were unfortunate enough to be captured – regardless of the fact that you were in a uniform – you would be killed: a clear breach of the Geneva Convention and a war crime.

The 'normal' war in North Africa was being fought along a relatively narrow corridor, rarely more than fifty miles back from the sea, which is where the roads and the towns and villages were to be found. Beyond that lay the deep desert, semi-impassable to armoured columns and with few roads or tracks worth talking about. LRDG had learned that by heading south and west, far into the desert, they could then, with luck, hook round and up and emerge undetected behind enemy lines. The strategic importance and relative impact of these raids – results achieved compared to resources involved – can be better understood when Carol Mather (who had been another ski volunteer) tells in his book how on one beat-up he was involved in, comprising ten officers and 100 men, the SAS and LRDG attacked the airfield at Fuka. Surprise was total and they 'burnt thirty aircraft, damaged more, and lost one man, a Frenchman, killed. The whole thing had taken fifteen minutes.' Compare that with 15 September 1940, the day of the last major engagement of the Battle of Britain. With most of Fighter Command up against the Luftwaffe, the British shot down sixty planes and lost twenty-eight. It was no wonder that SAS exploits were already legendary in North Africa by the time Geoff was having this conversation.

'Well,' Sandy Scrathley went on, 'David's got a thing going that is a bit more ambitious than his usual effort. We are starting off from Kufra with a largish mob, most of which will have a go at the docks and airfields at Benghazi while the remainder will attack the airfield at El Adem and the docks at Tobruk.'

'Where the hell is Kufra,' I asked, 'and where do I come in?'

'Hah,' he replied, 'we're taking a couple of Honey tanks with us to neutralise any destroyers in the port and, if you want it, the command is yours. Kufra is in the middle of the desert, about six hundred miles west of Wadi Halfa and about the same south of Benghazi. The Eyeties were there, but since we took it they have never bothered to try to get it back. It's a super oasis.'

'Well,' I decided, knowing that my chum Brian Dillon – he of the Mary's House conversation – would also be going along, 'OK. When do we start and where from?'

'The convoy leaves from Kabrit next Tuesday, but if you can't make it there are planes from Heliopolis every few days, flying in supplies.'

Well, of course I didn't make the convoy. The idea of bumping across the desert on my arse for 1400 miles when I could fly in direct in about five hours – Please! Anyway I was quite heavily involved with a delightful WAAF officer, the sister of one of my old school chums, and didn't fancy leaving her, or Cairo, a moment sooner than I had to.

In the event I barely made it to Heliopolis to catch my plane at 0500 hours. I had visions of flopping into a bucket seat, dozing off and trying to catch up on some badly needed sleep after my WAAF's attentions over the last three or four days.

It was not to be: the plane, a Lockheed Hudson, was already warmed up and the pilot was waiting for me.

'Wilson,' he said, introducing himself. 'We'd better be off. Hop in.'

I climbed in and was vaguely alarmed to realise that the entire fuselage appeared to be stacked with explosives and cans of aviation spirit.

As I buckled into the co-pilot's seat he tossed me a map. 'You had better navigate,' he said. 'I make it about four and a half hours on a bearing of 243 degrees. Here we go.'

We sailed along at about 10,000 feet over typical zero, nothing but desert landscape, and after four hours and thirty-eight minutes, and somewhat to my surprise, there was Kufra below us.

We circled to have a look at the runway, just an oiled strip in the sand, and started to come in. His approach, even to my eye, was much too fast. He gave her the gun and pulled away. Then he zoomed around for another run. I turned to him to make some facetious comment and froze. The man was sweating and pale green in the face. Oh shit, I thought.

We came down again just as fast but this time he kept her on the ground. We hurtled down the short runway, brakes screaming, hit a date palm with the port wing, spun around into the soft sand and buried the port engine.

'Fire!' he yelled, and disappeared. The starboard prop was still spinning and raising clouds of dust to add to my fear and confusion. I flipped off both mag switches, killing the electrics, and wormed my way out through a side door. Outside on the sand and about fifty yards away I reckoned that the plane had decided not to explode. So I sat down and waited for someone to arrive.

A Jeep came flying up, driven by a sergeant. He held in his hand a pint-sized fire-extinguisher.

'You all right, Sir?'

'Yes, I'm all right.'

'You look a bit pale.'

As he spoke I realised that I was, indeed, feeling a bit pale. Delayed shock, I suppose, but to my embarrassment I suddenly got the violent shakes and could do nothing about them. For long minutes I struggled to regain control over myself while the sergeant tactfully scanned the horizon.

'We had better go and pick up the pilot,' I said after a little while. 'He should know how best to get into that damn thing . . . I've got all my clobber in there somewhere.' I had suddenly remembered that in my kitbag was a bottle of whisky. The thoughtful and last-minute gift from my WAAF friend was sending me a very loud and clear message.

It transpired later that this was my pilot's first operational flight after a six-month grounding for 'operational fatigue', a euphemism for loss of nerve. My horrible luck to have picked that flight, I thought, and back to the funny farm for him, I supposed, poor bugger.

Kufra was indeed everyone's ideal of what an oasis should be: date palms and melon fields, brackish lagoons to float and sport in, and an abundance of pure sweet water just under the surface. It had been an outpost of Mussolini's Libyan empire, but its history went back into time as one of a chain of oases on the caravan route linking Chad with Egypt.

The two Honey tanks had already arrived on transporters and I set about getting to know their crews, testing the guns and the radios and going over their engines and tracks, as there was a long trek ahead of us. I figured that if they ever made it to Benghazi they would have to be abandoned there and destroyed. At their huge rate of consumption there was no way that sufficient fuel could be hauled along for the return trip.

As it happened, neither of them made it. The first one slid off a raised track within the oasis and immediately sank up to its turret into bottomless black ooze. I set off northwards, two days ahead of the main column, with the second tank and a 3-ton truck. We got no further than about ninety miles when something blew in its engine. I brought the truck back to rejoin the others and two days later we all set off in four-by-four trucks and Jeeps, about thirty-five vehicles in all, each mounting twin Vickers 'K' drum-fed light machine-guns.

With my small command gone I was now a supernumerary. David Stirling, however, was kind enough to allow me to tag along and said that he was sure that he could give me something useful to do. He was as good as his word – in a manner of speaking. I was allotted one sailor, a rubber dinghy, a grappling iron with thirty feet of rope, four magnetic limpet mines and as many grenades as I might choose to carry. My target was to be a cargo ship, lying alongside the dock.

Our route would take us due north into the hills and wadis to the south-east of Benghazi. On the way we were to bypass another oasis, Jalo, which had a strong Italian garrison. A day or so behind us would follow two companies of the Sudan Defence Force. They would take Jalo and hold it as a haven for us upon our return from beating up the port at Benghazi and the surrounding airfields.

Neat little plans seldom work in wartime, and this enterprise was beset with one misfortune after another. One of the Jeeps carrying a Royal Navy liaison officer ran over a mine and the officer was killed. Another of our officers, leading an assault on a small fort where the Italians had a radio station, was shot in the guts and later died.

Worst of all, we had lost the all-important element of surprise, though we were not aware of this at the time.

While the British disported themselves in Cairo and Alexandria, they little realised at the time how much of the country was deeply anti-British and, on the age-old basis that 'the enemy of my enemy is my friend', the Germans and Italians were passed a steady flow of information from their Egyptian spies, from waiters and cooks in the smart hotels and restaurants, through the Egyptian army and civil service and right up to the Egyptian prime minister, who was forcibly deposed by the British High Commissioner in 1942 on suspicion of being pro-Axis.

Most of the SAS and LRDG raids were small, and therefore security could be kept reasonably tight, but when Sandy had said that there was going to be a 'largish mob' on this one he had not been joking. So many men were involved that the forthcoming raid had been the subject of gossip and speculation in the bars and brothels of Cairo for weeks – even, let it be said, in Mary's House. No wonder the Germans and Italians were awaiting them.

From Kufra there followed a seven-day and -night drive north and then north-west, to Benghazi. Unaware of the danger, we spent a day or so concealed in various wadis, checking everything and awaiting a report by some dubious Arab who had been sent into Benghazi to spy. He reported back that the talk of the barber shops and cafés was of the forthcoming attack.

I shared a bivouac with Brian, Steve Hastings and Carol Mather. The latter, a doughty warrior and a talented rhymester, had been with me during the Chamonix skiing farce.

That afternoon, just before we set off for Benghazi, I noticed that Steve had produced a clean smart tunic from somewhere. He laid it out on the sand to get the wrinkles out and was polishing and affixing the Scots Guards buttons in their regulation groups of three. I was riveted! The man had been given the horrid job of attacking a battery of anti-aircraft guns with only a handful of men, yet here he was, his chances of survival extremely iffy, ready to die if he must, but by God, properly accoutred as a Guards officer. How absolutely splendid!

Carol strolled up. 'Here,' he said, 'David thinks we might need these.' He produced a handful of white pills. 'Benzedrine,' he went on, 'in case you fall asleep and forget where you are.'

We chatted for a while till Carol sniffed the air, looked around and poked me in the ribs. On the sand lay the perfect outline of Steve's tunic, in grey ash, the buttons perfectly positioned. A carelessly thrown cigarette butt, I suppose.

Poor Steve. His face crumpled in chagrin and dismay. Our laughter was not meant unkindly, but we fairly hooted.

On the night of 13 September we set off in pitch darkness down an extremely rough track. About three hours' driving brought us down on to the plain and, so far as I had any means of guessing, to within about ten miles of one of our targets, an airfield. The leading Jeep had its headlights on and I rode with Brian in another about 500 yards behind. In front of us appeared a white swinging barrier, which blocked the track. There were signs of a minefield on either side. Nothing moved, however, and we could neither see nor hear anything untoward. One of David's officers in the leading Jeep, Bill Cumper, got out and, silhouetted in the headlights, strolled over to the barrier and swung it aside. He doffed his cap and made a graceful bow into the darkness ahead. 'Let battle commence,' he said.

It did. On the instant.

There must have been half a dozen Bredas[2] and scores of rifles popping away at us. A truck and two Jeeps were set afire.

2   Bredas: Italian-made machine-guns which came in 8 mm and 20 mm sizes. Considered an excellent weapon. Captured guns, of which there were many, were often appropriated and used by British forces.

We were nose to tail along the track and we could not do much other than spray a few thousand rounds of tracer in reply.

Anyway, the situation was blown. Dawn was not far off and we were without cover on the plain. At first light we could expect dozens of warplanes to be swarming all over us. We split up and made for cover any way we could. Most of us had just made it up into the hills as dawn broke. And then the fun began.

The Italians put up Macchi 202 fighters with cannons, nippy little CR42 biplanes with machine-guns and two Savoia bombers. What's more, they had only to fly about thirty miles to refuel and reload. They kept it up the whole bloody day, picking individual targets when they could, but just plastering the hills and wadis regardless.

Brian and I had left our disabled Jeep on the floor of one wadi and had scrambled part of the way up the hillside. There we lay for many hours behind a couple of small rocks, hoping like hell that we wouldn't be spotted. Eventually we were – by the pilot of a CR42. He made three passes at us and, looking straight down his winking guns, I knew real terror. He couldn't quite make the angle for fear of hitting the hillside on his pull up, but each pass had been just that much closer. 'Bugger this for a lark,' said Brian, 'best get a bit further down the hill and split up.' This we did and he lost us, thank God.

As dusk fell we climbed the hill and reunited with the other chaps to tally the damage. We had lost quite a lot of our transport but, surprisingly, there were only two dead and four wounded – although the numbers of dead and wounded would continue to rise in the days that followed.

We laid up in the general area for a few days while David decided what should best be done.

He learned that the El Adem party – tasked to capture this enemy strongpoint which lay along their line of retreat – had also come to grief, and that the SDF (Sudanese Defence Force – Sudanese soldiers under mainly British officers who garrisoned many of the oases deep in the desert) had failed to take Jalo Oasis and its airfield, which was held by the Italians.

The plan had called for Jalo to be captured to stop the Italians counter-attacking and flying aircraft from it and cutting off our retreat.

There was nothing for it but to pack ourselves into our remaining transport and make our inglorious way back to Kufra. That journey took ten long days as we struggled back over the Great Sand Sea: lines of dunes like waves, some thirty miles long, sometimes with hard troughs at the bottom, some 500 yards long, others five miles. Exhausting work in the blasting heat of the desert as we had to push and dig the vehicles to get them up and over the soft dunes to the hard floor below. Finally, on 23 September we got back to Kufra and awaited the stragglers.

We had some revenge when, the day after getting back, six German fighter bombers, Heinkel 111s and Ju88s, suddenly appeared over the oasis to bomb and strafe. We shot one down with a 20 mm Breda and subsequently learned that none of the others had made it back to base. Peppered with machine-gun fire, they had all made forced landings in the desert through damage to their cooling systems or whatever.

After a week of indecision we took transport due east back to Wadi Halfa, whence the main party were to take a river boat back down the Nile to Cairo. I managed to hop on a plane as I was impatient to get rid of my beard and, more urgently, to discover whether my favourite WAAF had missed me as much as I had missed her.

I let myself into my WAAF's flat.

'Christ!' she said, looking a bit startled. 'What a sight! Come over here and let me feel if you're real. Hmmm . . . well, there's something here that doesn't seem to have changed too much.'

I slipped my hand between her legs. 'Feels a bit like my beard,' I observed.

She giggled and bit my lip. 'Down, you randy beast,' she ordered. 'You can stop the heavy breathing as this will have to wait for a bit. I have to get back to my office.'

'Well, if you must. Look, I'm off to Shepheard's to get this crud off my face. I'll try to get one of their best suites and we'll dine together and wallow in champagne.'

I had a few drinks in Freddie's Bar and wandered downstairs to the barber shop. This was run by a soft-fingered Greek called Nikko, who knew his stuff.

'Nikko,' I said, 'I'm tired and smelly.' I felt the crud on my face. 'I want a haircut, shave, shampoo, face pack, the works. And don't talk.'

God, the sheer bliss of total abandonment! I must have dozed off. He gently nudged me awake and I sat up in my chair. With my beard off my cheeks looked strangely pale, and sitting obscenely across my too short upper lip was a natty little moustache.

'What the hell's this?' I spluttered.

Nikko looked crushed. 'But, Captain, it is beautiful and it suits you.'

I regarded it. 'No it doesn't,' I decided. 'I think it makes me look like a bloody dago. Take it off at once.'

I got the suite I wanted, had a magnum of Bollinger sent up, ran water into one of those wonderful seven-foot Edwardian bathtubs and waited impatiently for my WAAF to show up.

She arrived at the trot and right on time.

Somehow it seemed a pity to get dressed for dinner so we had dinner sent up and then lay down to 'talk things over'.

She had, I soon learned, missed me very much.

Oh, and in case you want to ask, the SAS never tried to use tanks on a desert raid again.

That was one of David Stirling's dangerous strengths, his charm and conviction. He could make a man believe the impossible. A high-risk raid – attacking a properly defended port city – was full of short straws for the picking. Some reckoned that Geoff had picked almost the shortest of all those very short straws: two lightly armoured Honeys with 37 mm popguns taking on sundry warships? An interesting idea, but probably not the cleverest.

7

In the first fifteen and SOE

I had been granted some sick leave upon my return from Kufra and was spending most of this propping up the bar at Shepheard's.

One evening I struck up a conversation with an elderly civilian and, in the course of our chat, mentioned that I was at a loose end and looking for an amusing job. He questioned me casually and then kindly offered to mention my name to someone at General HQ he thought might be able to help. I thanked him, of course, and gave him my room number, but then dismissed him entirely from my mind. Two days later I found a note at the hall porter's desk asking me to report to a Captain Walker in Rustom Buildings, a part of GHQ Middle East.

I wandered along, thinking that perhaps my leave had been cut short, and in due course found myself in the office of this affable character.

'Ah!' he said. 'How do you do? Gordon-Creed, isn't it? Yes, well . . . enjoying your leave?'

'Yes, thank you.'

'Yes, well . . . I see you've got an MC. Forgive my asking, but where did you collect it?'

'Frigging around in my tank.'

'Oh. Quite. Well . . . where were you at school?'

None of your bloody business, I thought. 'Downside.'

'Oh really?' He made a note on his pad. 'We used to play you at rugger. Sherborne . . . Were you in the first fifteen?'

'I was, actually.'

'Jolly good. We must have a chat someday. Well, I've got your number, haven't I? Jolly good. Well I expect Major Blair will want a word with you sometime. I'll get in touch. Goodbye, old fellow.'

I drifted out and was back in Shepheard's in nice time for a pink gin session before lunch.

The following morning, in response to a telephone call from Walker, I was back in his office. 'Ah. Well. There you are. Jolly good. Major Blair won't keep you a tick, he's just in with the Colonel for a moment.' He beamed encouragingly at me.

A buzzer sounded on his desk.

'Ah. Well, it looks as though he's back again. Come along and I'll just trot you in.'

I followed him into the adjoining office and saluted.

'Good morning, Sir.'

'Hrrmph.'

Major Blair was evidently monumentally hung over. I now recalled having seen him cavorting around the dance floor at Madame Badia's nightclub the previous evening. He was a tubby little man with an expensive complexion and impressive moustaches.

'Gawd!' he said heavily. He reached for a glass of water, popped a couple of aspirins in his mouth and shut his eyes. A door slammed outside in the corridor. He winced.

'Now then,' he said fruitily. 'Let me see.' He gazed blankly down at a paper in front of him on his desk. 'Ah!' he said finally. 'I see you're a Papist. We had a Roman Catholic padre in my regiment once. Drank like a fish. Yes, well . . . I believe you want to see the Colonel?'

I looked blank.

'Well anyway, he wants to see you. Hang on a minute.' He rose carefully to his feet and went out.

What the hell is all this, I thought. What possible job could these nuts have to offer me? The door opened again and I stood up. Major Blair winked a bloodshot eye at me and held the door open for me to go through.

'Colonel, this is Captain Gordon-Creed. I believe you've already got his file.'

I went in and saluted smartly. He waved back.

'Ah. Good morning. Sit down, sit down. Smoke? Well now, do you think you'll want to come and work for us?'

'Well, Sir,' I hesitated. 'I'm afraid I have no idea what it is that you do.'

'Wassat? Good God! I thought . . .' he broke off and picked up my file. 'Yes, well. Where did you pick up your MC?'

'With my regiment, in the desert, Sir.'

'Hmmm . . . I see you were at Downside. I used to know it quite well. Played against you often. I was at Radley.'

'Oh really, Sir?'

'Yes. Were you in the fifteen by any chance?'

'Yes . . . front row.'

'Were you now? I played on the wing. Yes, well . . . to get back to business. We here recruit and train chaps to operate behind the lines in occupied countries for sabotage and so on. It would mean about six months' training at our various schools and a parachute course.'

'I see.'

'If you complete the training you will be held in a pool ready to be dropped wherever you might be needed. Probably Greece or Yugoslavia – unless you have specialised knowledge of some other country, that is. What languages do you speak?'

'My French is pretty good and my German is not too bad.'

'No Greek, or anything like that?'

'No, I'm afraid not.'

'No, well, never mind. I think you'll probably do.[1] I'll get the

---

1 Classic British army at work: establish that a man has certain useful skills, and then ignore them.

Brigadier to give you the once-over if he's free. Come along with me.'

The Brigadier, when I eventually saw him, gave me the rugger routine; asked me if I was enjoying my leave and dismissed me. I was to stay on at Shepheard's until I heard further from them.

I went somewhat thoughtfully on my way. On the face of it, these people might be just what I was looking for. I had had more than enough of tanks, and my little stint with the SAS had shown me that, while you could not ask for better fellows, I preferred the idea of being under nobody's direct command.

On the other hand, what about that parachuting? The thought of casting myself out of a perfectly good aeroplane had always been something of a nightmare for me. However, I felt that I wouldn't have to do it just yet, and anyway if others could do it I supposed I would be able find the courage to do it also. What a bore, though, that part of it was, and what a bizarre collection of people seemed to be in charge.

I waited in great curiosity for nearly two days. After lunch I was called to the phone.

'Captain Gordon-Creed?'

'Yes.'

'You will be at 17, Sharia Salsoul, Garden City by five minutes before seven this evening. Go upstairs and ring the bell of Flat 5 at precisely 7 p.m. Understood?'

'Yes, I've got that. Who . . .?' Click.

Now, of course, I was intrigued and wild horses couldn't have kept me away. At seven on the dot I rang the expensive-looking bell of Flat 5.

The door was opened instantly by an attractive girl, obviously English. She offered no greeting and motioned for me to step quickly inside. I followed her, with mounting curiosity and amusement, through a lavishly furnished drawing room,

into a bedroom and through a bathroom. Here was a stairway
leading down to the flat below. Down we went. The layout was
identical and I followed my guide back through the bedroom
and into the drawing room. She led me up to another door
and rapped twice. She opened the door and thrust me inside.

There was a bright spotlight shining right into my eyes and I
was unable to see beyond it into the shadows. I stood in silence
for long seconds and then – click – the spotlight went off. The
other lights came on and I stepped forward, blinking.

Behind a desk and rising to greet me was the same little
civilian gentleman with whom I had originally chatted in the
bar at Shepheard's.

He looked at me keenly.

I gaped at him like an idiot.

'Welcome to our organisation,' he said.

Today, SOE – Special Operations Executive – is appreciated for
what it achieved. Back in 1942 many were anything but sure of
its value. In February 1941, Air Chief Marshal Charles Portal,
Chief of the Air Staff, wrote a secret letter to Gladwyn Jebb,
private secretary to the Minister of Economic Warfare (MEW),
under which SOE came. It set out the RAF's position with
regard to helping SOE:

I think that the dropping of men dressed in civilian clothing
for the purpose of attempting to kill members of the opposing
forces is not an operation with which the Royal Air Force should
be associated . . . there is a vast difference, in ethics, between
the time-honoured operation of the dropping of a spy from the
air and this entirely new scheme for dropping what can only be
called assassins.[2]

Churchill, however, had other ideas. His slogan for the newly

2   Quoted in M.R.D. Foot's book, *SOE, The Special Operations Executive
1940–1946.*

created SOE was 'the Ministry of Ungentlemanly Warfare'. He believed that there was only one way to fight the Nazis and that was to behave as ruthlessly as they did. Although Portal and the RAF were persuaded to change their official attitude to co-operation, he and others in high command did not necessarily change their deeper objections to the method and effectiveness of this type of clandestine warfare. A bomber dropping bombs provided a direct cause and effect. That same bomber, diverted to dropping SOE agents, was not fulfilling its proper function of dropping bombs. That is the way some of those in command viewed SOE: an unnecessary distraction from the main war effort.

Hitler, as we have seen, designated them criminals. Even the 'honourable' Field Marshal Rommel is known to have referred to them as 'gangster commandos'.[3] They certainly used terror but would have objected to being called terrorists – a distinction we can struggle with today. Perhaps the biggest indicator that they were not terrorists in the modern meaning of the word is the huge efforts they and their bosses went to in trying to avoid the unnecessary deaths of non-combatants, either directly or by way of causing the Germans and Italians to take reprisals against the civilian population. Of course, cynics might well disagree with this distinction and point out that secret agents and saboteurs can only survive, let alone flourish, with the approval of the general population: get them killed and sentiment soon turns against you, however worthy your cause.

What is clear from the history of SOE written by M.R.D. Foot is that those selected were required to be ruthless: it was something

3 *Daily Telegraph* obituary of Colonel George Lane. Lane, a member of SOE, was captured on a cross-channel foray in 1944, testing for sea mines off a possible landing beach. Threatened with being shot, he instead found himself being interviewed over a cup of tea by Rommel in his headquarters. Despite talking about 'gangster commandos' – of which he was obviously one – Lane always believed Rommel saved his life by not handing him over to the Gestapo. He remained in a PoW camp until freed by the Americans.

those recruiters looked for. SOE operatives knew and accepted they might have to act beyond the Geneva Conventions. They rarely took prisoners – how could they? They were taught that traitors were to be summarily executed. They were playing by a dirty set of rules and, conversely, were under no illusions what-soever of the consequences of capture: no dropping their rifle or bomb and shouting 'I surrender' as sundry human rights lawyers beat a path to their prison cell to check they were being well treated and claim compensation if they were not.

Back then, facing the consequences of Nazi victory and knowing what their enemies were capable of, there was very little that was out of bounds. They certainly believed that what they were doing was entirely legitimate. After all, the conse-quences of failure would be nothing short of cataclysmic.

How can one describe one's feelings after such a scene? Torn by the desire to burst out laughing, at the same time I was conscious that something deadly serious might have been set in train. The first step had been taken which, unless I flunked the courses ahead of me, must inevitably lead to the moment when I would be thrown in at the deep end, as it were, to sink or swim according to my calibre.

Would I go into the field with proper training and equip-ment to survive and would I be of any use there? If captured, would I break down? Could I face a firing squad in a manly fashion? Once launched into some godforsaken country, would I ever get out again?

In my taxi on the way back to Shepheard's I wished I had someone to talk things over with.

I needn't have worried. When I got back I found the other bed in my room occupied by my greatest friend, John Proctor, who had just returned from South Africa where he had been recuperating from severe wounds received during one of our tank battles together. I was delighted to see him and, on learning that he was also awaiting a posting, lost no time in running him along that very next morning to Rustom Buildings.

Luckily John had also played rugger, and a few days later we departed, together with about thirty other aspiring agents, to our first spy school.

It was near Haifa, about halfway up Mount Carmel in modern-day Israel – but before leaving Egypt, Geoff was obliged to write to his parents on 8 December 1942 asking to be bailed out to the tune of £25. It was one thing to live for months in the desert, spending nothing, and then blow it all living the high life for a few days. It was quite another to take up residence in Cairo, as Geoff recently had. That required extra income and Geoff only ever had his fairly paltry army salary. Not for the first time, he was living well beyond his means.

I was in a desperate situation, unable to leave my hotel in Cairo and the bill going up every day!
[*He wrote:*]
My work is extremely secret and I'm afraid I can give you no inkling of what it is – however it promises more excitement than anything I have hitherto attempted!
'I wish to hell the goddam war would finish – I'm tired of being without my wife and liable to fly off the handle pretty soon. As for the army, I don't like khaki any longer and would like to dress in pink chiffon panties and kiss-me-quicks.'

Long experience of army courses has taught me that one can roughly judge their merits by the amount of physical training inflicted upon one for want of all other ideas. This course, John and I agreed, was an all-time stinker. The living conditions were abominable and the directing staff were, with one exception we thought, lazy and unimaginative and, I suspected, rather happy to hold their nice safe jobs.

I recall one of their better efforts. With great hoo-ha they laid on an exercise for us, quote: 'A testing and important exercise under realistic conditions'.

We were to land at night from rubber boats somewhere near Acre, a port on the coast, as infiltrating saboteurs. Thence, carrying a radio, a battery and explosives, we were to make our way undetected across the coastal plain and up into the hills and beyond to blow up a bridge. It was a total distance of about thirty miles, I suppose, and we had fifty hours within which to do it. They split us into two groups of ten and landed us about five miles apart. I commanded one of the groups and from my map had selected an Arab village up in the hills about ten miles from the coast as my first objective. I hoped we might be able to hole up there unobserved during daylight.

The surf was choppy and we all got soaked. We deflated and buried the rubber boats and set off on a compass bearing, each man toting about 40 lb of kit.

After a while we came upon a high link security fence which, in the pale moonlight, appeared to stretch for miles in both directions. I opted to follow it to the left, and we hadn't gone 200 yards when we were suddenly challenged.

'*Haltie. Oo go da?*' I heard a voice asking in unmistakeable Ki-Swahili – the patois of my boyhood in Africa.

Too late I saw a twitchy black soldier pointing his rifle at my guts. I had to think quickly before he got nervous and let the damn thing off. I figured he had to be from the King's African Rifles, who were often employed on guard duties.

'*Rafiki. Sisi rafiki.* Friends. We are friends,' I answered falling back into my boyhood language. 'Greetings. Who are you?'

'My name is Juma, Effendi.' He seemed greatly relieved. As was I.

'Excellent, Private Juma,' I said, taking his rifle. 'Can you come with us?' I said pointing. 'We need someone to show us the way across here.'

He obligingly guided us across the airfield, which those sods hadn't told us about. I then abducted the unlucky Private Juma and obliged him to carry the battery.

We arrived at the village at dawn, established radio contact and reported a prisoner in the form of one Private Juma of the King's African Rifles.

We lay up all day in a village and I studied my map. It looked like a longish haul over some pretty bloody terrain, which indeed it was. I was then struck with an excellent idea. I summoned the Muktah, or headman, of the village and politely, yet very firmly, ordered a camel with a guide to take us overnight to the next village, which was only about a mile from our target.

That most excellent camel carried pretty well our entire cargo without turning a hair and I was happy to trot along immediately behind it up the steep track, thinking how clever I had been. True enough, but every so often and out of a cloudless sky I received a refreshing spray of moisture in my face. I was unaware at that time that the Prophet Muhammad, fourteen centuries earlier, with a wave of his hand had so altered the anatomy of a camel as to make it piss backwards.

We arrived at our target with several hours to spare. We placed our explosives and decided to amuse ourselves a little. About forty yards from where the bang would be and in the direction from where my enemy, the Chief Instructor, was due to arrive, we sat and waited.

In due course a staff car drove up. The Chief Instructor was sitting in the front with the driver, and in the rear were two of his stooges.

The mine, when I exploded it, made an impressive bang and sent chunks of concrete flying in all directions. They bailed out as one man and hit the dirt, whereupon we sprayed submachine-gun bullets all around their feet.

When the dust had settled the Chief Instructor picked himself up. He was ashen and, I noticed, had a small gash over his right eye. It was bleeding quite nicely.

'What the bloody hell do you think you're doing?' he spluttered. 'You weren't supposed to actually blow up the culvert. Now you've destroyed the only road to God knows where and there'll be hell to pay. And what about the prisoner?' he went on, dabbing furiously at his forehead. 'Christ, his regiment has been giving me fits.'

'Sir,' I replied with a perfectly straight face. 'You never told us not to blow up the culvert and, as for the prisoner, he spotted us, so I had either to shoot him or bring him along as we were supposed to be infiltrating saboteurs. We destroyed the target you selected and, incidentally, you and the others are very dead.'

He glared at me through one malignant eye. 'You will submit a full written report for the Commanding Officer by 0900 hours tomorrow.' I did that and was summoned at around 1100 hours. I entered the Colonel's office and stood rigidly to attention.

'You may stand at ease,' he said after a short while.

He flipped over my report. 'I've read this, and, before I go any further I will tell you that I think you displayed admirable resourcefulness and initiative. However, this is not why you're here.' He paused and chose his words. 'It would appear that you are at serious odds with the Chief Instructor. He has intimated that you display a certain arrogance in your attitude towards him and a contempt for his authority.'

How true, I thought, but made no comment.

'My staff is dedicated to giving you the best possible training and I will not tolerate insubordination from anyone at any time. Is that clearly understood? Very well . . . I am not going to reprimand you officially but, for your own good, you had better change your attitude. That is all. You may go.'

I saluted and turned to leave.

'Oh, by the way,' he said, his eyes twinkling. 'I enjoyed that bit with the camel. You must have been specially blessed!'[4]

A long while later I learned that accounts of my later successes filtered back to the Chief Instructor, still on Mount Carmel. Suddenly I had always been his star pupil. And hadn't he done a splendid job training me?

Private Juma was returned safely to his unit . . . all smiles and richer by a month's pay in baksheesh from me.

John and I had one friend on the staff, a Polish officer. His unpronounceable name sounded like a foot being pulled out of a swampski and so he was simply known as Stan. He was a magnificent chap and a great gentleman.

Stan taught us explosives, their many varieties and different functions. He taught us about the setting and defusing of mines and booby traps. He instructed us in enemy weapons of all kinds and was in charge of the pistol and submachine-gun ranges. Towards the end of the course you were encouraged to select what was to be your personal weapon when you entered the field. Stan would then spend hours altering and moulding the butt so that the pistol or revolver, as the case may be, fitted your grasp absolutely perfectly. I chose for myself a Smith & Wesson .38 Special revolver, and under Stan's tutelage became surprisingly expert with it. John and I worked like dogs and passed out top among all the other students.

The survivors of the course, now twelve in number, left for Kabrit on the Suez Canal to become parachutists. I know the brave boys and other lunatics will tell you that there is nothing

4 I'm guessing here, but I suspect this is some reference/joke about being the unwitting beneficiary of the Prophet Muhammad's changing of the anatomy of the camel.

to jumping out of an aeroplane. They may be right. It must be a matter of temperament. All I can say is that I have made seven jumps and hated each one more than the one before.

They did their best to maim us during the first week of the course by making us jump off fast-moving vehicles and leap off terrifying heights. Then the dread time arrived. They would kick us out of bed at 0400 hours, when our courage was at its lowest ebb, in order that we could make our jumps in the calm of the morning, before the wind got up and made it too dangerous.

I had a veteran soldier servant who used to meet me on the ground with a flask of hot tea. I thought his sense of humour was a trifle offbeat. ''Orrible sight you was this morning, Sir,' he would say with great satisfaction. 'Arse over tip you came aht an I says ter meself, I says, Gawd, e's gonna 'it ther tail an cut 'isself in 'arf.'

However, I survived and came the glorious moment at last when, having made our final jumps, the twelve survivors were entitled to sew parachute wings on their uniforms. We had a week before our final school and John and I, feeling very doggy and proud of ourselves, took off for a few days' sailing in Alexandria.

Near Haifa (in modern day Israel) on the plain at Megiddo, which is the traditional site of Armageddon, stood an isolated house. This was the property of an American archaeological foundation, and here was installed the school where we were to learn the meat of our trade. This was a very far cry from the paramilitary establishment on Mount Carmel. Here the instructors were first-class professionals who took their work and their students extremely seriously. Many of them had themselves operated in the field, and they were keen to pass on their knowledge and experience.

One mistake, they were fond of emphasising, would probably be your last.

During the two months we spent in their charge we were never once allowed outside the grounds except when we were taking part in some exercise. This was no hardship as the school was comfortable and well run, the food was excellent and the work, to me at least, was utterly absorbing.

The course covered a wide range of subjects: wireless, codes, secret ink, lock-picking, breaking and entering, searching rooms and luggage, shadowing and eluding a shadow, poisons, disguises and, above all, interrogations.

Many, many hours were spent in establishing identities and cover stories and then breaking them down through harsh and sometimes brutal interrogation.

We were aware of Hitler's mandatory directive that all parachutists or agents of any kind, if captured in uniform or otherwise, were to be handed over immediately to the Gestapo for interrogation and execution. It was drummed into us over and over again that not only would our own lives depend upon our caution and attention to detail, but also the lives of many brave men and women who would be helping us.

Absolute perfection was demanded and no excuses were accepted.

I passed. (One perk that I hadn't reckoned on was that as a member of SOE I no longer paid income tax.)

Back again once more in Cairo, I learned the depressing news that John and three others had been rejected. Poor John went gloomily off to join a parachute battalion and subsequently got shot in the backside while jumping into Sicily. He really had the worst luck.

8

A feast in Greece

I was informed that I had been selected to open up an area in Greece where hitherto there had been no Military Mission. I would be sent in, if possible, during the next new moon period at the end of March 1943. My area was bounded on the south by the Gulf of Corinth – the inland sea that splits the main chunk of northern Greece from the Peloponnesus – and included the entire provinces of Parnassus and Dorice.

I studied the maps avidly and read many famous names of places which recalled my classical studies at Downside. Delphi, Agrinion, Thermopylae, Lamia – they were all there – the mountains of Parnassus, Giona and Vardhousia, the homes of the ancient gods. I set about learning as much as I could about the topography, communications and economy of the area, and I also learned by heart one sentence in Greek: 'I am a British officer and I do not understand Greek.'[1]

I met my wireless operator, Sergeant Bill Weatherley, who would jump in with me, and also the interpreter I had been allotted, an unprepossessing character named Simonopoulos. My operation was given a code name, 'FEROCITY', and I

---

1   When I went to fight the Argentinians I spoke no Spanish. I had a farewell drink with the father of a great friend, an ex-World War II commando and a man of action out of the Geoff mould. To survive this coming war, he advised, I needed to learn but two phrases in Spanish. The first: 'I surrender' (of no use, of course, to Geoff) and, the second: 'Two large whiskies, please. My friend will pay.'

was busied day after day in discussions about what my load should consist of and many other matters.

In those days parachute drops were made by a flight of Halifax bombers operating out of Gambut in Libya. Each machine carried in the bomb bays twelve large containers and, in addition, upwards of thirty packages could be dropped through a large hole in the floor of the fuselage. Through this hole also departed the parachutists. The drill was to make the first drop, which would include personnel, wireless set, charging engine and batteries, and then, once communications with Cairo had been established, to follow it up with a second planeload a day or so later.

Subsequent drops depended upon circumstances and averaged from one to four or five per month, according to the availability of aircraft and the demands from other theatres.

When the full moon period came around we all made our way up to Gambut, where there was a tented camp adjacent to the airfield. Here I met a dozen or more agents waiting to be dropped into Yugoslavia, Romania and Hungary. I discovered that I was low down on the list of priorities. The atmosphere in the mess, as might be expected, was subdued. Each man had plenty to occupy his thoughts. As the days passed the number of agents dwindled. We used to watch the great Halifax bombers lumbering off at around tea-time and would sometimes hear them returning as dawn was breaking.

There arrived one day a New Zealander, Donald Stott.[2] It appeared that he was to share my plane, but he was to be

---

2   Captain Donald Stott, as he was by this time, was one of the bravest of one very brave and tough nation: the New Zealanders. Born in 1914, by now he was already a veteran. As a sergeant in the Royal Artillery he had been wounded and captured on Crete during the catastrophic collapse of Allied forces defending Greece and its islands. In a PoW camp in Greece he teamed up with another countryman, Bob Morton – they were to become a team thenceforward – and the two stunned their captors by high-vaulting over the perimeter fence in daylight and escaping. Commissioned in 1942, Stott and Morton were parachuted back into Greece.

dropped a bit further north, where a Military Mission had been established under Brigadier Eddie Myers six months earlier. It was Brigadier Myers who was in overall command of SOE in central Greece.

Don already enjoyed a reputation for derring-do, a reputation I was subsequently to discover he thoroughly deserved. I can truthfully say that among the many brave men I have met, he stood out head and shoulders above all the others. It was a tragedy that, after many astonishing exploits, he lost his life when setting ashore from one of our submarines as he attempted an operation against the Japs. I lost a very true friend.

At the very end of the moon period our turn finally came. We would fly directly to Don's rendezvous where there was a reception party expecting him. We would drop him, together with a couple of containers and a few packages, and then return to the Mount Giona area and look for a signal of nine fires in the form of an 'F'. That would mean that there would be a group of some kind waiting for me.

There was a great deal of doubt about the very existence of my reception party. The only news was two months old and, while Cairo had rumours of a resistance group which was supposed to be forming in my area, they had no idea as to who they were or what they amounted to.

We took off. We had several hours' flying ahead of us and, once settled in, there seemed to be nothing to do other than catch up on some sleep. As we crossed the Greek coast there was some desultory AA fire and I went up front and sat in the co-pilot's seat. The beauty of the scene was breathtaking. The moon rode high and placidly. The mountains were covered in snow, and far below us twinkled a few scattered lights. I gazed and gazed.

Suddenly I was struck with fear. Must I really cast myself out into the night? During the months my mind had shelved the reality of this moment and now, when it was too late, all my doubts and fears came flooding back tenfold.

The pilot broke into my reverie: 'I'll start down now. You'd better go back and tell the other bod to be ready to jump in about twenty minutes. After he's gone you'd better come back up and see if you can recognise your signal . . . if we find one.' I nodded and went back to help Don into his jumping suit and parachute.

As the plane descended it began to bucket about in a most unpleasant manner. I started to feel sick. The RAF dispatcher removed the cover from the yawning aperture and we busied ourselves arranging things so that Don and the few packages going with him would make a clean exit from the plane.

The intercom squawked, the dispatcher listened, then grinned and gave the thumbs-up. This was it. Don settled himself on the edge of the hole facing the tail and I knelt behind to steady him. The plane gave a violent lurch which finished me and I threw up neatly all over his chute.

'Fuck you!' he said with feeling. 'Now the bloody thing won't open.'

The next moment the red warning light came on. He tensed. 'GREEN!' And away he went with a clatter and a bang. The rear gunner laconically reported the chute opened. I mopped my brow, still feeling ghastly. Bill Weatherley, who had been watching all this, was convulsed with laughter.

The plane was climbing again now and I staggered forward and plumped myself down by the pilot. He turned and grinned at me. 'Very nice drop,' he said. 'Right on the nose. Now for your lot.'

'How long?' I asked.

'Well, about twenty minutes to get there and then I can afford about forty minutes to look around. After that, I'm afraid, we'll have to go home.'

We arrived over the target area and almost immediately the pilot drew my attention and pointed downwards, arching his brows in interrogation. I could see signal fires springing up: seven – eight – nine – ten of them, in rather a ropey 'H'. I considered. We seemed to be well away from any town or road so it seemed unlikely that they could be decoy fires.

'Any good?' he asked.

'I suppose so,' I said. 'Anyway, I think we'll have a go. Just give us about ten minutes to get ready, will you?'

I went back to alert the others. I would go first, followed by Bill, then Simonopoulos.

A few minutes later, after the usual heart-stopping plunge, I was swinging in space. I looked down. The fires were a long way beneath me and appeared to be moving away fast. I guessed there must be a strong wind. I began to feel uneasy as I could see nothing but trees and craggy rocks to land on. Down I came, oscillating violently, and landed heavily in a bush on the side of a steep slope. Relief! Silence. The bomber roared over, making its canister run, and then climbed away, headed for home.

I felt very lonely.

Next moment I heard a shouting and a crashing coming towards me out of the night. Playing it safe, I drew my revolver and crouched behind my bush. The noise came closer and I could hear someone panting heavily. I peered around my bush and saw in the moonlight the figure of a man in uniform.

An Italian uniform.

As always when given a bad fright, my reaction was one of furious rage. No damned Eyetie was going to put me tamely in the bag.

I leapt from my bush and covered him. My intention was to use him as a guide to get me away from the immediate vicinity and then shoot him. After that I had no plan except to run like hell and hope that the other members of my party would do likewise. At least with our codebook safely in my pocket, the Italians would not be able to use the wireless transmitter (W/T) set to any advantage.

He spun around and his startled expression, clear in the moonlight, was replaced by a look of delight. He spread his arms wide as though to step forward and embrace me, but stopped short when he saw my revolver.

'I'm Greek,' he said. 'Are you English or American?'

'Don't move,' I said. 'I'm an Englishman. Why the Italian uniform?'

'Oh!' he laughed. 'I see. Yes, of course, but it isn't . . . it's Greek. You'll see the difference easily in daylight. I am Captain Lagouranis, late of the 5/42 Regiment of Evzones. There are about fifty of us here. Come along and meet our commander, Colonel Psaros.'[3]

I put up my gun and took his hand thankfully. 'You gave me a hell of a fright,' I said. 'There are two others with me. Are they all right?'

'I saw their parachutes. Don't worry, they'll be looked after and everything that was dropped will be brought up to our HQ. By God, I'm glad to see you,' he went on. 'We've been waiting here for weeks not knowing whether to expect you or not.'

We chatted together, partly in English and partly in French, as we made our way past excited little groups of men busy with the containers. Finally we reached a shelter made of pine branches where a man was standing beside a fire. He was middle-aged, rather portly and had a gentle manner.

---

3 Evzones: elite Greek troops and the precursors of today's royal guard. Colonel Psaros appears to have been notable in that he was not overtly political and was genuinely anti-German, as against other Greek resistance movements. If anything, Psaros was a republican but certainly no Communist, which was to be his undoing.

As I came up and saluted him, he smiled broadly and embraced me.

'Psaros,' he said. 'This is a happy occasion. Welcome to Greece! Were our fires all right? There was some confusion on the part of our contacts in Athens.'

I laughed. 'Well, they got us down here. How close are the Germans?'

'At least ten miles away across the mountains.'

'Any danger of their coming to investigate?' I asked.

'No.'

'Good. Well there should be ten large metal containers with coloured silk parachutes and twenty-eight packages with white cotton chutes. I'd rather nothing was opened until everything has been collected as certain of the containers carry the W/T set and other materials which are for us, as opposed to all the other stuff which is for you.'

'I have ordered everything to be brought up here unopened,' he said. 'Ah . . . here comes the rest of your party.'

Bill and Simonopoulos arrived with an excited escort and I made the introductions. The latter was in a high state of elation and I had to stop him making a speech.

I explained to Colonel Psaros that our first priority was to establish communications with Cairo and that, if we were successful in doing this, we could expect to receive another drop of supplies within a day or two.

Included in the drop which had come with me were 4000 gold sovereigns, and I immediately handed over a bag containing 1000. This was a no ifs, no buts fortune, especially in that place and at that time. The going rate of pay for an Andarte – a Greek partisan, who was expected to present himself fully armed and equipped for action – was one gold sovereign a month. That meant there was enough in that one bag alone to buy an Andarte army and keep it in the field for a good few months.

The rest of the load had comprised rifles, light machine-guns, ammo, boots, uniforms and medical supplies. We were all kept busy for the rest of the night sorting and stacking everything ready for distribution on the morrow.

On his first attempt the following afternoon Bill succeeded in raising Cairo on the W/T and we were warned to expect an aircraft that very night. The signal was to be twelve fires making an 'M'.

At around 11 p.m. a plane was heard approaching and, without thinking, I ordered the fires to be lit. The immediate and unwelcome result was a shower of anti-personnel bombs from a Heinkel 111. This was my first and last mistake of this nature. Subsequently our ears became tuned to the sound of our own planes and we never lit up until we were quite sure.

No one was hurt on this occasion, however. Barely had the German departed, after busily machine-gunning us for about ten minutes, when the Halifax arrived and made a perfect drop with a full load of weapons and ammunition.

During the next few days Psaros tried to instruct me about current conditions in Greece as well as giving me all the information he could about the enemy and their methods.

He informed me that there were several resistance organisations in the process of formation throughout Greece. His force was called the EKKA and was made up of republicans. He had no strong political inclinations and just wanted to fight the common enemy. Psaros told me that the only other military band in this area was known as the ELAS. The ELAS was the military arm of a hard-line Communist organisation called the EAM, which had direct links back to Moscow.

In my naivety I did not at first grasp the implications of these resistance organisations being affiliated to different and implacably hostile factions. It was inconceivable to me that the Greeks, with the enemy occupying their country, could put any consideration above that of simply killing Germans and Italians.

In time, I was to learn how sinister were the designs of the Communists and how they would stop at nothing to neutralise all other armed organisations. Their aim was to be the only resistance movement in the field so that, come the end of the war, there would be no one in a position to stop them taking over Greece. Nor did I know that Brigadier Myers (the head British honcho in Greece, who had his HQ to the north of me) and his staff were spending as much time trying to reconcile the various warring factions as planning raids on the Germans. It is true to say that the thousands of ELAS partisans contributed virtually nothing towards the liberation of Greece. Indeed, because their avowed intention was to enslave their own countrymen under the hammer and sickle come the end of the conflict, Greece was to dissolve into a vicious civil war that was not to end until 1948.

A few days later I was delighted to see Don Stott ride into our camp. He was accompanied by a bearded, sinister-looking individual going under the alias of Thiamundis. He was the commissar of an ELAS band of Andartes established on Mount Parnassus, to the east of us. Like all the commissars I met, Thiamundis was a professionally trained Communist organiser. A veteran of the Spanish Civil War, he had been sent to Greece by the 3rd International to get on and do his dirty work. I could tell that he was already put out by the evidence of weapons and supplies that I had brought to the EKKA, who they were to treat as their avowed enemy.

Don and I had a long discussion. During his escape from Greece he had got to know something about the Greeks – he said that he owed his survival to them – and the way things worked. He advised me that as soon as I felt able to stand on my own feet I should set up my own HQ and avoid, as far as possible, becoming identified with any one particular group.

Our mission was to fight the Germans, not to get dragged into Greek politics. I am thankful that I took his advice. On three subsequent occasions, the EKKA were treacherously attacked and disarmed by the ELAS, who kept their weapons and ammunition for themselves. The ELAS claimed that the situation would be resolved if only the EKKA would disperse or place themselves under their command. Psaros continued to refuse to comply, and eventually he and several of his officers were murdered by them in cold blood.

But all this was in the future. Anxious to get started in my work, I left Bill with Psaros for a few days and set off with Don and Simonopoulos for Mount Parnassus, as I wished to meet the ELAS commander and judge his attitude for myself.

Simonopoulos proved troublesome. He had developed a sort of *folie de grandeur* and was continually making noisy speeches and sounding off on his own account instead of interpreting my needs and instructions. Finally, in exasperation, I refused to allow him to accompany me further and sent him back to Psaros with instructions that he should be considered as under open arrest until I could obtain some guidance from Cairo as to his future. He was reluctant to go.

This was an awkward and potentially dangerous situation and one which was resolved when Simonopoulos failed to return from a short walk.[4] I confess that I was a little taken aback when I was told what had happened. But, as was pointed out, in the game we were involved in no unnecessary risk was justified: absolute obedience and loyalty was the only criterion.

---

4 Although Geoff is somewhat reticent about spelling it out, Simonopoulos was clearly killed. Geoff sent his draft manuscript to a wartime chum who wrote back suggesting that he play this episode down. After all, Simonopoulos would most probably have had family and Geoff was still alive: some would have said that he might have been complicit in murder. Foot's book on SOE is unequivocal on the subject: agents were taught that in this scenario – where a person threatened the safety of the group – there was but one option, and Geoff's men took it.

I replaced him shortly afterwards with Yotis Mariettis. He was to interpret faithfully for me and to remain my loyal friend and counsellor until the day I left Greece.

Easter must have been early in 1943. In any event I remember that I celebrated it with Colonel Psaros up on Mount Giona. We had received a few more supply drops and the morale of the EKKA was high. He explained to me that in Greece Easter Sunday was literally a 'feast' day and that his band of Andartes would observe it accordingly.

Shortly after daybreak our camp was astir. Each man greeted his fellow with '*Christos annestis*' – 'Christ has risen' – not just once but every few minutes, and red-dyed hard-boiled eggs were exchanged and eaten. Pits were dug and huge barbecue fires lit. Young male lambs were slaughtered and their hides cleverly removed like jackets to make future wineskins. Their intestines were thoroughly cleaned and stuffed into long sausages of chopped-up livers, kidneys, hearts, lungs and testicles. The carcasses were impaled upon young pine trees and the whole lot set to roast over the fires.

We all sat around salivating and swigging ouzo and a rough red retsina: a wine steeped in pine resin which, once one gets over the first shock, can be addictive.

It would be about seven hours before the lambs would be ready, and to kill time we sang and joked and danced those extraordinary dances in a circle to music provided by a variety of instruments. It was Oriental-sounding stuff, a legacy of four hundred years of often brutal Turkish occupation, but haunting enough.

Swaying a little, Colonel Psaros hoisted to a dead fir tree an enormous silken Greek flag which fluttered bravely above us to the cheers and tears of the company. He took the occasion to make me an honorary captain of Evzones, in the 5/42nd, his own regiment, and plonked upon my head an astrakhan shako made for him by his loving wife in Athens.

I was appreciative of the honour and made what I thought was a suitable little speech, which no one understood except Bill, who giggled tipsily. Later he said, 'I do apologise, Sir, but I thought you looked a proper Charley in that hat.' He was right, of course.

Lord, how we enjoyed those 'sausages' as mezze with our ouzo; how we devoured those lambs barbecued with their spices; how we swilled that retsina and stuffed ourselves with wholemeal bread, sheep's butter, yoghurt and ripe olives; how we sang and danced! A shepherd's lad of about seventeen, clad in the ancient garb of jodhpur-like trousers and a pleated frock coat – a truly beautiful youth with deep blue eyes and tight black curls, an Adonis – came shyly forward and, kneeling in front of me, offered in his cupped hands, with ineffable grace, all that he had to offer: a posy of spring violets.

I felt faintly embarrassed, but rather touched.

Come the dawn, our hangovers were monumental and Bill, for the first and only time, overslept and missed his scheduled W/T transmission to Cairo, causing some concern for our safety. I was hard on him, which was a little unfair as my tolerance for alcohol is only matched by two women of my acquaintance.

9

The unattackable viaduct

During the next few weeks I travelled continuously around my area keeping in occasional touch with Bill by runner – back in those days we used our radio more to communicate with Cairo than with each other. Bill was quite comfortably installed with his radio and his own interpreter in the village of Stromni to the north-west of Mount Giona.

I was busy looking over the railway line north of Parnassus when I heard that Colonel Psaros had been suddenly attacked and disarmed by Thiamundis, the ELAS political commissar, and his men. Unwilling to credit this fantastic treachery but fearing for the safety of Bill and the wireless set, I hurried back to investigate.

A few words are appropriate at this juncture to describe the methods of the Communists. People often wonder how a situation can come about where a tiny minority can rule a country, can hold it in slavery in fact, against the wishes of the great majority of its population.

The answer is, of course, through fear.

The pattern is always the same and I have seen it successfully followed in many countries. But, back then, it was the first time I had come across it and I still had much to learn. What had happened was roughly as follows:

When the Axis forces overran and occupied Greece there were thousands of patriotic young men anxious to strike a blow for their freedom, but they lacked both the materials and the organisation to acquire the means of resistance. This was where the Communists stepped in to seize their opportunity. They presented themselves in the image of a non-political resistance movement and raised the Greek flag in the mountains as a rallying point. They were organised into two sections. The controlling Committee, known as the EAM, operated in Athens and numbered among its members, apart from hardcore Communists, many prominent citizens and senior professional soldiers whose names were known to and respected by the public.

In the field their armed forces, or Andartes[1] as they were called, were known as the ELAS. Each band or company was jointly commanded by a triumvirate: a captain, usually a professional army officer, a commissar and a quartermaster. The two latter were always professional Communist organisers and, as they could outvote the captain, inevitably ended up constituting the source of authority and command.

Starting early in 1942 and with only a few hundred armed Communists, the ELAS proceeded to establish themselves in the mountains in various parts of Greece. However, it was essential that they controlled the villages so that they could obtain the supplies of food, mules and any other commodities they required. To achieve this they used to proceed as follows.

Having selected their target village they would assemble thirty or forty armed men and appear in the square. Here, beneath a Greek flag, they would make stirring speeches about the need for discipline, unity and sacrifice on the part of everyone if the enemy were ever to be driven from the country.

Warmly welcomed by the villagers, they would then recruit

1 The word comes from the Greek word *andartiko*, meaning 'guerrilla warfare'. The Greeks were masters of this type of warfare. They needed to be, having resisted their Ottoman Turkish overlords for centuries. To them the Germans were but another in a long line of murderous oppressors.

into their ranks as many young men as they could, binding
them with severe oaths. The next step would be a verbal attack
on the selfish complacency of the wealthier and more influential members of the community – this almost inevitably included
the schoolmaster and the village priest, whose reactionary attitude in the past, they would claim, had helped to bring Greece
to her present position of disgrace and defencelessness. Next,
specifically from among the village riff-raff they would select a
man whom they would appoint as *Epefthanos*, or their representative, to replace the former headman or mayor, and would
immediately put him in charge of the village telephone
exchange. Imploring the people to co-operate with the new
Epefthanos, they would depart with their new recruits.

There would then be an immediate split in the village. The
have-nots and the very young would support the new arrangement, whereas the well-to-do and the more influential, who
considered their own patriotism second to none and who naturally resented being usurped by a man known to be uneducated
and of bad character, would quickly re-establish the status quo.

A week or two later, back would come the partisans. The
leading citizens and sometimes the priest also would be
dragged out and denounced as traitors. Some would be
flogged, others hanged and the village would be collectively
punished by the levy of a heavy fine, in cash and in kind.

Thereafter, with the ever-present threat of the partisans a
few hours away in the mountains above them, the villagers
would be forced to toe the line.

Thus, piecemeal, was a large part of the country brought
under the Communist heel. They enforced savage discipline
within their own ranks, and once under oath any man who
realised too late who and what his masters stood for and who
tried to escape the trap was immediately executed. Such men
were often tortured first.

One can appreciate why the ELAS was determined to

prevent the existence of any armed non-Communist resistance groups to whom the majority of the defenceless Greeks could look for support. As might be expected, the EAM/ELAS tried for as long as possible to hide their true nature from the world at large and from the British Military Mission in particular. They wanted our weapons, money and supplies and we thought we needed their numbers to fight against the enemy. When our senior officers finally realised what was really going on and tried to explain this to our masters in Cairo they were told to get on with the job in hand. From Churchill down, the message was the same: we are only interested in fighting and damaging the Italians and Germans; we are not particularly interested in what might happen in Greece come the peace, not least because we are not going to be ruling – or be very interested in – Greece come the peace. What matters to the war effort is finding those who are most effective at fighting the enemy and equipping them to do so.

Fine in theory, and the ELAS could be thoroughly effective fighters when they were so minded, but when the powers that be in Cairo finally came to credit what we in the field had been telling them for months – that the ELAS never had the slightest intention of using British arms and equipment except to conduct an armed Communist revolution as soon as the Germans left the country – it was too late.

A bitter civil war was to ensue following the German retreat at the end of 1944, and it was only the timely arrival of British battalions from Egypt – with a little help from us lot – that prevented Greece from disappearing behind the Iron Curtain, like the rest of the Balkans.[2] And when I say civil war, I mean

2 When the post-Nazi world was being carved up between the Allies, Stalin agreed that Greece was to remain in the West. Somewhat surprisingly, especially given the way things were to turn out later elsewhere in Eastern Europe, he kept to his agreement. So, when the Communists did try to take over Greece in 1944, and on several occasions thereafter, Stalin did not send them the help they so badly needed. Had he done so, the ELAS/EAM could well have won the civil war and Greece with it.

war: in the fighting against the ELAS of late 1944/January 1945, we British lost 237 killed and 2101 wounded. Some allies they turned out to be.

But back to my story.

On my way I fell in with the head of our mission, Brigadier Eddie Myers, who as it happened was on his way down from his HQ in the high mountains to the north of me to visit and try to deal with this new crisis.

Eddie patched up the quarrel by threatening to cut off all further supplies to the ELAS unless all the material taken from the EKKA was restored. But what he really wanted to see me about was something different. He had received urgent instructions from Cairo and he wanted me to get involved in an extremely important sabotage operation: the destruction of the Asopos Viaduct.

There was only one railway line from Germany down to Athens. The Germans had been sending men, supplies and equipment south by train – upwards of forty trains a day at the height of the Desert War – to Athens and its nearby port of Piraeus. There they transhipped to Crete, and from there it was but a one-night trip across to Tobruk and North Africa.

There were three gorges where the line could be cut for a significant and worthwhile period of time – anywhere else and the Germans simply rebuilt the line or unblocked the tunnel in a matter of days. The British had destroyed one viaduct on their retreat from Greece in April 1941, but this had been rebuilt and was now heavily guarded. Brigadier Eddie had been specifically dropped into Greece in September 1942 to knock out one of the bridges over these gorges. The reason: to delay German reinforcements and supplies for the battle of El Alamein. Eddie had looked at the Asopos Viaduct and concluded it was far too chancy – given its near impregnable position a frontal attack would have required a large force of regular soldiers (unavailable), or a sneak attack along the railway line by a mass of irregulars (too chancy) or a really sneaky attack by a handful of picked men (too risky, as it meant descending an unexplored gorge).

He and the Andartes had, instead, attacked and destroyed the Gorgopotamos Viaduct in November 1942. This had been a full-scale attack involving masses of Andartes, who had neutralised the Italian garrison while Royal Engineer officers blew up the bridge.[3] However, come late January 1943, the viaduct had been cobbled back together using wooden 'piers' and trains were crossing, albeit slowly. Inevitably, the Germans were now guarding the Gorgopotamos in force.

Now London and GHQ Cairo again needed one of those three viaducts knocked out. They reckoned that the 'best' viaduct to attack was the Asopos, for three reasons: first, it had not yet been attacked; second, the Krauts reckoned it was 'unattackable'; and third, given where it was built – halfway up a cliff face – it would take many months to repair. Drop the Asopos and the Germans would have very major resupply problems throughout the Balkans and Greece.

With the expulsion of the Axis armies from Africa it became of urgent importance to German intelligence that they should know precisely where and when the Allies planned to make their attack on *Festung Europa* ('Fortress Europe'). The choices open to the Allies were:

1 invade Sicily;
2 invade the Italian mainland;
3 make a two-pronged attack, one wing of which would enter the Balkans via Salonika (on the eastern Mediterranean coast in modern-day Albania) and thrust up north through and eventually into Hungary.

3   The sad denouement, as reported by Myers in his book, *Greek Entanglement*, was that thirteen innocents from Lamia were taken to the viaduct a few days later and shot: sabotage could carry a very heavy price.

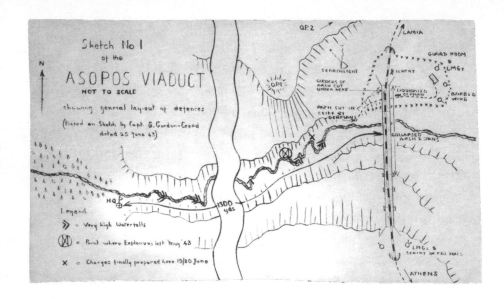

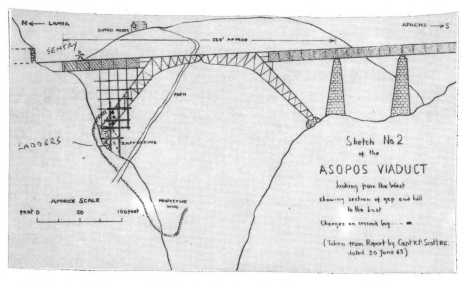

The Asopos Viaduct from below with the team's OP (Observational Post) marked on the cliffs above. Deemed unattackable by the Germans, the solution was to approach down a periously unclimbed gorge – the last place sentries thought to look.

It was known that Churchill was in favour of the last plan which had, among other advantages, the opportunity of lessening Russian influence in Eastern Europe come the end of the war.

The whole idea behind the operation was to make the Krauts think that Greece was our next port of call. Why, otherwise, go to such horrendous risks to do the otherwise impossible?[4]

We now know that the Sicily route was chosen, but we did not know that at the time and, back then, it was vital for the Allies to keep the Germans guessing and therefore forced to keep their forces dispersed to meet all possible eventualities. Had they worked out our plans they would have concentrated their forces in Sicily and destroyed the invasion on the beach.

So the British Military Missions throughout the Balkans were ordered to do all that lay within their power, through the various resistance movements and through their own resources, to sabotage the German war effort, with particular emphasis on the destruction of lines of communication. The maximum disruption was to be timed for May and June 1943, during the build-up to the Sicily landings.

After much deliberation it was decided on high that the main target in Greece was the Asopos Viaduct, on the railway line between Athens and Lamia to the north.[5] This viaduct

4   This is pure speculation on my part but, thinking about it, I wonder whether the team was not expendable. Drop the viaduct and – result! The Germans horrendously inconvenienced at a key moment and evidence that Greece was where the Allies were going to attack next. Fail to drop it – doubtless getting killed in the process – and it would still get the Germans thinking: why would the Allies sacrifice a top-level sabotage team trying to do the impossible, unless it was mission-critical they succeeded? Their very failure would be further proof that the Allies were next heading to Greece. Cynical of me, maybe, but . . .

5   In fact, Brigadier Myers says that the instruction to drop the Asopos came from Cairo – perhaps he was clever and let the man who would be risking his life think he was the one doing the selecting rather than issue a near-suicidal order. The other two, Myers wrote, were now too heavily guarded for there to be any hope of success. Only the Asopos left any chance, however remote, and that was because the Germans believed it impossible to attack.

was chosen because, although it was the best guarded and the most difficult to approach, its destruction would completely cut all railway communication to the whole of the south of mainland Greece and the Greek islands for at least two months and would also prove the greatest embarrassment to the enemy.

There were also various political considerations. As I have already explained, a natural consequence of the occupation of Greece by German Axis forces was the emergence of resistance movements. By the end of 1942 there were three or four groups roughly organised, ranging from the vaguely right-wing EDES to the Communist EAM/ELAS. As you now know, it was the policy of the EAM/ELAS to suppress all other resistance groups with the object of being in a position, at the end of the war, to impose their form of Communism on Greece. To this end they embarked upon a campaign of terrorism directed not against the Germans but against the people of Greece in general and opposing resistance groups in particular.[6]

But at the time of these events, the real motivation of the EAM/ELAS was not apparent to those on the spot or indeed elsewhere. With typically cynical opportunism, the Communists had declared themselves entirely at the disposal of the Commander in Chief, Middle East Forces, for guerrilla operations. As a result, they continued to receive planeloads of equipment, arms and explosives from the British.

When the project of destroying the Asopos Viaduct was first put to the EAM/ELAS by Brigadier Eddie, they replied that they would indeed help. They said they would provide an attacking force of 100 men [*Brigadier Myers, in his book, says 1000 men*] and hold the bridge long enough for a British

---

6   Although Brigadier Myers stated in his book that he never quite knew who was really in control in the mountains, it was the EAM political command in Athens or local ELAS commanders.

demolition party to blow it up, much the same plan of attack that had resulted in the destruction of the Gorgopotamos Viaduct six months earlier. They went on, however, to impose the condition that, owing to the hazardous nature of the operation, the difficulty of approach, the strength of the guard and the near proximity of a full battalion of German troops, they would require considerable extra quantities of arms and ammunition. Specifically, they needed heavy mortars and machine-guns.

So important was the Asopos project considered that, with great difficulty and only by depriving other theatres of operations, all that the EAM/ELAS demanded was supplied during the months of April and early May. The actual attack had been slated for 20 May.

All preparations on the British side were completed when, on 18 May, the EAM/ELAS dropped their bomb: the job was too dangerous and they would have nothing to do with it.

I will never forget the look of incredulity on Brigadier Eddie's face when he heard the news, nor the scathing throat-lashing to which he treated the two Communist leaders.

After they had gone and we were all in the deepest gloom, I suggested to Eddie that I take Don Stott along with me to have a look at the prospects of achieving by stealth what we had hoped to effect by force.

Clutching at straws I suppose, he agreed. Two days later Don and I set off with as much rope as we could scrounge.

At this point I propose to leave the narrative and to describe the bridge, its approaches, guards and so on.

The Asopos River has its source in a small glacier on the north face of Mount Giona (8235 feet). It cascades several thousand feet to the valley bottom and runs due east for several miles before plunging into a formidable gorge. This gorge, which no one had ever yet managed to penetrate, took the river, now an icy raging torrent, down a distance of about a mile and a half in a series of waterfalls, sluices and whirl-pools, dropping a further 1000 feet before debouching out of the mountains and on to the plains.

It was at the highest and narrowest point of the gorge that the Athens–Lamia railway line came straight out of a long tunnel through a mountain, crossed the gorge by way of the Asopos Viaduct and plunged directly into another tunnel on the far side. From the centre of the main 150-foot span to the river bed at this point was a height of about 200 feet, while the cliffs on either side soared upwards for a further 600 feet. An assault down the aforementioned gorge was assumed to be impossible.

It was reckoned that the only feasible method was to capture a train and drive it, full of Andartes, down the line and seize the viaduct in a surprise attack. The engineers could lay their charges and blow the structure. Everyone would then disappear back into the mountains.

Clustered about the tunnel mouth on the north side were the huts of the German guards, the searchlight and machine-gun positions, all heavily barbed-wired and mined. The guard consisted of a detachment of fifty men commanded by a sergeant, who were drawn from a battalion that was billeted in a village back down the railway line some three miles south of the viaduct.

The bridge had been built in 1912 by a firm of French engineers and was considered a magnificent feat of engineering. It also just so happened that a copy of the blueprint had been lodged in the British Museum. A copy of this was already in our possession. We used it to plan not only where to place the explosives for maximum effect but also how to fashion and shape the charges in a form which would enable us to place them quickly on to the main girders and get away.

The evening of 20 May saw Don Stott and me making camp under some plane trees at the mouth of the gorge. We were purposely avoiding villages where we might otherwise have slept, as we were particularly anxious to avoid the occasion for gossip and speculation about our intentions which could, in time, have reached German ears.

Early the next morning we made our way carefully along the top of the gorge to a point from which we were able to look directly down upon our target, the bridge. Through our field glasses we were able to observe every detail of the defences and the movements of the sentries. We were particularly intrigued to notice that the Germans were starting to erect scaffolding around the abutments on either side of the bridge. Evidently some repairs were about to be made.

The more we studied the place the less we fancied our chances. The obvious approach was from the plain to the east, but naturally all the defences were sited to guard against an attack from that direction. To scale down the cliffs from where we were lying was physically possible with enough rope, but it was in full view of the defences. We toyed with the idea of capturing a rail trolley, loading it with explosives, running it on to the bridge at night and exploding it with a pull-switch. The problem was that, while we would destroy the rails, we were most unlikely to drop the bridge. The only way to do that was to blow the bridge's supports.

We eventually decided that our only hope was to attempt to get down the impassable gorge. Then, under cover of darkness but with enough moon to help us see but not be seen, we would have to scale the 200-foot cliffs up to the abutments, climb on to the main structure, do our stuff with the explosives and escape back up the gorge. How long it would all take and whether it was even possible we would have no idea until we explored the gorge.

I have marked OP (observation point) on the sketch (page 126) to indicate the spot from which we were making our recce. From here it looked to us that the north-face cliffs offered our best chance of getting to the bottom of the bridge. Having decided this we made our way back to camp, stripped off and, carrying all the rope we had with us, gingerly entered the torrent of ice melt and began to swim and clamber down the gorge. After a very short distance we came upon our first obstacle, a formidable waterfall about thirty feet high. This we negotiated with ropes, only to meet another a little further on.

It was obvious now that we would require a hell of a lot more rope and a few extra hands, not to mention waterproofing for the explosives and fuses.

We decided to pack it in and get back to Eddie with our report. And so, almost exhausted, badly cut about and frozen stiff, we brewed up and then set off through the night for the seven-hour trek back to Stromni.

We found Eddie anxiously waiting. We were able to tell him that, providing he could get us enough rope and whatever else we needed, we felt it was worth having a go. We all agreed that nothing of our intentions should be made known to the gallant partisans.

Operation Asopos was now given the official code name of 'WASHING' and was also granted top priority on W/T (wireless transmissions).

I sat down with Don and sent Cairo a list of our needs, which were chiefly several thousand feet of good quality climbing rope, brown army gym shoes, navy blue shorts and T-shirts, non-glossy waterproof sheeting to wrap the explosives in and, finally, several dozen best quality 'French letters' or condoms. Whatever Cairo might have thought was our reason for demanding these last, we knew from experience that they were the ideal things for waterproofing fuses and detonators. Get those wet and, come the time, they would not work.

We figured that we would need an attacking party of four

plus a further two men to help with the porterage and running the camp. With me, therefore, besides Don, came two sapper (Royal Engineer) officers: McIntyre (known as Mac) and Scott. For the other two I chose Sergeant Khuri, a tough little Palestinian Arab from the Pioneer Corps, and Lance Corporal Charlie Mutch, a dour giant of a man who was an escaped PoW and whom we had collected from the mountains some time previously.

By mid-June everything had arrived safely and, having first extracted the promise of a case of Scotch whisky from Eddie as a reward for success, we set off secretly during the night of 21 May to make camp under the plane trees at the head of the gorge.

Charlie Mutch was in charge of our four mules: Brown Job, Black Job, Bloody Maud and, his special favourite, a misanthropic bitch named Pearl.

Marching all through the night, keeping well clear of villages and the business end of Pearl, we arrived at our campsite at first light. I lost no time in taking Mac and Scott up to the OP and was rather disconcerted to find there clear evidence of a recent enemy patrol, in the form of their refuse. However, we all had a good look at the bridge and were delighted to see that the scaffolding was coming along nicely. This was to play a decisive part in our later success.

Back down to the camp to make ourselves as comfortable as we could and to rest up in preparation for our start down the gorge on the morrow. It was chilly and the place was alive with scorpions.

The next four days were a nightmare I would prefer to forget. Each day we would crawl out of our blankets, brew up something hot and shiver our way into that damnably icy river, and each day, after hours of swimming, climbing and struggling, we would get a few yards further down the gorge. The force of the current was terrifying, and we knew that a slip would almost certainly mean death by drowning or by being battered over a forty-foot waterfall.

We took it in turns to swim ahead with the rope, belayed by the others, until it was possible to clamber on to a rock further downstream and make fast for the others to follow. As we progressed we left ropes secured as lifelines all along the way.

One incident, which might have been tragic, gave us all a laugh. Don, who was leading at the time, missed his footing, lost the rope and was swept around a corner and out of sight. When, with my heart in my mouth, I got to the corner and peered around it, I saw him safe and sound standing on a rock on the other side of a foaming circular maelstrom about twenty yards wide. The only way to him was straight across. The noise of the torrent was such that to shout was pointless so I made signs to him to ask how deep the pool was. The bastard put his hands at thigh level and so, sucker that I am, I plunged fearlessly in – into about twelve feet of water.

Don was convulsed. We then enjoyed our little comedy together as Mac and Scott in turn peered around the rock and went through the same pantomime about the depth, each one disappearing arse over tip.

All the time the gorge was getting narrower and narrower. It gave you a most unpleasant sensation to be able to touch both sides with your arms, as you could sometimes look straight up at those beetling cliffs soaring hundreds and hundreds of feet above. I had been startled by occasional loud cracks, like pistol shots, which sounded over the noise of the torrent. I was not too comforted when I realised that they were caused by small rocks falling down from the heights above.

We made fairly steady progress day by day and were getting to know our way back up very well, shinning up the ropes left in places where they were necessary. This was important, as after the attack we would have to escape up the gorge in the dark, and probably in a hurry as well.

On the fourth day, when we estimated that we must be about three-quarters of the way down, we hit a snag. The gorge narrowed to nothing. The torrent rushed down a high smooth corridor of rock, smashed around a huge boulder and vanished over a fall, the height of which we had no means of judging.

We saw no means of tackling this problem because, hard as we looked, we could find no projection around which we could belay a rope. This was a moment of near despair, until Don had a brainwave. If we cut down a substantial tree with a bole, say, of about eight inches width and a length of about eight feet, perhaps we could jam it across the gap. Once it was in position the current would keep it in place. This we could use as an anchor for the rope, and once we could get a look over the fall, perhaps we could find a way down.

I made the finding of two suitable trees the next day an excuse for giving everyone a rest in camp. We were all nearer to exhaustion than we realised, and a whole day of sunbathing, eating and drinking and never mentioning the river, except to curse it, worked wonders for our morale. Don and I did make one last trip up to the OP and were able to bless the industry of our enemies: the bridge, abutments and spans were covered with scaffolding.

That night around our campfire was something special; we all got slightly plastered and sang the songs that young soldiers sing. Mac had a particularly sweet voice and entertained us with a little ditty that went:

> I took my wife for a ramble,
> A ramble down a country lane.
> She caught her foot on a bramble,
> A bramble, and arse over bollocks she came

Singing:
Hey, jig-a-jig, shag a little pig.
Follow the band.
Follow the band all the way.

This catchy little number stuck in my brain and I sang it to myself all through the climb down the waterfalls and for weeks afterwards.

We decided also that as we had to spend the next day getting the trees down the river we might as well carry the made-up explosive charges down the river as far as we could while we were about it. We would find a spot for a cache.

The tree jam worked like a charm and we found ourselves able to negotiate the considerable fall to the south side. However, we had used up all of our rope, and if the going continued as it had we were going to need plenty more to get to the bottom. Also, the moon was well on the wane and we were going to need some ambient moonlight to be able to see to fix up the explosives when we came to making our final attack; it goes without saying that artificial light was not an option as we would have been spotted by the guards in a second, nor did we want too much moonlight as, once again, we would have been equally easily spotted.

If that were not enough, a couple of the men were suffering severe lacerations to their hands and knees from the constant buffeting of sharp rocks. It was time to get back to base and order up the extra rope we needed.

We reported back, and more rope was ordered and duly dropped by parachute although all this, obviously, took time.

A month later we had our rope, the moon was right and we were ready to try again. We set off and got to the top of the gorge on 15 June. Don then did a lone recce using all the rope we had already laid, and managed to get all the way down the gorge to the bottom. We had our route down.

Come the morning of 19 June, we found ourselves looking up at the bridge. In great excitement we scanned the cliff above us, and it appeared that it was going to be much less of a problem than we had feared. We were going to have to hump the dynamite up to where the supports rested on the rocks and from there climb the conveniently placed scaffolding to where we would tie on the explosives. We could see a series of ledges and even rough tracks leading upwards – the Germans had even been kind enough to cut routes through the barbed wire so their workmen could get to the base of the scaffolding. Withal, having no head for heights, I was thankful that the ascent would be at night and in the dark.

On regaining camp that evening I sent off Charlie Mutch with two of the mules. They were now redundant and likely to slow down our escape march. The rest of us spent the day resting. Charlie returned in the evening and, poor fellow, while saying 'hello' to his chum Pearl was kicked in the ribs by Bloody Maud. A lesser man would have passed out on the spot. Even tough old Charlie was so shaken that we decided to leave him in camp the next day, where he could be most useful getting everything packed up and ready to leave the moment we returned.

On 20 June the five of us made our way quickly down the gorge, picking up the explosives from the cache on the way. Once we had our ropes securely in place it was amazing how rapidly and with what confidence we could move around and over obstacles that previously might have taken us the better part of a day to master (it also helped that we were extremely fit). Finally we parked ourselves behind the last bend, which hid us from the bridge.

Now we had a longish wait until dark which, if I remember rightly, was about 8 p.m. (local time). In Greece, because it is much further south than Britain, not only does night come much earlier but the period of dusk is much shorter: probably about thirty minutes tops. We spent the time going over the charges, resting and having something to eat.

There was a waning moon nearly in its third quarter. It was due to rise over the gorge, we figured, at about 11 p.m. We planned to start our attack just before 8 p.m., as it was getting dark, and hoped to have placed our charges, set our fuses and left before the moon added to our chances of being spotted.

Darkness fell at last and with it came bitter cold. We had spent all day in and out of the icy water and were dressed only in shorts and T-shirts; our only food had been cold bully, bread and river water. Just about 8 p.m. saw us shivering in the river, up to our waists, at a point under the bridge where we intended to make our climb. I had decided that Don and I would start up first and, if all went well, would come back down to the others and help them hump the charges. I had also decided that no weapons were to be carried other than coshes.

There were four principal charges of about 30 lb apiece made up on wooden battens in a shape to fit the main girders – made up previously, if you remember, from the British Museum blueprints. We also had several 'sausages' about two feet long, useful for wrapping around the secondary beams. All the charges would have to be connected up with Primacord and detonated by time fuse. We had decided on a two-hour delay. We had also decided that because of the soaking everything had been subjected to, it would be prudent to duplicate all the circuits to minimise the chances of a misfire.

I set off up the cliff with Don. As we climbed higher, now in full view of the guards should they happen to direct their searchlights downward, the noise of the torrent subsided and the stillness became deafening. The abutment, covered with the scaffolding, was now looming above and we made the shelter of it with no little relief. It was dark as hell and one could really only see something when it was silhouetted against the night sky. Feeling around, I was astonished to find a ladder lashed to the scaffolding and leading upwards. This I promptly climbed and, about twenty feet up, found myself on a wooden platform whence another shorter ladder led up to a higher platform. From there and within easy reach were the main girders of the bridge. This was going to be a pushover!

Halfway down the cliff to fetch the others, we met them coming up. They had made an intelligent guess and, anyway, were fed up with freezing in the river. At this point I sent Sergeant Khuri back up the gorge to warn Charlie to be ready and to help him, as I was not too happy about his rib injuries.

Up the four of us scrambled, making a terrible noise, and settled ourselves on the top platform with the charges.

Mac and Scott now took over, as the Royal Engineer explosives experts. I was horrified a few moments later to hear a resounding four-letter word from Mac: at some point since 1912 the girders had been boxed in and our carefully constructed charges would have to be completely remade if they were to be effective. High explosive becomes little more than hot air and noise unless the resultant blast is properly channelled.

'How long, for Christ's sake?' I whispered.

'Maybe two hours,' replied Mac.

Bloody hell, I thought. Every second we were stuck on that scaffolding, nowhere to hide, the risks of discovery increased. Lady Luck had been with us up until now but that could all change in a second. What was more, the moon would be well up by then and the chances of being spotted would be commensurately higher.

At this moment the guards chose to switch on two searchlights.[7]

We froze and sweated. I watched the beams lazily searching the cliffs above, stabbing down into the gorge and glancing fleetingly over the bridge itself. Then, happening to glance upwards, I suffered a shock that nearly finished me. Not thirty feet above our heads stood a sentry. We hadn't even noticed the bugger!

I squeezed Mac's hand and gestured upwards. His reaction was to roll his eyes and cross himself. This struck me as so comical that I immediately fell into helpless giggles. Nerves, I suppose, but we all caught it and clung to one another until someone kicked a loose bolt with his foot and sent it plunging down into the darkness. The sentry would have to have noticed had he not been following the searchlight with his eyes.

Time wore on. Mac and Scott worked on the charges while Don and I helped where we could and watched the sentries. The moon came up over the mountains at 10 p.m. and we then had to time our movements with the clouds that were drifting across it. It was far too light for comfort. The sentry was bored. He stamped his feet, looked at his watch, gazed at the moon, had a good scratch and at one point broke wind with a force that must have gratified him. Poor fellow – his number was almost up.

---

7 There was obviously no set routine to the searchlight sweeps or the team would have conformed to them. On missions like these, 'routine' is good for the attackers, 'random' is bad. Just imagine yourself as one of those sentries. To find yourself tasked to guard a bridge in the middle of the Greek mountains you would have to be a fairly low-grade soldier. Chances are you just wouldn't be interested – and nor would a high-grade soldier, for that matter. You might have been stationed there weeks, or even months. You know there is no realistic threat as the bridge is built in such an extreme place that an attack is deemed impossible. The two-hour sentry 'stag' would pass all too slowly and you would, to use an old army term, be 'thumb in bum, mind in neutral'. Those searchlight sweeps were probably more about staying awake, and showing the guard commander you were awake, than looking for saboteurs about to blow up your bridge – not that Geoff and his boys would have known that.

Come 11 p.m. and there was another heart-stopping challenge when the sentries were changed and the new guard amused themselves by going through the searchlight routine for a while before getting bored and turning them off. Once all was quiet, Mac whispered that he thought one of the smaller 'sausages' had been left at the foot of the ladder. Down I crept and was feeling around when, happening to look round the abutment, I was horrified to see coming towards me, down the tiny track which led up to the guard huts, a cigarette's glowing tip.

It could only be our sentry boy. He now had to be off duty and taking a little stroll in the moonlight before turning in. I crouched behind the abutment and prayed that the silly sod would come no further. I took my cosh off my belt and waited with my heart pounding. Down he came, picking his way, dragging on his butt and pausing every so often to look up at the moon.

There was nothing for it. Every ounce I had went into that wallop on to his head and he went over and into the gorge without a sound. I sat down weakly and, as it happened, right on top of the 'sausage' I had come to look for.

Five minutes later and the job was done. It was just past midnight when the time-pencils were squeezed, releasing the acid to begin its work eating through the retaining springs. They were timed to release the little plungers in just over two hours' time.

On our way down the cliff we were treated to another display from the searchlights. These really frightened us. The job was done, but we badly wanted to get away and we were completely exposed should they happen to flash downwards.

Then we began the long climb back up the gorge and, by God, we were tired. Some of the higher climbs we almost didn't manage and the whole trip was taking us longer than we cared for. I remember that it was past two in the morning

and we were three-quarters of the way home and up to our
necks in a deep pool when a reverberating roar of sound
reached us over the noise of the torrent. We solemnly shook
hands all round and, taking courage from our success, made
good time back to camp.

Here we found Charlie, rather anxious as to why we were so
late. Pausing only to get into our dry clothes we set the mules off
hell for leather for home. On the way Don and I summoned our
remaining strength and climbed back up to the OP. At around 6
a.m., as dawn broke, we peered down. The entire main span and
both supporting arms had disappeared into a tangled mess of
wreckage lying 300 feet down in the river bed.

Later I was to learn that, so convinced were the Germans
that there must have been treachery, they shot their guard
commander and ten men with him – although Eddie later said
in his book that they shot the entire guard contingent.

It took the Germans four months to pass a train over the
gorge.

Even here there was a further and very satisfying twist. The
Germans immediately started repairing the bridge, putting
pressed labour to work: Greeks and Poles worked night and day
to repair the damage. Two months later they had the bridge
repaired, or so they thought. The first train they put over proved
otherwise when it, and the bridge, descended into the gorge.
Whether it was sabotage by the labourers or Kraut over-
haste to get the bridge repaired that was to blame, no one ever
discovered. I would like to think it was the former because, and
as taught at SOE school, you don't necessarily need to blow
something up to destroy it:[8] even slight changes in the mixes for

8   M.R.D. Foot recounts one stunning piece of noiseless sabotage. The elite SS
Panzer division, Das Reich, was based in southern France. To save on track wear
its tanks (as tanks do to this day) travelled any distance on transporters. The tanks
were obviously heavily guarded; the transporters not. On 5 June 1944 – the day

the concrete might have been enough to make a structure as extreme as the Asopos Viaduct unstable. Whatever, it took a further two months before the line was finally reopened.

Everyone, from the prime minister downwards, was delighted and the operation was judged a major strategic success. Together with the mass of simultaneous sabotage attacks going on all over northern Greece, it convinced the Germans that Greece was the target for the invasion of southern Europe, and they moved two divisions down from Yugoslavia to defend the coastline. They were still there a couple of weeks later, staring out to sea, when the Allies invaded Sicily on 10 July 1943. By the time the Germans realised they had been duped and the divisions had been turned around to head back to defend Italy, it was too late and the Allies were firmly ashore.

Everyone on the attack team received a gallantry medal: Geoff and Don won DSOs; the two engineer officers won MCs; Sergeant Khuri and Lance Corporal Mutch, MMs. Geoff's, and certainly Don's and probably the others', were 'immediate' medals, the best of their type that can be won: no ifs, no buts. Interestingly, and it is there on his records, his MC was an 'immediate' one as well. He was that sort of guy.

A reconnaissance Spitfire flew over and took photographs of the demolition. Remember that promised case of whisky? Our much-anticipated reward was, in typical military balls-up fashion, duly dropped and duly enjoyed by a surprised and deeply gratified British officer living some hundred miles away: he had not participated in our little party in any way whatsoever.

---

before D-Day – SOE and the French Resistance sallied forth into the rail yards and drained the axle grease from the transporter cars (which they later sold on the black market, turning a nice profit!) and replaced it with ground carborundum – an abrasive grease. Come 7 June, Das Reich was ordered to the Normandy battle and the tanks were loaded. The trains set off and every transporter seized up. The nearest alternatives were 100 miles north over rough roads and mountains, which the Resistance then contested. Das Reich finally got into action only on D+17. That's the sort of guerrilla action that may well have helped sway the final success of D-Day.

In Volume V of *The Second World War*, Sir Winston Churchill described the result: 'a vital viaduct on the main Athens railway was destroyed and other sabotage operations were successful. The result was that two German Divisions were moved into Greece which might have been used in Sicily.'

In his book *Greek Entanglement*, Brigadier E.C.W. Myers, CBE, DSO, wrote: 'There were many magnificent exploits during the war behind the enemy lines in the Balkans; but for sheer endurance, determination to succeed and pluck, there was probably no more gallant achievement of its type. Mr. Churchill himself, when he learned of the operation, also sent his personal congratulations.' Also, and more personal: 'Some months later I was asked to show them [the RAF photographs of the collapsed viaduct] to Mr Churchill. I still remember his gleeful chuckle.'

Those involved were:

Brigadier Eddie Myers
Leader of the attack party: Capt. Geoffrey Gordon-
    Creed, MC
Attack party: Capt. Donald Stott, Capt. Ken Scott, Capt.
    Harry McIntyre
Sergeant Michael Khuri, MM[9]
Lance Corporal Charlie Mutch
Mules: Brown Job, Black Job, Bloody Maud and Pearl.

---

9   Sergeant Michael Khuri, Pioneer Corps, had already won a much deserved Military Medal for his part in the spectacular destruction of the Gorgopotomas Viaduct in November 1941. Brigadier Myers describes first meeting Khuri – an escaped PoW – resplendent in the uniform of a British second lieutenant: better for obtaining food, explained Khuri, who confessed to being a private. In fact, better for wooing a local maiden, concluded a disapproving Brigadier Myers. Poor old Khuri: he had to give up the girl and badges of rank but was promoted to lance corporal. Such behaviour with girls was banned in Eddie's camp – Khuri would have had much more fun in Geoff's. In fact, from contemporary photos Brigadier Eddie's boys look more like band members of ZZ Top than British officers, all heavy beard and moustache. It is difficult to see them being very attractive to the local females, unlike the debonair Mister Major Geoff.

IO

All's fair

Geoff had no time to rest on his laurels. The order had come from GHQ Cairo for maximum sabotage during the months of May, June and July. All over northern Greece railways and bridges were being blown, telephones lines dropped. A German column was ambushed in one pass, which was then blocked. The Andartes held the ends of the pass for two weeks, under attack from two battalions of infantry, before melting back into the mountains. The Germans had no idea what had hit them: no wonder they decided that Greece was the Allies' next target.

In the south of Greece there was only one motor road running east–west. It connected Athens with the port of Nafpaktos at the western entrance of the Gulf of Corinth.

This road, starting westwards from Athens, forks left at Livadhia and, skirting to the south of Mount Parnassus, serves the towns of Delphi and Amfissa. At Amfissa it forks left again and runs around the south of Mount Giona to the small town of Lidhorikion. Thereafter, it runs generally westwards, following the Mornos river valley to Nafpaktos, crossing numerous reinforced concrete bridges along the way.

One such bridge – described by Myers as a 'large and important road bridge' – spanned a narrow gap between the mountains a few miles to the north-west of Lidhorikion. Here it crossed the river with a single span of 100 feet at a place where the road took a double hairpin bend. A few yards to the west of the modern reinforced concrete construction was an ancient, humpbacked masonry mule bridge dating from the days of the Turkish occupation, too narrow for a vehicle to cross.

Lidhorikion is strategically important to an occupying force as it commands not just the only route to the west, but also the valley running north between the mountain massifs of Giona and Vardhousia. The Italians maintained an infantry battalion in a fortified enclave on the south side of the little town, and from there they would, though only very occasionally, operate patrols against the Andartes.

Following the successful disruption of rail services by the destruction of the Asopos Viaduct a few days previously, I decided to blow up this modern 100-foot bridge. I would not only effectively interrupt all mechanised troop movements by the enemy from east to west, but also further convince them of a concerted plan of sabotage designed to isolate their forces in southern Greece when the Allies invaded the Balkans by way of Salonika.

I took off with my interpreter, Yotis, to make a reconnaissance. He was a splendid fellow, this Yotis. He had once been bursar of Roberts College in Athens, spoke half a dozen languages and, though distinctly portly and unwarlike, bore with me the rigours and dangers of clandestine life with great courage and fortitude. I was greatly attached to him. Heavily disguised as black-market spivs, we wobbled off on our ancient motorbike with me driving and Yotis perched on the pillion. I was clutching a cardboard suitcase containing several million inflated drachmae and thousands of evil-smelling cigarettes. If we were stopped by an enemy patrol, my role was to avoid conversation by tinkering with the bike and Yotis was to show all his gold teeth in an ingratiating smile and perform whatever was necessary in the way of bribes and smooth talk.

Around noon on a blazing hot day we rattled along, not

knowing what to expect when we arrived at the bridge but hoping that whatever picket was on guard would be having thoughts of an afternoon siesta.

Round the final hairpin we came, to be suddenly confronted with a roadblock. Our brakes were virtually non-existent. So, rather than annoy the Italians by ramming into the pole they had rigged across the road, Yotis and I simply fell off, to the huge delight of our enemies. They shouted with joy and stamped around while we sat rather foolishly on our backsides in the dust.

With everyone in high good humour, the examination of our identity cards was perfunctory. While Yotis was dispensing cigarettes and wisecracks, I was free to lean over the railings of the bridge and make mental notes of the dimensions of the beams, the siting of the pillboxes and the numbers of the guard. After about ten minutes we were waved on our way, minus half our cigarettes, but firm friends all round.

Demolishing reinforced concrete bridges can offer quite a few problems. What is more, we would probably not have too much time to spare over this job as, at the first sound of trouble, some of the garrison in Lidhorikion – only about three miles away – were bound to come running. As I read it, everything depended upon a quick liquidation of the picket and my having the explosives immediately to hand. I figured I could count on having a maximum thirty minutes to do the job and get safely away.

There was no shortage of explosives; we had recently received a drop. I decided that my quickest method would be to literally knock the bridge flat by using one cutting charge of gelignite against each pin where the arches met the abutment. This would have to be combined with a large pressure charge of twenty 20 lb cans of ammonal laid in a row across the top of the arch on the road surface and well tamped down with sandbags to direct the blast downwards.

The whole operation would require an eight-man attacking

party split into two parts of six and two; an explosives party of three; and a transport party for the explosives and sandbags of eight men and twenty mules.

My plan was to spend a day concealed a few hundred yards to the west of the target, filling sandbags and preparing the charges. At the proper time I would station two men with submachine-guns in ambush on the far side of the bridge, between it and Lidhorikion. They would also lay mines in the road. At last light we would attack from the west, along the road we had driven down. I expected any survivors from the picket to run back towards Lidhorikion and the garrison, where they would be caught in the ambush.

Once we were in control of the bridge two blasts of the whistle would bring up the mules at the trot and then everyone, with the exception of lookouts, would lend a hand with placing the explosives and humping the sandbags.

We had quite a problem in hiring that many extra mules to supplement my four old faithfuls because we could give no inkling of our intentions or reasons for wanting them lest we were betrayed. However, all was eventually co-ordinated and 30 June found the whole party concealed in good cover along the river bed.

The guard picket was relieved at 6 p.m. by the night guard, consisting of a corporal and eight men. Different men, I couldn't help hoping, from the lads with whom Yotis and I had played our little comedy on the motorbike. As soon as the truck carrying away the old guard had disappeared I sent off the two lookouts to prepare their ambush and bury four anti-tank mines in the road about half a mile away.

I allowed them twenty minutes. Then I collected my bravos and prepared to assault with submachine-guns. I figured that, with any luck, the noise of their fire might not be heard in Lidhorikion, whereas the blast of light machine-guns and grenades would certainly bring the garrison running.

We straggled slowly up the road with our guns concealed under shepherds' cloaks and driving old Bloody Maud in front of us. She carried a heavy load of sandbags but in the fading light they might have been anything. As we got to the pole across the road we were challenged and a soldier came forward to examine our identities. I let him have a couple of rounds in the guts. There then ensued a notable fusillade and confusion as my boys, with their blood up, blazed away at the pillboxes and the bridge regardless of the attempts of our surprised and terrified enemies to surrender. One incredibly lucky fellow broke away and fled in the direction of our 'long-stop'; the others died on the spot.

Old Bloody Maud, unflappable veteran, never turned a hair throughout and merely amused herself by snapping viciously at the other mules as they came crowding and jostling out of the darkness in response to my whistle.

Twenty minutes of frantic work and the charges were in position. I was almost finished with the Primacord circuits, the lads were stacking up the sandbags and the mules had trotted off to safety. Suddenly Yotis, on lookout and a bit over-excited with it all, heard someone approaching up the road from the direction of Lidhorikion. He shouted a challenge and blazed off with his gun. The answer was a storm of abuse and a description of his personal habits and those of his ancestors that left him speechless. Of course, it was those damn fools from my ambush party. Apparently the lone Eyetie, fleeing the pillbox, had come past them with his ears pinned back and going like the clappers. But both my heroes had forgotten to release their safety catches and he had got clean away. They had been walking towards us, reviling their luck and one another, and quite unthinking of the danger they were running into. Luckily for them it had been old Yotis they had met, because his slugs had gone high.

I lit twelve inches of safety fuse and we scampered off around the corner. There followed a crucifying bang, and when the dust settled we saw to our satisfaction that the entire 100-foot span was lying in the river bed below. Moreover, the ancient humpbacked mule bridge, built across the defile long before, remained intact for the locals to cross on foot, or by mule, which was what we had intended all along. No enemy vehicles would be passing this way for quite some time, which is also what we had intended.

We debated whether to lay an ambush for the column which would come to inspect the damage. I decided against this, however, as someone might get wounded and it would be a real problem to evacuate them come daybreak, when the Italians would be swarming angrily all over the place.

We did hear quite a good bang from one of our mines about fifteen minutes later. This was followed by a lively display of Verey lights behind us as we sweated off, well content, into the darkness, chaffing poor Yotis on his marksmanship.

And that for the time being was the end of our assault on the enemy. Come 11 July and the successful invasion of Sicily, the command came from Brigadier Eddie to ease up on attacks for the time being. The aim had been achieved in diverting those German divisions from where they were needed. All that further sabotage would now do was risk inviting unnecessary reprisals on to the civilian population.

Yanni Mastangakis and his wife Sophie lived in a tiny house right on the road a mile or two to the south of Lidhorikion. He had been a road foreman with the Public Works Department and was invaluable to me. He supplied me with blueprints of all the roads in my area showing the culverts, retaining walls and bridges. Sophie was no slouch either. From her parlour window, she kept a census of all enemy traffic that passed her door. They were good people and I often spent the night with them during my travels.

One evening, as we sat over our simple meal, I could sense that Sophie had something on her mind.

'Mister Geoff,' she said finally, 'what is your other name, your family name?'

'Gordon-Creed, Sophie. Why?'

'Gordon? Ah . . . the people were right,' she breathed.

'What do you mean?' I asked.

Her eyes grew round and she lowered her voice reverently. 'Mister Geoff, are you . . . are you a *lord*?'

'A lord? Good heavens, no,' I laughed.

'Mister Geoff, the people are saying that you are a descendant of Lord Byron and that is why you have come to Greece to liberate us.'

Thus was I stuck with it. The Greeks are incurable romantics and the fantasy of another Lord Byron carrying the torch of freedom in the mountains was irresistible.[1]

Finding myself the object of hero worship I naturally took every possible advantage that I could when it came to obtaining sometimes hard-to-get services and commodities. In my area it soon became a matter of patriotism for the villagers to supply me with mules, fodder and information.

There was, however, one considerable disadvantage to my position. When one is 23 years old, supremely fit and endowed, perhaps, with a better than average supply of hormones, living a life of total celibacy can become tiresome. Resplendent upon my lordly pedestal I guessed that, were I to team up with

---

1   In Greece, Lord George Byron, the famous Romantic poet, is still considered Britain's best export. He joined the Greek freedom fighters in their war of independence against the Turks, adding international glamour to their cause, if no notable fighting skills. He died of a fever in 1824, not far from where Geoff was fighting. His legacy spread to Britain and Greece alike. A number of Geoff's fellow SOE men were Greek classicists, fighting, *à la* Byron, for the cause of the birthplace of democracy (*demos*, the Greek word for 'the people').

some willing maiden, I risked making deadly enemies of a dozen others. In my world of fear and intrigue, jealousy might cause one of them to betray her rival and thus me. Much as I longed to, it would be a foolish risk to take.

What is more, I knew that there was huge disapproval among the likes of Brigadier Eddie at any concept of us British 'consorting with the locals'. One of his officers had had a narrow escape when three girls had been brought to his camp, offering him and his men a good time. He had placed them all under arrest while he delved into their past. One had turned out to be an Italian spy and ended up paying the price against a nearby wall; the other two had been forcibly 'retired' from their previous line of business for the duration of hostilities. All of which seemed a trifle extreme and certainly something of a waste. Anyhow, whatever I got up to would have to be kept very quiet from Eddie.

An elderly friend of my French great grandmother used proudly to introduce his wife thus: '*Permettez-moi, vous presenter ma femme, ci-devant maîtresse de Lord Byron*' ('Excuse me. Might I introduce my wife? She used to be Lord Byron's mistress'). Somehow I felt that such broadmindedness and tolerance would be unlikely to go down well among the Greek villagers. It was particularly galling for me, as I knew damn well that Bill, Yotis and the rest of the lads never passed up the opportunity for a jolly tumble.

I well remember one summer's day stopping for a drink at a cool spring just outside a village. A pretty girl was on her knees, filling her water pots. Her sleeves were rolled up and she was letting the icy water flow over her brown arms, revelling in the sensation. She was suddenly beautiful for me and my desire for her almost choked me. I hurried blindly away. Clearly I needed to arrange something soon or I might commit some foolish and possibly disastrous indiscretion.

Khrysso is a prosperous village overlooking the olive groves of Amfissa. Here, in a splendid house, lived George with his young and pretty wife Maria. George was very fat and a very great coward. Poor fellow, he was nervous of the Italians, frightened of the Communists and simply petrified of the Germans. At the drop of a hat he would leave Maria to guard the house and take off for a funk hole he maintained in the roof of one of his barns.

He was a good-hearted fellow all the same, and would take our leg-pulling about his yellow streak in good part.

However, I was getting the germ of an idea.

One evening of severe thunderstorms I collected Yotis and rode into Khrysso on the motorbike. We pulled up at a ramshackle inn which overlooked George's house.

'Now then,' I said to Yotis, who had guessed what I had in mind. 'This is where you earn your keep. Rush into George's and tell him we've been tipped off that the Krauts are coming to question him about reports of a British officer being seen in his house. Make it convincing. If he takes off for the hills you can shove off . . . but come and pick me up early tomorrow morning.'

Yotis ran down the hill and began hammering frantically on the door. He was admitted and a few minutes later George came flapping out clutching a blanket and a lantern, and disappeared into the pouring night.

A few minutes later I walked down the hill and tapped on the door. Maria opened it and looked at me in alarm.

'Mister Geoff! Quick, you must go. The Germans are coming. They're coming for George.' She was pale with fright. 'Mister Geoff,' she squeaked. 'You . . .?'

I looked steadily back at her and smiled. For long moments she stared back, then realisation dawned. The alarm in her eyes gave place to an expression of mixed outrage and delight. She gave a breathless little laugh and stepped forward. She put her hands behind my head and drew me fiercely downwards, looking deeply into my eyes.

'You . . . you devil, Geoff!' she said.

Hours later, as we lay sleepily relaxed in George's enormous battlefield of a bed, I thought of the poor fellow freezing in his funk hole – probably awake and starting at every sound.

'Goodness, what a shit you are!' I thought to myself happily.

It was late one warm summer's evening when I approached my encampment. It lay in a pine forest a few miles to the north of Pendayoi, quite an important village about six miles to the north-west of the bridge over the Mornos which I had blown down a while previously.

Weary and fed up with the constant squabbles and intrigues of the various Andarte factions, I had given myself a week's holiday by the sea on the north shore of the Gulf of Corinth.

Here, in a little village I had lazed in the sun, swum in the sea and gossiped and drunk with the fishermen. By way of keeping my hand in, so to speak, two of them had rowed me one fine night across the ten miles of water to the Peloponnesus where few Andarte bands operated – there were too many Germans and the countryside did not lend itself so readily to guerrilla warfare: too many roads, not enough mountains. There we had placed charges under the railway line which ran along the north shore from Patras to Corinth.

Refreshed and once more ready for the fray, I toiled the last few hundred yards up the hill with thoughts of a good draught of wine and a session with Bill to catch up on all the W/T traffic that must have arrived from Cairo during my absence. I was spotted some way off and a crowd of my lads came running down the hill to meet me. Excitedly they ran up and thumped me on the shoulder. 'The Eyeties have packed it in!'

They were all shouting at once: 'Just heard it on the radio. There's an armistice or something.'[2]

This was terrific news indeed! We were all immensely elated and felt that here, at last, there was concrete evidence that the tide of war was beginning to swing our way.

But I knew immediately that I had a clear duty to do something about the Italian garrison at Lidhorikion. I would have to enter under a flag of truce and try to bluff and parley the commander to surrender to me before the Germans could bring pressure on him to stand firm or bring up their own troops to replace him.

There was no time to lose. I sent off runners with urgent messages to the commanders of the nearest ELAS and EKKA bands, explaining my intentions and urging them to move at once with every man and gun they could muster to surround the town and to demonstrate in strength. My plan was to demand the immediate surrender of all heavy machine-guns, light machine-guns and mortars, together with all their ammunition.

I would guarantee safe conduct and would permit personal weapons to be retained against a possible breach of faith by the ELAS. I would also provide an escort to guide the whole battalion northwards over the mountains towards Albania and eventual evacuation by sea back to Italy.

Pausing only to snatch a quick meal I collected Yotis, an Alsatian deserter whom we knew as 'Bill the German' and half a dozen members of my small bodyguard, including Nikitas their captain, and set off for Lidhorikion. We arrived there early the following morning.

As news of the Italian surrender was by now generally

---

2 Announcement of Italian armistice, 8 September 1943: the very word 'armistice' carried the poison of so much future misunderstanding. While many Italians felt they had not 'surrendered', the Allies assumed they had. That left the Italians in Greece with the problem of whether to fight on with the Germans, join the Allies or just give up altogether and go home. There were Italian soldiers of all different persuasions in Greece in 1943 and, for the Germans, the not inconsequential question of who got to keep any discarded weapons.

known, the town was in a ferment of excitement. Greek national flags, long hidden, were flying bravely over a dozen buildings and the people were congregated in excited groups. The Italians were reported to be standing to, under arms, ready to defend themselves.

I made my HQ in the house of one of the leading townsmen and planned my next move. I realised only too well that if anything were to be achieved I would have to act fast.

The Germans had a small garrison at Nafpaktos, to the west, some seventy miles away. But reinforcements arriving from that direction would have to de-bus three miles down the road, at the bridge I had blown, and would therefore be vulnerable to attack. A more likely source of German interference, I thought, would come from the east where there were largish garrisons at Levadhia and Amfissa, just over sixty miles and thirty miles distant respectively. I was anxious that the Andartes should place themselves across the only road that gave the Germans access to Lidhorikion.

I sent a letter via a small boy to the Italian battalion commander to announce that I proposed to visit him under a flag of truce at 1100 hours to discuss the terms of his surrender. I then sat down to await the arrival of the Andartes commanders whom I had urgently summoned.

The only one to appear by 1030 hours was an EKKA officer who, immediately after I had explained my intention to enter the enclave, began to put forward arguments against my so doing. He was convinced that it was suicidal and that I would certainly be trapped and shot.

This likely possibility was naturally very much on my mind. I had no need of this prophet of doom shaking my resolution to attempt what I knew was my duty. As he went on and on, I eventually lost patience with the fellow and snapped: 'If things go wrong, who is going to get shot – you or me?'

'You.'

'Well then, for Christ's sake hold your tongue or, if you can't bear to watch, get the hell out of here!'

He subsided, abashed.

It being now ten minutes before my deadline, I borrowed a large white tablecloth from my host and had Nikitas tie it on to a pole. I collected my little group and we set off rather nervously towards the roadblocks marking the boundary of the Italian fortified position. Dear old Yotis's knees began to knock together, and I could hear him muttering fervent prayers to some obscure Bulgarian saint whom he always kept in reserve for moments of particular danger. It was all rather unnerving. As we marched through the town, the people fell aside to let us pass. Some started to weep and cry out that we shouldn't risk our lives. Others were praying loudly and calling down blessings upon us.

Then a great silence fell.

We had about a hundred yards of open road to cover. As the distance steadily lessened I could plainly see the Italians huddled behind their machine-guns.

At five yards I halted the party and went forward alone up the barrier. In a loud and, I hoped, confident voice I demanded to see an officer.

There was an NCO in charge. He sent someone running and in a few moments there arrived a young and very dandified officer who introduced himself as the Adjutant. I explained my purpose and demanded that I and my party be escorted to his commanding officer.

He was very curious and very polite. He ordered the barrier drawn aside and in we all marched to the guardroom. We waited there about ten minutes, making small talk with the Adjutant while the Colonel, I suppose, discussed with his officers this unexpected advent of a uniformed British major[3]

3   Geoff was promoted to major, temporary, unpaid (typically!) shortly after the demolition of the Asopos Viaduct.

escorted by horrible-looking cut-throats. It transpired that my note had never reached him.

Then the second-in-command arrived to escort us to the commanding officer.

We marched behind him deeper into the enclave and suddenly, to my alarm, we were confronted by the sight of a German W/T truck and about fifteen fully armed and extremely hostile-looking Krauts. Here was a totally unexpected development and one which I did not like one bit.

As we all paused involuntarily, poor Yotis set up a gabble of prayer which must have roused every saint in the calendar, but there was no going back. Completely ignoring the Germans, who were rather nonplussed at the sight of my white flag and Italian officer escort, we continued firmly into the battalion office. I left Bill the German outside with the boys and the flag to keep an eye on the Kraut truck and sat down with Yotis, Nikitas, the Italian colonel and six of his officers.

We were very formal and very polite. The Colonel was fat, shifty-eyed and highly perfumed.

I put my proposal to him. He looked very doubtful and asked how I thought I could make a safe-conduct effective when, in his opinion, all Greeks were liars and highly treacherous. I replied that he had my word of honour and that I personally would make one of their escort as far as Albania.

He was the picture of indecision as he sat and shuffled in his seat. Eventually, he said that he could really give no reply until he had received orders from his superiors. (Here was tragedy! At this very moment, had I but known it, the Italian divisional commander, General Infante, was surrendering to the British Military Mission in the Pindus mountain area up north.)[4]

---

4 Myers reckons that, in northern Greece, about twelve thousand Italians surrendered to the Andartes and their British liaison officers: General Infante's Pinerole Division alone comprised 7,000 men. Things started well enough, with

I then told him that if he refused to honour the armistice signed by his government, I would report him over my W/T to GHQ Cairo as a last-ditch fascist and he would be held responsible for the deaths and casualties which his regiment must inevitably suffer on attempting to break out of Lidhorikion. I then went on to tell him that I already had a thousand men surrounding the place and would have twice that number within forty-eight hours. May God forgive me the thumping lie!

At this interesting point Bill the German stuck his head around the door and announced that he had overheard the German corporal order his men to 'make sharp zir hand grenades'. He also said that, ever since we had arrived, they had been frantically radioing from their truck.

I immediately stopped the meeting and demanded that the Colonel himself go out and put a stop to the signalling and also scotch any ideas that the Germans might have of attacking me and my party.

'Colonel,' I said rather grandly, 'I am here under a flag of truce and our countries are no longer at war. Your honour demands that my flag is not violated. If it were to be,' I added hopefully, 'you would certainly be hanged as a war criminal.'

He got my point and quickly went outside to soothe the Germans. I think they had their suspicions that their own surrender was also being negotiated.

However, on resuming, I was unable to budge him from his stand that he could do nothing without orders. He asked for twenty-four hours' grace, after which he hoped to be able to give me a favourable answer.

---

the Division fighting the Germans alongside the ELAS. However, and tragically, the ELAS realised that armed Italians might be a threat to their postwar plans for a Communist Greece. The collapse in the alliance began with the ELAS first breaking up the Italian Division, then 'borrowing' their equipment and, finally, disarming not only them but also all other non-Communist Andartes. The result was a brief foretaste of the civil war that was to break out a year later and during which one New Zealand liaison officer and a number of Greeks were killed.

I had perforce to agree, so we shook hands all round and prepared to leave.

As I left the building the German corporal marched smartly across and gave me a cracking salute. 'We will respect your flag of truce, Herr Major.'

'Very decent of you,' I murmured politely, with vast relief in my heart.

We then formed up and, feeling rather naked in the rear, trailed off back the way we had come. As we reappeared, smiling our relief, there arose a great shout. Rose petals were showered over us and we were kissed and embraced and compared loudly with the great heroes of the past.

Above the pandemonium I managed to make myself heard. I told them that the war was far from over and implored them to contain themselves and not provoke German reprisals. At that very moment, as if to emphasise my words, two ME 109Fs[5] appeared over the town. One of them dropped a message with a streamer into the enclave. Smart work, I thought, to have fighters patrolling in response to a W/T call for help sent out only about forty minutes previously.

It was now obvious to me that the Germans would attempt to reinforce their detachment during the night and that they would do so with sufficient force to prevent the Italians surrendering, as they doubtlessly preferred to do. At all costs, the Germans were going to have to be held off for at least forty-eight hours – I gave no credit to his request for twenty-four hours – while the Eyeties dithered.

But where were the bloody Andartes? Even a platoon of thirty men could hold the defile where I had blown the bridge. And a couple of hundred men with mines and machine-guns

---

5 ME 109: Messerschmitt 109, the workhorse of the Luftwaffe's fighter command and, like the Spitfire, produced in different variants. The 109E was used during the Battle of Britain. The 109F was an improved variant that appeared in 1941. The 109G, introduced 1942, was mass-produced until the end of the war.

could make it extremely rough on a large column trying to come in by road from the east. There were a dozen perfect places for an ambush.

But no – such units of the ELAS and EKKA as had responded to my call fell to squabbling over the division of spoils which were not even theirs yet. They refused to operate together and they refused to operate separately, in case while one lot was away the other might pinch all the loot. They were prepared to do nothing at all except swagger around the little town and play the hero. Realising the danger, I nearly went frantic and implored them not to miss this wonderful and last chance. To no avail. Their officers scoffed at the likelihood of any Germans arriving.

Sure enough, that night a column of only eighty Germans arrived from Nafpaktos, de-bussed unopposed at the bridge and force-marched into Lidhorikion. The next morning, from a small hut just outside the town where I had spent an uncomfortable night, I had the mortification of watching through my field glasses as 100 Germans disarmed the 500 Italians and trucked away their weapons.

I retired to Pendayoi, disgusted and furious. I was beginning to realise more and more that, were anything worthwhile to be achieved, it would have to be achieved out of our own resources and in spite of some of the Greeks I was forced to work with.

That afternoon about a quarter of Lidhorikion was burnt to the ground and many lost their lives.

I I

Ambushing trains

They are an odd mixture, the people who inhabit Greece. Somehow, and despite endless centuries of Ottoman and, before that, Frankish occupation, oppression and miscegenation, some of the ancient and heroic genes have survived. In the mountains I have known tall men of classical beauty both dark and very fair, who despite lacking any form of education retained an air of dignity and good breeding. Meeting them, I sometimes wished that I could have been around some two and a half thousand years ago when their ancestors – those giants among men in Athens – were not only talkers but doers and set the pattern for civilisation as we know it in the West.

Their women are something else. Conditioned from birth to a subordinate role in life, they seem to have retained qualities of courage and self-sacrifice all too often lacking in some of their menfolk.

It must have been in early July when I decided to visit Galaxhidion at the invitation of some prominent burgher of that town. I sent word by runner to expect me and a small party by such and such a date and duly set forth from my mountain to keep the appointment. It was extremely hot. As we straggled the last few miles along a track that led by the sea I did a very foolish thing. In my pride of youth and fitness and thinking myself indestructible, I drank from a verminous well.

The aforementioned burgher had laid on a civic welcome

in my honour. After an hour or two's rest in the house of a wealthy retired sea captain who had kindly offered to put me up, I found myself ensconced as the guest of honour at a banquet in the city hall. It was following the usual pattern of toasts and windy speeches when suddenly my guts were gripped as in a vice. I barely made it, mumbling apologies, into the lane outside. There, the bottom literally dropped out of my world.

Have you ever had dysentery? The real thing, I mean, and before antibiotics? If so, you are lucky to be alive.

Within twelve hours I was so prostrated I could barely move. Within twenty-four hours, tipped off by who knows who, a small party of Germans arrived, looking for a British officer.

They hit the town in the small hours and, barely conscious, I was carried out of bed by my host and his pretty 18-year-old daughter. Without time to get me away from the town, they persuaded me to jump down into their outdoor privy, into a midden of human shit.

The daughter, Zoe, jumped into the midden with me. For eight solid hours, enduring the stench, she cradled me in her arms, kept my head from sinking and muffled my groans while the Germans were searching the house. She crept out for water when the coast was clear, and finally got me back into the house and bathed all the shit off me. I was beyond caring, but she nursed me devotedly for ten days thereafter until my guts had recovered somewhat. It was eighteen months before I was fully recovered.

In my heart and in my memories there will always be an extra special place for Zoe. On the other hand, I would bet that if that poor girl ever thinks of an Englishman, she will think of you-know-what and heave her heart out!

Could you blame her?

★　　★　　★

Mountains do funny things with acoustics. We are all familiar with the echo effect of the human voice, but when the source is a machine-gun or a mortar bomb the sound goes wild. It reverberates and bounces around and is very difficult to pinpoint.

My HQ was now established in a villa outside and above the town of Galaxhidion, roughly halfway along the north coast of the Gulf of Corinth. One morning we were initially alarmed and then irritated by a sustained fusillade of machine-gun fire from the general direction of Amfissa – as the crow flies only about twelve miles away across the Bay of Itea. I sent one of my men, Elias, to go and have a look and report back. He was back within a few hours, and very put out he was too.

About thirty Germans under a corporal had set up targets against some olive trees. They had been blazing away at them to the great detriment of the trees, which were not only about a thousand years old but, to my man's horror and fury, just happened to belong to himself and his family.

The olive tree is as valuable to a Greek peasant as a prized camel is to a Bedouin Arab, or more so. Each individual tree is known, pedigreed and bequeathed to the next generation as a nearly perpetual source of oil and firewood. To have one tree, far less scores, wantonly vandalised was not to be tolerated.

I sympathised but was nevertheless surprised at the extent of the furious indignation expressed unanimously by the rest of my bodyguard after Elias had finished sounding off. Given the strength of my companions' feelings, I felt obliged to express our disapproval although, given the probable consequences, I was reluctant to stir up a hornets' nest so close to home. I had not forgotten that Cairo did not want us unduly irritating the Germans at that precise moment.

Nevertheless, we took my boat, ten of us, with light machine-guns and two anti-tank mines. On impulse, I also took the makings of a booby trap: a pull-switch and a detonator linked to an anti-personnel mine. It was an evil thing which sprayed lethal hardware everywhere when triggered.

Guided by Elias we arrived at the olive grove at first light. There was a bit of a track and a considerable amount of refuse left over from the previous day's shooting. The problems for a successful ambush were lack of cover and finding clear fields of fire. I did not want this to become a shoot-out among the olives between their professional soldiers and my irregulars, as there would have been only one outcome. I therefore decided to attack the truck the moment it halted and before the Germans could disembark.

I divided my men into two sections and hid them among the trees about 100 yards to the rear of where the truck had parked the previous day. I checked all their sights and told the men not to open fire until I did and then to keep firing until two of their magazines were spent. We sat down to wait and hope.

Just before 9 a.m. we heard the rumbling and grinding of a heavy diesel truck approaching. Standing up in the back and packed like sardines were the German target-shooting party. The truck halted. I remember seeing the whole group lurch forward just as I opened fire. I suppose that about a thousand rounds riddled that vehicle and we counted twenty-nine dead.

From the mess I took a few passbooks for unit identification purposes, while my men looted the bodies of wristwatches and whatever else they could find of value. I booby-trapped the body of the corporal and we headed off, carrying all the weapons and ammo we could handle.

The Germans were vastly annoyed. Ever anxious to prove they were doing something useful for the war effort, the ELAS claimed credit for the attack. This suited me very well, as by then the enemy already had too many scores to settle with me.

★   ★   ★

As mentioned previously, it was several months after the destruction of the Asopos Viaduct before the Germans managed to restore rail traffic between Athens and the north.

When I learned that the trains were running again I decided to resume my attacks on the line. So I carried out a series of recces with one of my officers, Alan MacGregor. The prospects for success were not rosy even though we had fifty miles or more of line to choose from. True, there were a couple of juicy viaducts, but they were in open country and impossible to approach by stealth. The line was constantly patrolled with railcars, and the road, which ran parallel, was also patrolled by small detachments of soldiers, both motorised and on foot.

The Germans, now determined to keep the line open at all costs, were in a nasty mood. All the villages on or near the line either had troops billeted in them or were visited daily. What is more, proclamations had gone out threatening dire reprisals against the villagers should any sabotage occur in the vicinity of their homes.

We made an attack one night and succeeded in derailing an engine and five coaches. We did this more or less as an experiment to see how the Germans would react.

They did several things very promptly. First, I was mortified to see that they had the line repaired and cleared for traffic again within eight hours. They achieved this with the aid of a large breakdown crane mounted on a flat car and by rounding up several hundred villagers and putting them to work under guard. Second, they seized ten hostages and publicly executed them. Third, they declared a curfew on all neighbouring villages and made the breaking of it punishable by death. Fourth, on each important train they put two engines, one in front and one in the rear. In front of the leading engine they pushed an empty freight truck to explode any mines on the line, and behind the rear engine, which was driven by a German, they pulled an open truck in which rode a section of infantrymen armed with machine-guns and mounting a searchlight. Fifth and finally, they increased the number of blockhouses on the line and doubled the guard at the small railway junction at Kastelli. There they kept the breakdown crane and had their repair workshops.

Clearly, therefore, pinprick attacks such as we had just made were simply not going to be worth the price. I wrote to the German commander in Levadhia, where the hostages had been executed, and told him that I would see to it that he would himself be executed as a war criminal for his atrocities. His only reaction was to double the already enormous price on my head and to threaten to execute fifty hostages the next time there was an attack on the line.

I was in a quandary. Obviously the war must go on, but if innocent people were to suffer for my actions then at least my attack should bring about a worthwhile result. The key to success, as I saw it, lay in destroying the crane. I knew that, apart from the one at Kastelli, there were no others nearer than Athens to the south or Lamia to the north. If I could catch an ammunition train and the crane together then I felt the line might be kept out of commission for a week or ten days. If this were to happen at a time when it was vital for the Germans to have the line open, then it might be justified to risk the lives of the hostages, but not otherwise.

We set ourselves to plan and prepare. To MacGregor I gave the job of making a detailed study of about twenty miles of line running eastwards from a village near the line named Kato Agoriani. I allowed him two weeks for this as I wanted accurate information, not only about the line itself but also on the guards and patrols. I needed to know of every culvert and bridge, every embankment and cutting, every spot where there was cover, a footpath or a crossing. From all the information he collected I hoped to be able to choose the best place to attack.

When MacGregor had gone, Yotis and I repaired to Kastelli as I wanted to take a discreet look at the crane and also to enlist the help of the station master.

We arrived in the evening on our motorbike, carrying our usual assortment of 'trade goods', and pulled in at a small inn by the station. As there were plenty of Germans around, I thought it prudent for me to keep well in the background and leave it to Yotis to sound out local opinion and get the feel of the place. I retired to the back of the room and buried myself in an old newspaper. Meanwhile Yotis spread his wares and began to exchange gossip with the half-dozen or so labourers and gangers who were sitting around drinking.

I listened to the talk. As was to be expected, the men were depressed and nervous. The Germans, it appeared, were very edgy and trigger-happy after our last attack and there was much resentment being expressed over the execution of the hostages. There was also criticism of the Andartes, who were being blamed for my rather abortive effort. It had provoked the Germans into savage retaliation and there was obvious apprehension and anxiety for the fate of fifty more hostages whom I now learned had already been taken. I could expect no help from these fellows – probably the reverse.

Without much hope in my heart I was about to send Yotis off to find the station master when the man himself chanced to arrive to tell his men about some duty or other. From my seat in the corner I studied him covertly and liked what I saw. He was a fine-looking man with an air of authority and I had an instinctive feeling that here was a man of courage and reliance.

I called Yotis over and told him to bring the fellow across

when he got a chance to buttonhole him. A few minutes later
the gangers filed out and Yotis spoke quietly with the man. I
saw him dart a curious glance in my direction, pull out his
watch and consider for a moment or two. He shrugged, then
spoke to Yotis and the two of them rose and came across to
where I was sitting.

'This is Mr Georgiou Papadoulos,' Yotis said. 'He can give
us about twenty minutes before the next train is due to come
through.'

I took his hand. 'I think perhaps we had better go through
into the back room where we shan't be disturbed,' I said, and
when we were settled, 'You'd better tell him who I am, Yotis.'

'This is the Englishman, Major Geoff,' said Yotis.

Georgiou gave a slight start. 'So you are Mister Geoff,' he
said slowly, staring hard at me. 'I knew you were not Greek, of
course, but I thought you might be an American airman.' He
held my eyes with his. 'Your name is well known, by God . . . and
the Germans – have you any idea what they're offering for
you?'

I nodded.

'By Jesus!' he said excitedly and stood up abruptly.

For a moment I thought I had misjudged my man and stood
up also, ready to tackle him if he was going to make trouble.

Instead, he placed his hands on my shoulders and his eyes
fairly blazed. 'By Jesus,' he repeated. 'By Christ, I am proud to
know you. You have caused these swine more trouble than all
those fornicating partisans put together.' He spat and walked
swiftly to the door and looked out. 'It's all right,' he said,
coming back, 'but you must be careful . . . these people . . .' he
shrugged expressively.

'I know, Georgiou,' I said, sitting down again. 'One can't
blame them for being afraid after what has happened recently.
This is why I want to talk to you. I need your help.'

'Anything, anything,' he assured me fervently. 'They can't

harm me, those bastards. I've no family to protect and I could escape to the mountains tomorrow if anything should happen. I would have gone before, but I didn't want to find myself forced to become a damned Communist.'

'Good,' I said. 'You may well end up having to join us in the mountains. Now, listen carefully. I want to blow up your breakdown crane and also close the line for at least ten days. To do this I'll have to destroy an ammunition or a fuel train. Now then, have you any means of knowing in advance what the various trains are carrying?'

'Yes, I can always know that,' he replied. 'The trains are marshalled at Lamia and I can get advance information by telephone. But the crane . . . that will not be easy. They guard it like a virgin!'

'Yes, I know they do,' I said, 'but we're going to get it all the same. Right then, we'll make our preparations and will keep in touch. We'll let you know when we're ready and then it'll be up to you to let us know when to expect a suitable train. OK?'

He nodded.

'Just one thing, Georgiou,' I added. 'Not a word to anyone. You understand? Not one word or hint to anyone at all. If we pull it off and you have to run for it, I'll supply you with all the money you need to lie low till after the Germans leave Greece. But all our lives will depend upon your discretion.'

'Never fear, Mister Geoff, I'll do my part. Now I must go back to my station.'

We shook hands warmly and he smiled. 'It would never do to have someone complain about the station master, would it?'

Well pleased with the result of our visit, Yotis and I retired to Ano Agoriani, a small village a few miles to the south of the line and well up the slopes of Mount Parnassus. Here we waited for ten days while explosives and mines were brought forward by mule from my dump on Giona.

Meanwhile MacGregor was completing his recce of the track, and in due course he arrived. He had done an excellent job but, having studied his maps and drawings and listened to what he had to say, it was all too clear to me that there was no spot that seemed to offer likely possibilities for an orthodox attack. I would have to think again.

There would have to be three explosions, I decided. The main charge would destroy a large culvert as the leading engine of the target train passed over it, and the crane would be sent to clear the line. The second explosion had to destroy the crane at some point on its way south to clear the wreckage. The third had to cut the line beyond all the wreckage to prevent the Athens crane coming up from the south and working from that end. The aim, if you remember, was not to close the track for months as we had done with the viaduct – no one could even get near those viaducts any longer – but to close it for seven to ten days: just long enough to cause major disruption at a critical moment.

The first and third explosions, I hoped, could be managed without too much difficulty, but the trick was going to be to catch the crane. This charge would have to be exploded manually as the crane passed over it. Fog signals or other pressure devices placed on the line would clearly be of no use, as the rails would be subjected to special scrutiny by the repair gang as they made their way towards the wreckage with their beloved crane.

To explode the mine manually meant that someone would have to be actually on the spot to do it and, as that someone would have to be me, I figured a lot more thought was called for. I had no intention of being caught red-handed.

As explosives are heavy in any case and my charges would have to be fairly hefty affairs, it would be necessary to have them concealed in position some time before the actual attack. With the line patrolled as heavily as it was, this presented quite a problem. I decided to call upon our new friend the station master once more, as it looked as though I would have to become a railwayman for a day or two.

I explained to him our problem of finding a suitable site to place the explosives and, after giving the matter some thought, he suggested that he supply us with workmen's documents. These he would obtain from the Germans and they would show that we were employed as gangers. Then, armed with our passes and the proper tools, we could walk down the line one Sunday, when most of the shifts were off, and try to find what we were looking for.

I thought this an excellent idea and told him to go ahead. We supplied him with photographs to go on the passes and, a few days later, carrying the damnably heavy and unfamiliar tools over our shoulders, Yotis and I staggered off down the line. We hadn't been walking more than a couple of miles when we were met by a small rail trolley carrying two Germans. They stopped to examine our passes and relieve us of a few cigarettes and then resumed their patrol. An hour later they repassed us on their return trip, but this time ignored us.

We walked on and on without finding any likely spots. I was beginning to lose hope when I noticed, lying abandoned by the side of a culvert, a few battered old steel drums. These, it turned out, had once contained cement. They gave me an idea. Calling to Yotis to help me, I rolled a couple of rusty drums into the mouth of the culvert at the point where it ran under the line.

'There we are,' I said. 'Now we'll just bait these with a few cigarettes. If the fags are still there in a few days' time, we'll know whether anyone has bothered to look into them or not. With any luck the Krauts are so used to seeing these things lying around that they pay them no attention.'

Rather heartened, we pressed on and, finding more drums

by other culverts, we treated them the same way until we had used up all our cigarettes.

We turned and began to retrace our steps towards Kastelli. We were pooped after tramping such a long way under the weight of those infernal tools, and I thought it quite in character to flag down the trolley when next it passed. We told the scowling Germans a tale about an urgent repair necessary to the line so they invited us aboard and we rode back in style. Georgiou's eyes nearly popped out of his head when he saw us arrive.

We were hard put to contain our impatience until the following Sunday when we could walk the line again to inspect our little trap. When the day came, to our delight we were able to recover our 'bait' intact. If our luck held we should now be able to stack the barrels with high explosives and leave them undisturbed until such time as we had selected our target.

The next phase was going to be tricky enough, owing to the sheer quantity of explosives required. Determined not to spoil the ship for a ha'p'orth of tar and because I was going to need pressure as opposed to cutting charges, I decided that the mine for the train would be a 200-pounder. For the crane, because the culvert I was going to place the charge in was smaller and fitted the barrel better, thus guaranteeing a more compressed explosion, I figured a 60-pounder would suffice.

During the following three nights we brought the charges, made up in 20 lb units, down from the mountain from Ano Agoriani and concealed them in the barrels. We had several near escapes, almost detected by road and rail patrols, but by keeping a sharp lookout and lying flat in the ditches and long grass whenever danger approached we completed the job to my satisfaction.

I rigged the main charge so that it was to be detonated by a railway fog signal. It would be Mac's job to nip up and place it on the line during the minute or so between the passing of the patrol trolley and the arrival of the train which would set it off.

I decided to set off the crane charge by means of a pull-switch and a long cord running from the culvert to my place of concealment. I dared not risk burying the cord for fear of leaving traces, so everything – fuses, switches, detonators and cord – were all bundled into the barrel with the explosives.

So far, so good, and I informed Georgiou that we were now waiting to hear from him with news of a worthwhile target.

At this point fortune took a hand. Two days later, on 15 September, we heard on our wireless the news of the successful occupation by our forces of the islands of Kos and Leros. Mussolini had garrisoned these and other islands in the south-east Aegean, back in those dark days of semi-perpetual defeat, as part of his grandiose dream of a revitalised imperial Italy. Our forces – not enough of them as it turned out – went ashore with the purpose of denying the islands to the Germans, who were busily replacing surrendering Italian garrisons. Our boys teamed up with the Italians, who if they had ever had much love of the Germans certainly had none by now, as the days following the official Italian surrender had seen some appalling massacres of Italian soldiers.

On the island of Cephalonia, the Italians had lost 1300 men in the battles that developed when they refused the German demand that they surrender. Murder had been added to insult when, having run out of ammunition and raised the white flag, they saw their former allies execute 5000 Italian prisoners of war.[1] On Corfu the Krauts excelled themselves and

1 This infamous massacre of Italian PoWs on Cephalonia provides the background for Louis de Bernières' famous novel, *Captain Corelli's Mandolin*.

massacred all 280 of the Italian officers on the island. They shoved their bodies on to a ship, took it to sea and dropped the lot overboard. If they hoped that, somehow, no one but the fish would notice, they miscalculated.

In Kos, when it was all over and the Germans had retaken the island and made prisoners of the British and Italian defenders, the Italian commander and ninety of his officers were shot. If anyone wants to accuse people like me of fighting dirty I suggest they read these statistics and then come and have the discussion.

Now, following our occupation of Kos and Leros, the German counter-attack came immediately. Squadrons of Stukas and Heinkels were flown down to the airfields in the south of Greece and there was a huge increase in rail traffic over 'our' stretch of line as the necessary fuel and bombs were rushed down to supply them. This was our chance.

In great excitement, Georgiou informed us that during the next few days his information was that no fewer than twelve special trains, carrying aviation spirit and bombs, were scheduled to pass through Kastelli, bound for Corinth.

I naturally wanted to catch one of the early trains in order to trap the others behind the wreckage, but I was also obliged to attack during night or early dawn. I told Georgiou that at all costs he must get further details.

In order to be on the spot, Yotis and I moved into Kastelli and waited while he obtained a schedule and timetable by telephone from his opposite number in Lamia. By early evening the information was in our hands. Studying the timetable I could see that we would be obliged to let the first two and possibly a third go through unmolested as they would pass too early. The one I selected would take in water at Kastelli at around 3 a.m. and should arrive at the mine before 4 a.m. If it all went well and if the repair gang turned out smartly – and Georgiou swore that he'd make damn certain it did – I should be able to catch the crane on its way to the wreckage just before dawn.

We snatched a quick bite, bought two bottles of brandy and roared off on the motorbike to tell Mac to get ready to do his stuff.

The mines were about three miles apart and, to save time, I dumped Yotis and took Mac to within a mile of his position. I gave him one of the bottles for company and told him that once his mine went up he was not to hang around. He should make his way to Ano Agoriani, where I would meet him. We would then decide when and where to set the third mine.

I was getting a little nervous as it was well past curfew time and I still had to get the bike and myself back to my own position. However, using a tactic that had served me well before, I waited in some bushes by the side of the road until a motorised patrol passed that was going my way. I then rode quietly along behind them, without lights and in their dust, until we reached a point opposite my culvert. There I peeled off and hid the bike in the ditch.

It was about 8 p.m. and I had a long, long wait ahead of me. I started to make a hole in the brandy.

At 10 p.m. the first of the special trains came through. From a long way off I saw its headlight, a blazing bright light that at first did not appear to be moving. It gradually approached, lighting up the countryside in a cone of fierce white that left me feeling remarkable naked, and forced me to crouch flat, like a rabbit. As it clanked and crashed past I peered cautiously up from my cover and counted ten or twelve tanker cars only. I was glad that I hadn't chosen this one to blow up.

At 1 a.m. the second train passed: eighteen trucks, some tankers and some laden flats. This looked more promising. I moved up and nearer the line to wait out the remaining hours.

During all the time I'd been waiting so far, I had been surprised to count only three patrolling trolley cars, so evidently
only the normal guard schedule was being kept. I sent up a
prayer that Mac had noticed this too and would not delay putting his fog signal on the line too long, lest he ended up being
picked out in the train's searchlight.

At 3 a.m. I went up to my culvert, got out the cord and connected it to the pull-switch. I removed the safety pin and
carefully unrolled the cord until I reached my ditch about
forty yards away.

The road where the bike was hidden was about seventy
yards to my rear. After I had yanked the cord and exploded
the mine I would have to run like hell for the bike and ride
flat out back down the road for about three-quarters of a
mile. There I would turn off up a small track. This led about
half a mile up the mountain to nowhere before finally peter-
ing out.

If I should happen to meet a motorised patrol during that
ride it would just be too bad. I would have to ditch the bike
and hope to escape on foot.

At 3.30 a.m. the brandy was half gone and it was damn
cold. There was a thrumming on the line and a trolley passed,
coming from Kastelli. I could make out the muffled forms of
three soldiers as they trundled along, with their flashlights
playing on the lines about thirty yards ahead of them. Certainly
there was no danger of them spotting my cord.

I kept my eyes towards the west looking for the first sign of
our train and, sure enough, within a few minutes saw the
gleam of the searchlight. I was very much closer to the line
this time and lay very low as she thundered up. It seemed as if
the earth was shaking, and I lay in my shallow ditch with my
heart pounding with excitement as she hissed and clanked
past. I dared not look up but, by counting the sounds of the
wheels, I figured she was at least as long as the previous train.

I let out my breath. If Mac had done his stuff I should hear the bang within ten minutes.

I sat and sweated and prayed. The minutes dragged past.

There was a vivid flash in the sky to the east. I jumped to my feet and, moments later, there came the rumble of a heavy explosion.

'Bloody hell!' I thought. 'That's going for it, Mac!' I kept my eyes in the direction and saw what I was hoping to see . . . the whole sky lighting up as the tankers caught fire. Brighter and brighter grew the light, and then came a terrific flash and the cracking roar of an enormous explosion. We had been lucky: our train had been carrying bombs as well. They would have heard that bang at Kastelli, and I hoped that Georgiou was doing his stuff to get the crane on the way.

Fifteen minutes passed and two truckloads of soldiers came tearing down the road towards the wreck. I waited anxiously, in a sweat. If the crane waited until daylight to come out I was sunk as I couldn't possibly stay where I was after dawn broke.

Another twenty minutes passed and I was getting really worried. In a half hour or so it would be starting to get light and I would have to set off my mine, leaving the most important part of the operation undone.

I left my ditch again, crawled to the track and laid my ear to the line. Ah! There was a definite something on the way. Then I realised that the crane, which was pushed by a small shunting engine, probably would not have a searchlight and would be depending on a rail trolley to inspect the line ahead.

Within five minutes a trolley came past packed with soldiers flashing their torches and, a minute or so behind them, trundling rapidly, making a great puffing and fuss, came the shunting engine with the crane rocking along ahead of it.

I knelt on one knee and braced myself. As the front bogies of the crane reached the culvert, I yanked the cord. A split second later up went my mine with a roar. I ducked. A hunk of metal sang wickedly over my head and the crane leapt off the track and was rolled over sideways by the engine as it continued to push for a few yards. Then it too fell off the rails and rolled over on to its side. There was a brief silence and then someone began to scream in agony, probably the unfortunate engine driver or fireman.

I didn't wait to see. I fled for the bike and rode like the wind down the road. I rounded each corner with my heart in my mouth, but luck was with me and, reaching my turn-off, I went crashing and bucketing up the mountain as far as I could. Then, having hidden the bike behind some boulders, I set off across country for Ano Agoriani, where I expected to meet Mac.

It was mid-morning before he arrived. It had been his first sabotage operation and he had been unable to resist the temptation to stay and watch the results of his efforts. It had been most spectacular. The mine had completely destroyed the culvert and blown the leading engine clean off the track. The rear engine, unable to stop, had then pushed truck after truck into the wreckage, which had instantly caught fire. Although he had been about 200 yards away, he had been knocked over by the blast as the truckloads of bombs went off. In addition, so far as he could judge at least 100 yards of track had been totally demolished.

Mac was insistent that he be allowed to set off the third mine and, against my better judgement, I let him go off with the remaining explosives. He was spotted approaching the line by a patrol, wounded and captured. He was eventually executed.

The Germans made superhuman efforts and, largely because we had been unable to prevent the Athens crane from arriving, managed to clear the line within eight days. However, I like to think that we achieved something in that the nine trains trapped behind the wreckage were ten days late in getting to their destinations, thus taking some of the heat off our chaps in Kos and Leros. Not that it did much good in the end: the Germans recaptured both islands.

Georgiou very wisely joined me in the mountains, but not before he had thoroughly sabotaged the telephones in Kastelli. We could have done with a few more of his calibre.

The schoolboy: Geoffrey Eckstein, before
changing his name to Gordon-Creed.

1942, Cairo or Alexandria. Indulging in a spot of R&R back from the fighting
with fellow officers of 2 Royal Gloucestershire Hussars.

The Western Desert 1941–2 with 2nd Royal Gloucestershire Hussars.

A waterless shave.

'*L'Hirondelle*' (a Mark VI Crusader tank). GG-C won his MC in her, but she was soon destroyed: it was the first of a number that were to be destroyed under him in action.

GG-C and crew with their Honey tank, bedding down for the night.

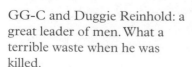

GG-C and Duggie Reinhold: a great leader of men. What a terrible waste when he was killed.

The Asopos Viaduct from below with the team's OP (Observation post) marked on the cliffs above. Deemed unattackable by the Germans, the solution was to approach down a previously unclimbed gorge – the last place the German sentries thought to look.

Sergeant Bill Weatherley, GG-C's radio operator throughout his time in Greece, at one of their parachute dropping grounds, high in the mountains.

From left to right: Brian Dillon – he was i/c of the area to the East and a good neighbour and friend; Don Stott – the bravest of men, he was tragically killed later in the Far East and Harry McIntyre, one of the two Royal Engineer Officers on the Asopos raid. They had to, first, shape the explosives, then haul them into position and, finally, set the time fuses. The resulting explosion demolished the structure to spectacular effect.

Taking a break from the vicious fighting behind the lines in Greece. As Geoff himself described this picture: 'soaking up the sun and relaxing by the sea.'

Greek fisherman.

Greece – vermin riddled hovels.

In cavalry (yeomanry) mode. SOE operatives usually wore their army uniform or a version thereof. The support of local priests was of great importance.

A couple of Greek mountain men.

1 June 1944, GG-C (with pipe) about to finally leave Greece for good with a group of rescued pilots – mostly Americans.

June 1944, back to the luxury of Cairo after the squalor of Greece. Lunch with King George and Queen Frederica of Greece.

The very end of the war, Germany 1945.

1947. Beirut was a paradise after war-ravaged Britain.

In party mode.

Kenya 1956: the great white hunter with his prize: his second wife Belinda. She came through arrivals of Nairobi airport but never made it to the departure lounge.

Camden, South Carolina, USA circa 1980. In his sixties and still breaking hearts.

Circa 1950. General Farid Chehab, Lebanese spymaster and Deputy Head of Interpol: Geoff owed him his life after the war, but would never say why.

12

Thank me anytime you like

'Oos' fookin' fooker's this fooker?'

'That fooker's my fooker's fooker. So fook off!'

And thus a perfect understanding was established between two British soldiers as to the ownership of an item of an officer's equipment.

I have been intrigued and amused by the differences and preferences of various nationalities in their choice of invective. Anglo-Saxons and Germans are boringly prone to repetitive 'fucks', 'buggers' and 'shits'. The French invoke the name of God. The Spaniards are subtle and viciously wounding, while the Greeks, at least to my ear, are the most offensive.

I remember an occasion when I was marching with my entire entourage of between thirty and forty men from an area I no longer considered secure to another location. Our route took us through a certain large village which, on our approach, we were warned was occupied by a foraging party of Italians. Not caring to draw attention to ourselves I decided to make a detour and this we did. Presently, we found ourselves by a spring about 500 feet above and 1200 feet away from the nearest houses. We sat down for a rest and a smoke.

One of my bodyguards, Michaelis, a cocky little shit for whom I had long entertained a cordial dislike, suddenly gave tongue. 'Fuck the cross!' he exclaimed. 'Look at that pederast.'

We looked in the direction he was pointing and saw an

Italian soldier holding a flapping white chicken by its legs and obviously bargaining with some old crow of a village woman.

'Major Geoff,' said Michaelis, 'let you and I each take one shot at that bastard and we shall see which of us is the better man.'

I couldn't allow myself to be faced down, so agreed. I took a German service rifle from one of the boys, Michaelis having his own, and we both lay down, aimed and waited the order to fire from Yotis. I thought that it was a damned difficult shot. Not the 500 yards distance so much, but the fact that it was downhill made the target area very much smaller, nor did it help that it was not my rifle and thus not zeroed in for me.[1] But, making as I thought the proper allowances for wind and elevation, I aimed to hit my man somewhere about the middle.

'Fire!' said Yotis, and I squeezed off. The chicken, held three inches in front of the Eyetie's balls, exploded in a cloud of feathers. A split second later Michaelis fired and the Eyetie collapsed with a bullet in his thigh. He yelled and flopped off along the ground until he found shelter behind a hut.

Those oafs my bodyguards fell around in heaps laughing, and Michaelis was fair bursting with pride and self-glory.

A little miffed, I gave an order to continue the march and, walking along in front, had to pretend not to hear the exquisite witticisms and hearty guffaws as bloody Michaelis elaborated on my prowess as an intrepid slayer of poultry. About half an hour later it so happened that a blue jay, a fairly common bird in that part of Greece, flashed across our path

---

1   Soldiers go to the range to practise and improve their shooting. What may not be so obvious is that even the best of shots needs to keep his rifle 'zeroed': ensuring that the sights are set so that when he aims at a point, that is where the bullet strikes. Every person holds a rifle differently, thus each soldier should shoot with his own 'corrected' rifle. Geoff's shot may have been perfect, but with the sights either set for another man or – and as likely – perhaps knocked off 'true', he stood less chance of succeeding.

about thirty yards in front of us. For no reason that I can think of I drew my personalised .38 Smith & Wesson in one beautifully smooth movement and fired from the hip. Again there was an explosion of feathers, this time accompanied by a stunned silence from behind. Without breaking step I blew down the muzzle and nonchalantly replaced the revolver in its holster. Strolling up to the remains of the unlucky jay I found the two blue pin feathers and, sticking one in my cap, I took the other up to the gaping and, for once, speechless Michaelis and handed it to him.

Smiling into his eyes I said pleasantly and in English, 'Try that for size, you smart prick!'

He recovered. 'Bugger the Virgin!' he muttered. 'I suppose you can also walk on water?'

'What do you think?' I replied.

This monumental fluke earned for me a quite unjustified reputation as a deadly shot with a handgun and the story spread far and wide, losing nothing, needless to say, in the telling.

An unexpected dividend from it all came to me a few months later when an attempt was made on my life by a crazed Greek regular ex-officer of extreme right-wing opinions, who incredibly had come to the conclusion that I was secretly a Communist sympathiser.

Anyway, one late afternoon I was strolling along with Yotis and Nikitas, one of my bodyguards. We were many miles from the nearest enemy and, so far as we could feel safe and relaxed in our circumstances, we certainly did. The three of us, with myself leading, were walking down the mountain track leading from our camp down into the little village of Episkopi where we had thoughts of sharing an ouzo or two and perhaps a few glasses of wine, as was our daily wont. Suddenly from an outcrop of rocks about 300 yards away and to the right came a burst of machine-gun fire. I heard that ugly crack of a very near miss just above my head and dived headlong for cover with Yotis and Nikitas. We lay flat behind some rocks and regarded one another in shocked surprise.

'Christ!' I said. 'That was close. What the hell's going on? There can't be any Krauts within miles – or can there? That was bloody deliberate, goddammit,' I continued, beginning to feel that familiar flow of adrenalin that always follows a fright in my case. 'Let's get the sod . . . Yotis, you stay put and try and hold his attention. Wave your hat or something. Nikitas, you've got your Schmeisser – work around to the right. I'll go left, so watch out for me if you shoot. Come on.'

I only had my revolver and the cover on my side was patchy, so consequently I had covered only about two-thirds of the distance when I heard a short burst of fire from Nikitas. I jumped up and ran like hell towards the sound. When I arrived panting and pale with fury I found Nikitas already standing over a man he had wounded in the buttocks and legs. A German light machine-gun was lying beside him. I kicked the gun away and pointed my revolver at his head.

'All right, damn you,' I spluttered. 'Who are you and why did you try to kill me?'

He was bleeding fairly badly but was not desperately hurt. His loathing for me showed plainly on his face. We got his story disjointedly and with much prodding from Nikitas, who was making great play of stropping his knife against his boot: an embittered royalist, ex-captain of Evzones, a patriot crazy with frustration and worry at what he saw happening to his country, he was convinced I was part and parcel of the Communist plot.

Puzzled at how he had managed to miss me at what had been virtually point-blank range, I examined his LMG and found the silly bugger had the sights set at more than half a mile.

'As a matter of interest,' I asked, 'why did you open fire when I was so far off? You could have cut me in half if you had waited until we were closer.'

'Major Geoff,' he replied, 'I knew that if I let you get within pistol shot, I was a dead man. What are you going to do with me?'

'I'll send a mule up from the village,' I said, feeling rather sorry for the poor chap and my rage having subsided. 'I'm keeping your gun and you'd better keep well away from me from now on.'

It was shortly after the fiasco at Lidhorikion, when we had so narrowly failed to take the surrender of the Italians, that the ELAS struck for the second time at the EKKA. Colonel Psaros – my old chum from my original parachute landing – had taken his band for training high up on to Mount Giona and was encamped in some shepherds' huts which were only used in the summertime. My own HQ was established a few miles further down the mountain to the south of him. Here, in an enclosed little valley, I had an excellent dropping ground.

I made a trip up to Anatoli to tell Brigadier Eddie what had happened at Lidhorikion and was returning to my HQ along a track down in the valley between Mounts Giona and Vardhousia. As I had to bypass Lidhorikion, my way led up Mount Giona by way of Psaros's camp. From there I would descend the mountain to rejoin my men.

It was a long and arduous climb. Halfway up, I heard distant machine-gun and rifle fire ahead of me. A little way on, I ran into a small picket of ELAS Andartes guarding the path. I guessed what was happening and my heart sank at the perfidy of these swine. It had been barely six weeks since they had given their solemn word to obey the directives from GHQ Middle East and to refrain from all hostile acts against each other. They had promised to direct all their energies against the Germans and Italians.

The rearguard were obviously both astonished and put out to see me. They rose to their feet and stood in sullen and embarrassed silence, fingering their guns as I approached. I was conscious that I was myself in a position of great danger because I was a witness to their treachery against their fellows. I also knew that I could very easily be removed by an 'accidental' bullet. Nonetheless, I had an obvious duty to find out what was afoot and also to protect my HQ and wireless set.

'What's up, boys?' I asked, forcing a cheerful look.

Silence.

'Well?' I said sharply. 'Come on, let's have it.'

One of them shuffled. ''Ares' Andartes are disarming Psaros,' he muttered.[2]

'I see. Well I should be grateful if one of you fellows would come with me and show me the way to where Ares is. How about you?' I pointed to the man who had spoken.

He hesitated a moment, then shrugged and stepped out ahead of me. Two hours' steady climbing brought us to a cow dominating the pastures on which the EKKA had been encamped. The battle was over and the place was swarming with armed partisans. I recognised the bearded Ares sitting on a rock with some of his officers. I made my way over to him.

'This is a bad business, Ares,' I said.

'I have my orders,' he lied cheerfully. 'The central committee of the EAM has decided that there is no need or room for

2 Ares was the pseudonym of the political commissar who had caused trouble when Geoff first landed. This Communist commander, apparently once a schoolmaster, had a reputation for cruelty. He met his end in 1945, fighting Greek government forces during the civil war that followed the German retreat. He was decapitated, and his head was put on a stake and displayed in the village square of Trikkala.

any Andartes other than the ELAS. These people are welcome to join us if they like. Psaros has run away.'

'Is my wireless set all right?' I asked.

'We have no quarrel with you, Major Geoff . . . Just so long as you don't interfere with us,' he added.

'You realise what the consequences might be when I report your actions to Cairo?'

'We can do without your arms and your money,' he retorted. 'Report whatever you like to Cairo. If they send paratroops against us we shall deal with them!'

'I don't suppose that will happen as we came here to fight Germans, not Greeks. Now if you'll give me a pass to get through your lines I'll be on my way. Incidentally, if you have any wounded I will be glad to supply your medical officer with whatever I have in the way of supplies.'

He grunted, scribbled a few lines and handed me his pass. 'The doctor will go with you,' he said. 'There are a few wounded.'

As I turned to leave, he spoke again. 'Give my regards to Mr Churchill,' he sneered.

I turned and looked steadily at him. 'Thank you, I might just do that.'

I was glad to get away. I reached my HQ two hours later to find my men all quite safe, albeit somewhat alarmed.

It transpired that the ELAS had surrounded the sleeping EKKA during the night and had attacked at first light. Colonel Psaros, naturally loath to fight his fellow countrymen, had retired and abandoned most of his stores and ammunition.

When the news of Ares' second attack on Psaros became known, the Central Committee in Athens cynically repudiated all responsibility. They renewed their protestations of good faith to Cairo and even went through the pantomime of condemning Ares to death for his 'disobedience'!

Much to my disgust, as I could see how this was going to

end, I was ordered to re-form and rearm the EKKA. But, acting on my own initiative, I suggested to Psaros, when I found him a week or so later, that I should supply him only with easily concealed weapons such as pistols, grenades and submachine-guns. It was only a question of time before he was attacked again. I also advised him to disperse his field force and move them back to Athens. There he should wait 'underground' to combat the Communist threat at a later date. Tragically, he could not see it my way and refused. In March 1944 Ares attacked him in overwhelming force, and this time murdered him and several of his officers in cold blood.

The ELAS doctor who had accompanied me back to my HQ observed that we were encamped in a pleasant spot with shade and a good spring. He asked if I minded his moving the wounded down to where we were. I replied that so long as he brought any wounded EKKA as well I would be delighted.

In a short while I had a dozen or more men on my hands suffering from a variety of wounds, none of which were too serious. The doctor was rather a good fellow and we subsequently became quite good friends. A few days later, after we had bedded down our patients and were thinking of our supper, a heavily laden mule came trotting around the corner. Yotis caught it and for a few minutes we speculated about the identity of the owner. Looking back up the track in the direction from which the mule had come, I was surprised to see, striding into view, none other than Brian Dillon, the very man who had first introduced me to Special Forces all that time ago – a lifetime ago, it seemed to me – in Mary's House in Cairo. I had assumed that he was still in the desert with David Stirling and the SAS. Concealing my delight I let him approach and greeted him:

'It would be you, wouldn't it? I suppose your creditors ran you out of Egypt?'

He grinned broadly. 'Whew! That bloody mule goes like a train. Well, you old fart, how are you?'

'Scratching along. What on earth brings you here?'

'I bust my pelvis in one of David's shows,' he replied, 'and, what with the war packing up in North Africa, I thought that I'd come and keep you out of mischief.'

'Well, I couldn't be more pleased,' I said and meant it. 'What's the idea? Are you supposed to be staying with me?'

'Only for a week or two to learn the form,' he said. 'Then I'm supposed to go on and open up the Mount Helicon area. We'll be neighbours anyway.'

We had much to discuss and I was delighted to have him with me over the next three weeks or so until, having supplied him with a guide and an interpreter, I waved him on his way eastwards towards Helicon.

Brian was to remain in Greece right up until the end in 1944, and was to play a significant part in the operations which finally led to the defeat of the Communists during the civil war. He was a very fine type of regular soldier whose services, in my opinion, were never accorded their proper due.[3]

Galaxhidion was a rather charming and decaying little port serving the western approach to the Bay of Itea in the Gulf of Corinth. A thousand or so feet above and well outside the town was my villa HQ. There we spent many of the daylight hours receiving and transmitting to Cairo such intelligence, political and military, as came our way.

---

3 Dillon was awarded the MBE. The general view was that his exploits had earned him a serious gallantry medal many times over. However, by the end of 1944, when the regular British army was in control of Greece, the role of SOE was now, in the words of Colonel Christopher Woodhouse – initially Brigadier Myers' second-in-command and thereafter in command of the British Mission to Greece on Myers' departure in late 1943 – viewed with anything from 'patronising indifference to fury and contempt'. Gallant SOE operatives were seen as 'irresponsible schoolboys playing Red Indians at other people's expense'. History, as ever, was being rewritten and this time at SOE's expense.

The evenings were another matter and, bored after a day on the W/T, Yotis and I would often descend into the town to pass the time with various citizens with whom we had become friendly. Several of them had pretty daughters, but pretty or not they were all of them beginning to look more and more attractive to my famished eye. There was definitely a problem. Having broken the ice, so to speak, with Maria – fat George's wife – I naturally saw her as often as was practical. But as she lived across the bay and several dangerous miles further on, I was often finding that weeks went by before I could make the journey.

There was no way that I would be stupid enough to contemplate the seduction of one of Galaxhidion's untouched and zealously guarded daughters. As I complained to Yotis: 'There must be some girl around here who's not a virgin. We need to find someone. We could put her on the payroll as a secretary . . . Actually, we could use someone to type out those surrender and safe-conduct leaflets that we thought of distributing among the Italians and Germans.' This was an idea of mine to irritate the German high command. The truth of the matter was that we were hard pressed to deal with the few deserters who did come over to us – we were always short of food, for a start – and we could not have coped with a rush of them.

Yotis nodded and flashed his gold teeth.

A few days later, looking rather pleased with himself, Yotis arrived at the villa, where we were busy decoding messages.

'I've got one, Major.'

'Got what?' I asked obtusely.

'A secretary.'

'Have you, by God. Any good? What's she like?'

He took a deep breath. 'Good,' he said. 'In fact, very good. In fact, Major, you are in for a surprise.'

'Well, well,' I said, beginning to feel a small twitch of antici-
pation. 'When and where do I meet this surprise?'

'She lives in one of those big old houses with her widowed
mum and kid brother,' said Yotis, 'I said we'd be down and
take supper with them. Her name is Eleni. She types after a
fashion and also speaks quite a bit of English and French.'

'Sounds perfect,' I said, pleased. 'Er . . . do you think,
she . . . er . . .?'

Yotis rolled his eyes.

I spruced up and took from our stores a few pounds of tea
and sugar – rare commodities indeed in Greece at that time.
At around 7.30 p.m. we presented ourselves at the door of the
large and crumbling old house belonging to the widow
Papadapolous. Yotis did the honours.

'Kyria Papadapolous,' he said, 'may I present the British
Major Geoff?'

I bowed over her hand politely. I saw a pale, rather ravaged
face but withal one of dignity and with some remaining traces
of past beauty.

'Please enter,' she said. 'This is indeed an honour. May I
lead the way?'

We followed her up the stairs into her drawing room, which
was large and gloomy and furnished in typically wealthy Greek
taste: massive furniture with drapes and antimacassars,[4] the
walls adorned with dozens of horrifying pictures and
portraits.

'What a nice room,' I said, looking around and wondering
whether I ought to have brought something with which to
fortify myself.

'Thank you,' she murmured. 'Please sit down. My daughter
is preparing a little refreshment for you, but in these hard

4   A linen square draped decoratively over the top of a chair to prevent it getting
stained: an ingenious invention given the Greek predilection for copious lashings
of hair oil.

times, you know . . .' Her voice trailed away. I winked at Yotis to produce our tea and sugar.

We sat making the usual silly small talk when the door opened with a rush and Eleni bounced in carrying a plate of some sweet concoction made from jam and also, thank God, a decanter and glasses.

'My daughter Eleni, Major Geoff.'

Whether I am right or wrong I cannot be sure, but I believe that over the years I have come to recognise certain character-istics in faces that denote extreme sexuality. Slightly buck teeth for example, a certain shade of slatey blue eyes and a longish, slightly pinched nose. There are others. Written down like this it doesn't sound too attractive, but nevertheless, and ignoring the more obvious 'chemistry' that one encounters from time to time, I have found that a girl with one or more of the above traits will usually prove to be a most enthusiastic bedfellow.

She was a tallish girl, I noticed, with a superb figure, gor-geous chestnut hair to her shoulders, perfect teeth and, need I say it, slatey, big blue eyes and a slightly pinched nose. She radiated energy and friendliness.

'My daughter has just returned from spending nine months in Athens,' said Mrs P, 'but life is so difficult now we thought it better for her to be with me.'

'Well, I'm delighted,' I said gallantly. 'And yes, thank you very much, I would like a glass of liqueur.'

We chatted away animatedly. Eleni was hopping around like a ping-pong ball as she looked after us, and I was hard put to it to drag my eyes away from her as she moved from one to the other, pouring drinks.

We went in to supper. Poor Mrs P had obviously scraped the bottom of the barrel to do honour to the occasion and I was suddenly conscious of the real hardships facing one in her position. Hopeless inflation having rendered her annuities and savings valueless, the poor soul was literally surviving by bartering her treasures and possessions one by one in exchange for food.

'Well . . . that was delicious,' I lied over a discreet burp. 'I really must thank you. You can have no idea what it means to me to be welcomed into a civilised household after living in the mountains for months and months with only ruffians for company.' I was laying it on a bit. 'Don't you agree, Yotis?

Yotis nodded.

'Now then, Mrs Papadapolous. I understand that Eleni types? Believe me, I am desperate for someone to do part-time work for me and, with your permission, I will employ her at ten gold sovereigns a month.'

Poor Mrs P went quite pale – as well she might: I could have had ten fully equipped and eager Andartes at my beck and call for the same monthly price. However, 100 Andartes could not have begun to supply what I had in mind. What the bean-counters back in Cairo would have made of my scheme I neither knew nor cared. Whenever they felt the urge they could head down to Mary's House or any number of similar establishments. Stuck in Greece until Lord alone knew when, I didn't have any such option.

'But . . . but, Major Geoff, that's a fortune!' she stammered. 'Eleni would be honoured to do your typing for nothing. She couldn't possibly accept such a sum.'

'Mrs Papadapolous,' I said seriously, 'I will get Eleni a type-writer and, from time to time, will ask her to do certain work for me. You must realise that there will be risks, deadly risks, if word should reach the enemy about her activities. In the circumstances, I can only look upon ten sovereigns a month as a token payment. If you have no objection,' I added cunningly, 'I should like to feel free to drop in here discreetly after dark to discuss things with Eleni and possibly have a hot bath.

Naturally, we will supply anything you might need from our own stores.'

I was not surprised when Mrs P broke down. 'Excuse me, Major Geoff,' she sniffed, 'you cannot know . . . Since my husband died and now this terrible war . . . I think you are an angel sent from heaven!'

Having thus disposed of mundane affairs and our meal being over, Mrs P suggested that Eleni show me over the house. We excused ourselves and, leading the way with an oil lamp, Eleni showed me the house floor by floor. It was surprisingly large and, typically, had no plumbing whatsoever.

'My bedroom,' she announced offhandedly. Somehow I found myself inside – or was I pushed? Anyway, she placed the lamp down on a table and spun round, her eyes blazing. 'Geoff!' she said and, taking me by the back of the neck, gazed avidly at me and at the same time did a funny little up and down dance. She began to breathe heavily through her nose, and the next thing I was aware of was what felt like six inches of tongue exploring my tonsils. Even before I could come up for air I felt her fingers busy with my flies. Perhaps I made a half-hearted attempt to defend myself, but I doubt it. Anyway, within ten seconds, she was down on her knees in front of me being extremely and expertly busy.

Finally: 'You are like a god,' she said flatteringly, albeit inaccurately.

'Wow,' I thought, putting myself together again. 'Something tells me that I've really landed with my arse in butter this time!'

The whole thing couldn't have lasted above eight minutes.

Eleni picked up the lamp, smiled and kissed me. 'Thank you, Geoff,' she said softly. 'Perhaps we should go down now.'

'Thank *me*, for Christ's sake!' thought I. 'You can thank me any time you damn well like!'

We rejoined Mrs P and Yotis downstairs. He caught my eye and permitted himself a half smile.

Walking back in the dark up towards the villa I fell over a stone. 'Fuck it!' I said, then, 'Holy shit, Yotis, she's one in a thousand. Anyway I'm committed, so you had better find her a non-Greek typewriter and a loaf of bumf and carbons and we'll play it by ear until we know her a bit better. I must say, though, I thought her mum was a super old bag.'

Eleni proved to be something special: a devoted, ingenious and unselfish lover. So much so that I must admit I soon became rather besotted with her, and this damn near cost me my life.

As I explained, in order to give her some pretence of work I had composed leaflets addressed to enemy soldiers, urging them to surrender and promising safe conduct and refuge in the mountains. About three thousand of these things were typed and distributed. We netted as a result no Germans and about forty Italians who were, in the event, nothing but a damned nuisance and a liability, as their value to their own side was obviously nil and now the responsibility for feeding and hiding them devolved to me. However, our success, such as it was, had evidently touched a nerve and the reaction when it came was sudden and alarming.

Because water, particularly on the coast, was usually in short supply, many of the larger houses including that of Mrs P had cisterns to catch rainwater built into their cellars. I had peered into Mrs P's cistern: a nasty black hole about sixteen feet deep, wide and high and containing, at that time, about four feet of murky-looking water. The only access was through a manhole about two feet square. On its cover usually stood a wooden bucket with a rope attached.

One evening, at about 9 p.m., Yotis and I were sitting with Eleni, going over proofs of a propaganda leaflet we had dreamed up. Eleni's little brother, a 9-year-old horror, came flying in.

'Germans!' he gasped. 'Hundreds of them. They're searching all the houses, looking for typewriters.'

We sprang to our feet, white-faced. How the hell could this
have happened, I thought numbly. It was a good forty-mile
drive from the nearest German garrison at Amfissa. Normally
we received immediate warning in code over the telephone
should there be any signs of enemy movement. I realised that
any attempt to flee would be suicidal as the Germans, being
no fools, would have every exit from the town blocked up
tight. As we gazed at one another in sick alarm there came a
thunderous knocking at the front door.

'Quick! The cistern,' said Eleni. I grabbed the typewriter,
Yotis the paper and carbons, and we fled helter-skelter into
the cellar as the knocking was repeated. We tumbled down
with a mighty splash into the water and crept into the furthest
corner, clutching typewriter and paper. Eleni hurriedly
replaced the manhole cover, leaving us in the pitch and smelly
darkness.

'Yotis,' I whispered urgently, 'for God's sake keep absolutely
still. Don't even breathe. If they look down and see the water
rippling we've had it. They'll just chuck down a couple of
grenades.'

The next thirty minutes were the worst I had ever spent.
Supposing, I thought, we had left something incriminating
upstairs. Or what if Eleni and the old lady were taken off for
questioning, leaving us with no one knowing where we were
and with no means of getting out of the cistern? We could
die a dog's death. Alternatively, as they often did, the
Germans might just set fire to the house, or perhaps they
might work on little brother till he squealed. Charming
prospects all!

Suddenly my heart almost stopped as the manhole cover
was lifted letting in the light and I heard Eleni's voice say:
'Look!' At the same time, she managed, apparently

accidentally, to drop the bucket and rope into the water. She thus achieved two things: she ruffled the water and, having disposed of the rope, discouraged any curious Kraut from lowering himself down to take a look.

As it was, a torch flashed briefly into the depths, someone grunted. '*Nichts darin, Herr Leutenant*,' and the cover was replaced.

I let out a long breath and gave Yotis's hand a fervent squeeze. We had no words.

What seemed like hours later, the manhole cover opened again. 'Geoff,' came the blessed voice of Eleni. 'Are you all right? They've gone . . . you can come out.'

'How?' I asked. 'The bloody rope's down here.'

'Oh. I forgot. Wait a minute. I'll get some string and pull it up and fasten it on to something.

Getting out of the trap was extremely difficult. I made it, but old Yotis simply lacked the arm muscle. Eventually we made him stand in the bucket and we all hauled him up. Everyone was near collapse from mental and physical shock.

'Christ! Eleni, you're a genius. How many of the sods were there?'

'Three and an officer, I think.'

'Did they give you a hard time? How did you get them out of the house?'

She looked me straight in the eye and shrugged her shoulders.

I gaped. 'Eleni! . . . No you didn't! *All* of them? Oh Jesus, what can I say?'

I took her in my arms and held her close, trembling.

'Oh Geoff! Geoff!' she cried, and wept helplessly.

'Don't, my love, my darling – please don't,' I begged her, near to tears myself. 'Hush, my baby. It's over and it never happened!'

Gradually, as I comforted her, her sobs subsided. After a while I smacked her on her bottom.

'Come on, sweetheart,' I said. 'Blow your nose. I'll go and fetch us all an enormous drink while you get that little brother of yours to fix us a hot bath.'

13

Texan beef and a traitor

Towards the autumn of 1943 I had my HQ in a pleasant valley a few miles to the north-east of the village of Pendayoi on Mount Vardhousia. I had been rather inactive over the previous two months, suffering from another virulent bout of dysentery which could have been cured had Cairo thought to include some explanatory literature along with pills they dropped at my urgent request.

A move to a secure winter HQ was much on my mind but I had, as yet, no specific ideas as to where to go. Pendayoi was now being visited fairly often by enemy foraging parties. Also, the village attitude towards the war in general and my proximity in particular left a lot to be desired. Miserable buggers, I thought, and Yotis agreed with me. I prepared to move but had it in mind, if occasion presented itself, to cause the enemy some slight bother in the hope that they would mount an expensive attack against me – after I had left. If Pendayoi should happen to catch some grief as a consequence, thought I, well, so be it.

Our W/T schedule at that time was daily at 10 a.m. One morning I was sitting with Bill Weatherley – my long-suffering sergeant radio operator, who had been dropped into Greece at the same time as me and whose job it was to keep me in contact with SOE HQ in Cairo – listening to him tapping away when, rather to my surprise and alarm, a Fieseler Storch[1]

---

1 Fieseler Storch: designed in 1936, an exceptional short take-off and landing scout plane.

came sneaking over the high hills from the west and proceeded to circle my valley. Bill cut transmissions at once, but I suspected that the damage had been done.

Sure enough the little plane circled and circled, probably taking photographs of our camp and dropping ground, which was quite close by. I resolved to move within twenty-four hours and went immediately into Pendayoi to negotiate the hire of the ten or so extra mules we would require to carry away our considerable supply of stores and explosives. My intention was to take off with Yotis, a few of my bodyguards and old Bloody Maud immediately after tomorrow's transmission. I would set off travelling as rapidly as I could to a site near to my original landing place on Mount Giona. There, I knew, I could find water and fodder. Then I would reconnoitre south-west towards the coast and pick a village, difficult of access but not too indescribably primitive, in which we could pass the winter. There would, of course, have to be suitable terrain for a dropping ground within a reasonable distance. Bill with the W/T set, charging engine and all the rest of the clobber would follow within a day or so.

I was awakened as usual the next morning by my little dog, Angelface. This heralded the arrival of a mug of morning tea and a can of hot shaving water. It was a beautiful, sparkling morning, as I recall.

Acting on a hunch I sent for Nikitas and told him to bring six of his best men on the double. 'Boys,' I said, 'if I know anything about Germans, that Storch will be over again at ten this morning. He came over that ridge at about three hundred feet. If we pull our fingers out and move now we should be able to make it up there in time to surprise the bugger. I'll take the Bren. You blokes take a Breda each. Only one mag each, as if he comes we are sure to get him and if he docsn't wc'll havc humpcd a lot of wcight up that bloody hill for nothing.'

I then told Bill to start sending a bogus transmission from 9.30 onwards until something happened.

We fairly sweated up the slopes and arrived at the col with about twenty minutes to spare. I spaced the men out at approximately hundred-yard intervals and threatened to murder any man who let his gun off before I did.

We saw and heard him coming from about three miles: doodling along as cool as a cucumber and evidently homing in on Bill's carrier wave. He was going to pass me, dammit, about three hundred yards to my right. But that would bring him slap over Nikitas, the brightest of my men and a dab hand with his Breda. When I judged him to be within a couple of hundred feet of Nikitas, I opened up with my tracers. A lively fusillade ensued and the little plane simply plummeted to the valley floor and exploded. Evidently this time he had brought along a small bomb or two.

My men went berserk, and I thought it expedient to ham it up a bit and embraced the ecstatic and rather smelly Nikitas. 'You are a hero . . . a true hero, my friend. This deed will go down in history. *Zito Hellas!*' I yelled.

Enormously pleased with ourselves we swaggered into camp and wallowed in the congratulations showered upon us. Nikitas made the most of his 'finest hour'.

Before I left with Yotis, I urged Bill to lose no time in getting started as the Germans would be certain to react rather swiftly to our latest impertinence. Yotis and I with our small party made it to the pre-agreed rendezvous without incident: a march of about seventeen hours. Two days later: no sign of Bill and the wireless. I began to worry.

Eight hours later he staggered in, distraught and utterly exhausted. Marching by night, Bill and his party had been ambushed by a German patrol whose first volley had killed the mule carrying my W/T set. Three of my bodyguards and two mule drivers were also cut down. Bill took off into the darkness away from the Verey lights – quite rightly – as he had our all-important codebook on his person. The rest of my bodyguards also took off without firing a shot, abandoning all the hired mules together with most of my stores and supplies. The lucky Kraut in command probably got a promotion.

We all had a hard time avoiding active patrols over the next thirty-six hours. I was temporarily out of business, as it took a week to get the bad news to Cairo via another station further north and another three weeks before another W/T set, code-book and batteries, etc., were dropped in.

Poor Bill had visions of disgrace and a court martial: silly bugger. When it was all over, I recommended him for a Military Medal, which he most deservedly received.

I later paid generous compensation in gold to the families of the mule drivers who had been killed and also for the mules which had been killed or captured.

But at the time I made them very depressed when I told the assembled villagers how much I was looking forward to re-establishing my camp in the same spot, come the spring.

For months and months the sound of an aircraft had only meant danger and caused me to seek cover or hurriedly to cease W/T transmissions. The only sight of a friendly plane had been the silhouette of a heavy bomber glimpsed fleetingly at night against the moon as we waited, hearts hammering lest we were ambushed, as it dropped us vital supplies. So imagine the thrill when, one morning in the autumn of 1943, I recognised the long-forgotten roar of many bombers approaching.

Rushing excitedly out of the villa I could count twenty – no, forty – silvery bombers roaring eastwards above me at 20,000 feet. The American air force, now based on the captured Italian airfields at Foggia, was paying the first of many visits to the enemy airfields at Eleusis. The squadrons of B-25s were escorted by long-range P-38 fighters, and it became a common spectacle to watch the vapour trails of the dogfights taking place as the Germans attacked with their squadrons of Messerschmitt 109Fs and Gs.

There began, too, a steady trickle of shot-down American airmen coming through my HQ. I used to keep them for a few days and then, when their numbers warranted it, would organise a party of mules and guides and start them off on their long trek northwards, towards Albania and eventual repatriation to Italy.

As one or two of these lads had received injuries of one kind or another, I organised a group of young ladies in Galaxhidion into a nursing service to care for such cases. I had leased an empty house, scrounged beds and cupboards and, so far as I could from our slender resources, stocked the medicine chest with drugs.

One morning we were sitting idly in the sun when, from the scream of diving aircraft, our attention was drawn to a single P-38 pursued by two German 109s. The poor chap was certainly in trouble. With one engine smoking he was diving almost vertically for the waters of the Gulf, while behind him the killers weaved, firing short bursts of cannon. I had him in my glasses and could see his frantic efforts at evasive action. Poor sod, I thought, you've certainly had it!

As he neared the water he tried unsuccessfully to level out and went in at an angle of about twenty degrees, hitting the water with an almighty splash. His plane flew into pieces and for a short while the fuel burned on the water. His pursuers, satisfied, climbed back up into the fight.

I took a bearing on the smoke and, having nothing in particular to do that morning, thought I might as well run out the five or so miles in my small caique[2] and search for a body or

---

2 Traditional Greek motor-sailer, from 5 to 70 tons weight, used for coastal trading or fishing.

wreckage that might identify the pilot. We used always to radio back to Cairo details of airmen rescued or killed. Cairo would in turn inform the USAAF: a small service, but one which was greatly appreciated.

Within a couple of hours, therefore, we were cruising around in the general vicinity of the crash when my skipper, Thalassinos, having the sharper eyes, pointed to a blob in the water. As we approached we could see this was the body of a man supported by his Mae West.

'He's alive, by God!'

'Balls. He couldn't be.'

'He is, I tell you. There . . . look, he waved.'

'Christ! I believe you're right.'

A few minutes later, with much sweating and effort, we hauled aboard a very large and groggy American. We gaped at one another.

'For Christ's sake,' the American said. 'A Limey!'

'Are you hurt?'

'Yeah . . . Ah guess. Mah laig feels bad.'

'Let's have a look . . . Skipper, beat it for home. We've got a customer for the hospital.'

I stripped him. He had a deep, clean gash in his right calf muscle and bad contusions around his thighs and shoulders where he had burst through his safety harness. But he seemed to have no other damage.

'See if you can pee,' I said, fearing internal injuries. He obliged. Nothing wrong there. 'I simply can't believe it,' I said. 'I saw you go in.'

'Jeez,' he said, 'the last thing Ah remember was ma airspeed showing 380 and the shells of those sons-a-bitches popping all round me.'

Marvelling, we legged it for home and soon had him tucked up in bed, where he slept the clock round. I radioed off his particulars that evening and the following day strolled down from the villa to have a look at him. I had to fight my way through a throng of happy little nurses and there he was, the dog, lying back like a lord. I chased the girls out.

'Well, Chuck, how's it going?'

'Jeez, Major, wadda set-up ya got here. Say, thanks fer pulling me out. Say, kin you get word to ma outfit?'

'All done.'

'Jeez, that's great. Boy, am Ah stiff! Kinda shook up, Ah guess.'

'Chum, you ought to be dead. I've brought you some fags and some Scotch. I've got nothing for you to read at the moment, I'm afraid, but anyway you should be getting all the rest you can. We want to have you on your feet for Christmas.' Christmas was about sixteen weeks away and we had planned to have a large bash as a break in our rather austere routine. I asked the 'nurses' to leave him in peace and to feed him as often as he felt like it.

Chuck made a rapid recovery and was soon getting about with the aid of a crutch. He was also, I noticed, putting on weight and becoming remarkably sleek. In order to facilitate the dressing of his wound and also because we had no room for him in our tiny villa HQ, I had allowed him to live down at the hospital, where his meals were prepared by a devoted little harem.

Three days before Christmas I was surprised to find Chuck at the villa. He had limped the two miles up the hill and was breathless and sweating from the effort.

'Hi, Major.'

'Wotcher, cock . . . This is a very pleasant surprise.'

'Ah bin thinking, Major. I guess Ah reely orta be getting started along back ter mah outfit.'

I cocked an eye at him. 'What's the panic? You don't want to miss the party, do you?'

'No, gee . . . but, well, Ah just guess Ah orta to be getting started. You know how it is.'

'No, I don't know how it is. I'm damned if I want to have to send off a guide and a mule now. My boys are looking forward to their Christmas piss-up, dammit. If you feel strong enough you can start off two days after Christmas. It'll give me time to make arrangements.'

'No . . . Well gee, ya don't understand. Ah jest *gotta* get goin'.'

'Ho-ho-ho,' I thought. 'Come on Chuck,' I said. 'Come clean. I suppose you're trying to tell me that you've caught the clap from dipping your wick?'

'Well, Ah don't know what that is, but that Maria . . . Well, she kinda took a fancy ter ma pecker and Ah guess she kinda gotten herself knocked up.'

'Oh Lord. Are you sure? D'you mean to say she's missed her whatnot?'

Chuck nodded glumly.

'Hell's bells,' I said. 'I'm afraid this might prove a bit awkward.'

It was inconvenient, but I had to agree that the sooner he was on his way, the better. One of my bodyguard volunteered to forego the party and we organised mule, rations, money and letters to show to any Andarte commander he might meet en route. He dossed down with us that night and set off at first light on the morrow.

He hadn't been gone two hours and I was sitting down to my breakfast when Yotis stuck his head around the door.

'You've got visitors, Major.' He had a peculiar expression on his face.

'Who are they and what do they want?'

'I'm afraid you'll have to see them,' Yotis said, trying to control himself.

Puzzled, I went outside. Six pairs of eyes regarded me; three pairs were red and swollen with tears, three pairs blazed with outrage and fury.

'Good morning, Maria.' Ssnnfff.

'Good morning, Helen.' Nnff.

'Good morning, Zoe.' Sob.

'Good morning, gentlemen. What can I do for you?'

'Where's the American?'

'I'm afraid he's gone.'

Babble! The three girls burst into loud sobs, the three papas into invective and threats.

'Gentlemen,' I said. 'Believe me . . . He really has gone. Come inside and we'll talk this matter over.'

'Right. Stop your snivelling, you damn whores, while we talk with Major Geoff.'

So, leaving the woebegone little group of foolish virgins outside, Yotis and I settled down with the fathers to see what could be done in this embarrassing situation.

Bursting and aching with suppressed mirth, we had to endure a two-hour tirade about the infamy of Chuck, the dishonour to their name and, especially, the disastrous fall of the value of their daughters in the marriage market. For my part, I essayed a moving speech about a heroic young airman, lonely and far from home, who had merely responded to their kindness and hospitality. They were not impressed.

'#**&%! . . . the randy goat! We are abused. You must get him back and make him marry Maria.'

'Your Maria is a whore like her mother. He shall marry Zoe.'

'No . . . It must be Helen!'

'Gentlemen, gentlemen,' I begged, fearing bloodshed. 'He can't marry all of them, can he? We must accept an unfortunate situation and make the best of it.'

Eventually, I gave each father twenty-five gold sovereigns in compensation and to assuage their damaged pride.

After they had gone, I was struck with a sudden thought. 'Where did Chuck say he was from, Yotis? Do you remember?'

'Texas, I think. Why?'

I sighed, thinking of a dirty joke I had once heard about the size and quality of Texan beef. 'That's something you wouldn't understand, old fellow.'

Just before I finally left Greece I stood proxy at the baptism of three little Chucks. It cost quite a lot as I felt obliged to pay for all the wine. But, for the memory of such a man, it was worth it!

For eight months of the year the climate in Greece is magnificent. Glorious springs, sweltering summers and long cool autumns. The winter, when it arrives, does so with a bang. Savage storms are frequent, the cold becomes intense and the snow line descends to about 3000 feet.

All this presents a grave problem to the resistance fighter. The conditions are so severe that he is forced down by the cold from the comparative safety of his summer encampments in the mountains and must find shelter for those four months in villages if he is to survive.

Obviously he must pick a village which is not too accessible, or the risk of a surprise attack by the enemy would be too great. There are also pressing problems of supply: food for himself and his men; fodder for the mules; gasoline for his charging engine for the wireless; communications, water and fuel for heating. There are many factors which limit his choice.

The majority of mountain villages in Greece are, at the best of times, just a collection of vermin-infested hovels, and after two or more years of war and privations the conditions of poverty and squalor in the vast majority of them were really horrible.[3] I had settled myself in a small villa and an aban-

---

3 By the time of the eventual German withdrawal from Greece, in October 1944, the Greeks were literally starving, their economy destroyed by two and a half years of occupation, food requisitions and resistance. It is reckoned that, had it not been for the Allies pouring emergency supplies into the country in the autumn and

doned monastery above Galaxhidion. It was a rather charming, decaying little place looking across the bay towards Itea and with a fine view of Mount Parnassus.

From a security point of view it was certainly not ideal, but there were various escape tracks leading westwards along the coast and there was also a safe anchorage for my caique, which I kept ready at a moment's notice.

We lived undisturbed by the enemy and in relative comfort until February 1944. My gang of ruffians had grown to quite a size. There were couriers [*used for running messages to other Andarte groups*], my bodyguards, W/T operators, interpreters, men to care for the mules, shot-down airmen and a sprinkling of Poles, Russians and other odds and sods, mostly deserters from German labour battalions. Among these last was a strapping young Sudeten Czech named Franz.[4]

Some months previously, needing enemy unit identifications, I had shot up a truck on the Amfissa road and had put him in the bag. He was, after all, not a German and seemed rather a good fellow. So, rather than turn him over to the Andartes to have his throat cut, I had kept him with me on parole – a sworn promise – not to escape. He was a powerful fellow and very useful about the place, and after a while he took an oath of allegiance to the Allied cause. We came to trust and like him and relaxed our watch.

One foul night of bitter cold and blizzard he slipped away. He was not missed until morning. I was dismayed and shocked and reproached the soft streak in my nature that had led me

---

winter of 1944, there would have been mass famine. At the time of writing this I have just read about a Greek count who is saying that the 2010 Greek financial crisis – and German bail-out – is directly attributable to what happened to Greece seventy years ago. Old memories and enmities die hard . . .

4   The Sudetenland was that part of western Czechoslovakia which bordered Germany. Its population was mainly German. It had been annexed by Hitler in 1938, with the connivance of the Western Powers, anxious to appease Hitler's territorial demands. That would have made Franz a natural enemy of the Germans, theoretically at least.

to spare his life in the first place. Now both my own life and the lives of my men were in the gravest danger. At the very least I might lose my W/T set and all the stores, weapons and materials that men had risked their lives to drop to us by parachute over the months.

We set frantically to work. The explosives, the weapons and the ammo were rushed off about a mile away into some little-known caves down by the sea. The W/T set, two batteries and the charging engine were hidden in another cave and the foodstuffs, fodder and clothing were loaded aboard the caique. I laid numerous booby traps and anti-personnel devices on the tracks leading up to the villa, and by nightfall everything I could think of for our security was done. We were stripped down to our personal weapons and bedding. Each man had two tins of bully and half a loaf of bread in his pack, and I had the four mules saddled and standing by to leave at a moment's notice with the cooking pots and bedding.

I set listening watches as night fell, but as the night wore on I became more and more uneasy, sensing we were in acute danger. Finally, at about 4 a.m., I got up and went outside. It was black as hell and all I could hear was the wind blowing keenly. I made my way 100 yards down the hill towards Galaxhidion and sat down out of the wind to watch and listen. I must have sat there for two hours and could faintly see the dawn beginning to light the peaks of Mount Parnassus, 6000 feet above me, when I thought I heard the noise of trucks faintly on the wind. I shut my eyes and strained with my hands cupping my ears.

There! By God I was right. I searched with my night glasses in the general direction of where I knew the road led into the town from Amfissa. Minutes passed and then I caught a tiny flash such as might be made by a shielded torch. It was enough.

I dashed back up the hill and roused the boys. Within

minutes they had tumbled out and were lashing the bedding rolls and pots and pans on to the mules. By now, through my glasses, I could just make out the dark shapes of numerous vehicles halted together on the outskirts of the town. A few minutes more and our mules, led by a mutinous Bloody Maud, were trotting off westwards to safety. Within minutes too, 80 mm mortar shells were dropping all around us as the Germans, realising that they had failed to take us by surprise, began attacking us at long range.

At this point I was not too worried as I did not think it likely that they could have mounted more than a company for the attack at such short notice. I was soon to learn my mistake!

With two of my bodyguards, Nikitas and Christo, I remained behind. From a rocky hillock about 600 yards away, and from where we had an excellent view of both the villa and the rolling countryside behind us to the north, we sat down to observe.

We watched them advancing in open order – well spaced out in case they were attacked – up to the villa.[5] I observed with delight as one of them got blown up by a booby trap. After a while I saw them dynamite both villa and monastery.

And that, with any luck, should be that, I thought; perhaps they'll pack up now and go home.

But this was not to be and I was rather put out to observe them re-forming their line and beginning to make their way towards where we were hiding. Time to leave. I sat up and looked around to see if the mules were still in sight.

Christ! About a mile away, well spread out and coming

5 Well-trained soldiers will always move well spaced out unless there is some pressing reason why they should be bunched together. That way, when they come under fire they are more difficult to hit. A burst of machine-gun fire will take down one man, not five. The individual rifleman will have to adjust his position to shoot at the next man, which takes time, not slightly shift his aim to get off the next shot. The same goes for tanks and armoured cars: they should always be well spaced out, for the same reason.

towards us from the north, was another line of beaters. That's what comes from underestimating one's enemy.

The caique was away down the coast, its diesel engine thumping flat out. I reckoned the mules should get away OK, but it looked as though we three were trapped. We would have to play hide-and-seek with these sods, lie doggo while they beat over us and then leg it back north-east away from the others and not in the direction we would be expected to run. I thought of an olive grove about three miles away.

On the principle that a hiding place that took my eye would also attract that of an intelligent enemy and should therefore be avoided, I signed to the other two to follow. We scuttled off, using dead ground until we hit about an acre of marshy ground in a shallow depression on a small plateau.

This was it. 'Dig! Dig for your lives!'

With our knives we raised up slabs of peat and matted grass right in the middle of the swamp. Beneath, we exposed icy water about a foot deep. I made the other two lie flat and covered them as best I could.

I then sneaked on hands and knees for a quick peek. There they were, the buggers, advancing straight towards us, well spread out and still about 500 yards away. I scuttled back to my own water hole and warned the others to expect a longish wait. On no account must they stir until I gave the word.

Christ, the cold! I could feel the icy water seeping into my clothes and boots, and something was exploring my left ear.

There we lay for what seemed like hours. What the hell was going on? Why didn't they come?

Then we heard it – thud-thud-thud, silence. Thud-thud, closer now. Thud-thud-squelch, very close now. A curse from a soldier who got water in his boots. Would he continue across or go around? Squelch, squelch, thud-thud, a bit further off now. A shout from someone to keep in line, and then silence.

After another age I squinted cautiously out of my right eye and took stock. Telling the others to stay put I crawled a few yards, peered over the rise and saw, thank God, large Krauts stumping off away from us, towards the sea.

Time to be off, I decided, in case they decided to beat back again. I roused the others and we ran off, stumbling, soaked to the skin and almost paralysed with the cold from a biting wind. It was still only about 8 a.m., and if we didn't find shelter where we could dry out we could be in serious trouble before the day was out. On we ran, gasping and cursing and almost crying with the agony of the cold. Suddenly I had doubts about that olive grove. It was just the kind of covert to attract a fugitive and therefore just the place to lay an ambush.

I called a halt and gasped out my fears to Nikitas. He agreed and suggested that, instead, we make for some small caves he knew which lay about three miles further on. They were right down by the sea and across the main road leading north out of Galaxhidion.

We pressed on, using every bit of cover we could, and were quite soon faced with the crossing of the road. Here we paused. There was a good fifty yards of open ground on either side of the road without a vestige of cover, but on the far side there were gorse bushes which looked quite attractive. One at a time, then.

Christo went first and bolted like a rabbit into cover.

I told Nikitas that when he got across he was to make his way up to a small knoll which should give him a better view of the road. He was to signal me from there if it was all clear for me to cross.

He shambled off and just made it before a half-track came rattling around the bend, followed by two trucks full of soldiers. I lay for a while and then, getting a discreet wave from Nikitas, jumped up and made for the road at top speed.

But at this moment Nikitas popped up from his cover and made frantic gesticulations. Oh shit, I thought, he was waving me back, not forward. I flew, touching the ground about twice in fifty yards, plunged head-first into a culvert that just happened to run under the road right in front of me and lay there gasping.

A minute later and there was another rattle-rattle, clank-clank as another half-track passed over me. I squirmed through the culvert and peered out for another signal, got it and scampered as fast as I could to land in a heap beside my two companions. I could see they were trying their damnedest not to laugh. They controlled themselves while I wheezed and puffed and cursed them both in round Anglo-Saxon terms, but the memory of my inspired sprint was eventually too much and they started to roll around helplessly.

We had been just in time. As we watched, a further three truckloads of soldiers halted along the road in front of us. They piled out and started to beat away from us towards the olive grove.

It seemed to me that we were better off where we lay rather than crouching in some damn cave. At least here we could see the enemy in case we had to run for it again. We were sheltered from the wind, and the sun was beginning to shine a little and dry us out. We sat and watched. We stripped down and cleaned our submachine-guns, and each ate a tin of bully.

The long day wore on. I wondered how the others had fared. Occasionally we heard shots and shouts in the distance, but no one disturbed us. As our spirits rose I began to think about getting our own back for an uncomfortable and harrowing day.

It occurred to me that if we made our way about another three miles up the road we would come to a defile where the road began a long series of 'S' bends and climbing hairpins, leading back eventually to the main Amfissa–Lidhorikion road. This was the way the Germans had come and this was their only way back home. At the end of a long day I would expect them to be tired and relaxed, and certainly not expecting any retaliation from the quarry they had chased and failed to take. Why not, then, shoot up the last vehicle in the convoy and then leg it off into the night?

The more we thought about it the more the idea appealed. And so, keeping to the seaward side of the road in case of trouble, we made our way rather stiffly to the spot I had in mind.

Here the road took a sharp left-hand bend around a spur cut into the side of the hill. There was a nice valley running westwards in the direction we would want to run and there was a long view down the road, which should enable us to spot the last vehicle. There was cover in the form of a rockfall which had dumped two large boulders in the ditch. By and large, it was perfect.

We sat and waited. It began to get dark and I started to worry that the Germans might have decided to stay overnight and, perhaps, burn down the town at their leisure on the morrow: just the sort of act of spite they were capable of.

Then at last there were headlights. The first to pass was a staff car, probably with the column commander hurrying off home. It was a pity to let *him* go, but we dared not risk it. We crouched behind the boulders. Two half-tracks passed and a truck. Then there was quite a big gap. Two more half-tracks and then three trucks close together. Still no good. Don't tell me that's the lot? No. This looks like our boy right at the end: a Volkswagen.

'Ready? Half a mag only, right!'

We jumped up and let fly at point-blank range. The little car gave a violent swerve and crashed into the ditch a few yards ahead. We ran up. Driver dead and an officer dying in the rear seat and . . . what's this? Can it be? There was another man next to the driver who seemed familiar. Nikitas dragged him around to the front of the car where the single surviving head-light was casting a glow.

It is! It's good old Franz with blood all over his nice new uniform from a wound in his shoulder.

We goggled at him. Franz goggled back. Then his mouth worked and he began to yammer at us in deadly fear.

Nikitas recovered first. He quite slowly and without a word took out his knife, leaned down and cut his throat from ear to ear.

14

How a man desires to kill

To experience utter enchantment you should be up on the south-west slopes of Mount Parnassus in the late springtime. A thousand feet or more below will lie the little towns of Delphi[1] and Khrysso, ablaze with cherry and plum blossom, and you will look across the Gulf of Corinth to a breathtaking panorama of snowy peaks in the Peloponnesus. The sun will warm your face and you will fill your lungs with great draughts of the purest and most sparkling air imaginable. Frequently, among the pine forests, you will come upon hidden meadows lush with grass and a million wild flowers. Encamped by a limpid spring you will certainly meet a shepherd or two happily engaged in making cheese from goat's or sheep's milk . . . and yoghurt: thick creamy stuff in wooden pails so different from the anaemic rubbish sold nowadays in little plastic cups. Baby lambs and goats, guarded by savage hairy dogs, frisk and gambol and shepherd youths still play the mournful, simple melodies on their pan pipes. And so it was when the world began.

This is how the arrival of spring felt to me. We lost no time in moving out of the vermin-infested hovels in which we had been forced to spend the rest of that winter and head back up into the mountains.

We encamped in a well-concealed spot in lean-to shelters

1 The site of the Oracle of Delphi and today – as for many thousands of years – a popular tourist destination.

made from pine branches. Our dropping ground was less than a mile away. For the time being there wasn't very much to do as I had not yet received my full requirements of explosives and other stores that were essential to my future plans. And so I was content to take it a bit easy and watch my mules grow sleek and fat.

Sometimes, at the close of a particularly halcyon day, glass of wine in hand and the aromatic scent of woodsmoke in my nostrils, listening to the cheerful exchange of insults being bandied around the company, I would be hit by the unreality of it all.

How could man desire to kill anything and so defile such perfection? I would carry the mood sometimes for a day or more and would then be brought back to ugly reality by the sight of a German troop convoy or, more usually, by the sound of their bloody planes, fitted with W/T intercept, circling my mountain and trying to pinpoint my station. Hatred would well up into my heart: hatred for a race which had welcomed as its leader a madman bent on world domination.

I acquired another godchild; I seem to collect them.

I was walking northwards one day across the mountain, heading towards a certain village. There I wished to meet a fellow who supplied me with reasonably accurate information about enemy dispositions along the railway line, my next intended target. On the way I chanced upon a middle-aged peasant seated upon a rock beside a tiny patch of land he was cultivating.

Naturally I responded to his greeting, offered him tobacco and sat down beside him – keeping carefully to windward – to hear the latest news and gossip. I was about to wend my way when I was startled by a strangled sort of squawk coming from the bushes behind me. As I looked over my shoulder I heard another louder gasp and could see what looked like a bundle of rags heaving around. Wide-eyed I looked at my companion. He kept his eyes straight ahead quite impassively. Then . . . 'What is it, woman?'

There was a longish silence, then, 'A son.'

A look of quiet satisfaction came over his craggy face. He got to his feet with great deliberation, took his battered old pipe from his mouth and said: 'Well done, woman. We will do no more work today. Wrap him up carefully and follow us down to the village. Major Geoff will take a glass of wine with me.'

Well, of course, half the damn village took wine with Major Geoff – gallons and gallons of it, in fact – and I daresay there is still in Ano Agoriani a strapping young man who wonders from time to time how the hell he came to be christened Geoff.

By the late spring of 1944 the war was starting to go well for the Allies. The Germans were on the defensive, fighting hard and losing rearguard actions both in Russia and in Italy. They could also shortly expect a full-scale invasion across the English Channel. It was obvious, therefore, that they would soon be obliged to withdraw their forces from such outlying theatres of war as Greece and the Aegean or run the risk of having them cut off by a Russian thrust through Romania and Hungary. The Germans were already in considerable difficulties with their lines of communication to Greece, as these ran through Yugoslavia where Marshall Tito controlled the activities of large numbers of highly active partisan forces.

Our task in Greece was clear. We would have to establish dumps of explosives in suitable places along the main German escape routes leading northwards from Athens and the south of Greece so that, when the time came, we would be able to inflict as much damage and delay on them as possible.

Owing to the mountainous and impoverished nature of our

part of the country, the roads north were very few. A glance at the map will show how easy, on the whole, was our task as saboteurs.

In the two provinces of Parnassus and Dorice that I commanded, the ground was particularly well suited to partisan operations. The few roads ran in and around the mountain massifs where, by then, I was not only well established but had numerous excellent aircraft dropping grounds. My good friend and neighbour to the east of me, Brian Dillon, was not so fortunate – if you remember, it was Brian who had got me involved in that SAS beat-up on Benghazi in Mary's House, back in Cairo what now seemed a lifetime ago. Brian had stayed on in the SAS until he too joined SOE and was assigned to Greece. In his area of operations, which went all the way to the eastern seaboard of Greece, there was only one large mountain, Helicon, where he lived. To his north stretched a wide cultivated plain. It was garrisoned at strategic points and well protected by motorised and mounted patrols of Germans and Italians. Every time he moved off Mount Helicon he was at risk, whereas I could move around my mountainous domain with relative peace of mind. The moment the Germans headed into our mountains we usually had enough warning to make ourselves scarce. (Thank the Lord that the Germans had not invented helicopters, as they were to change the dynamics of guerrilla warfare entirely.)

The northern boundary of Brian's area was the Gulf of Chaleris, which is on the east coast of this part of Greece. Skirting its eastern seaboard for much of the way was a road that ran through a low range of hills. As this road was a secondary one and was dangerous to approach, it had not hitherto received his attention. Now, establishing explosives dumps in these hills became his priority.

From time to time Brian and I used to exchange visits. We usually made the trip to each other's camps by boat along the

Gulf of Corinth. It was my misfortune to be staying with him, enjoying the salubrious air of his mountain retreat, when he decided to make his first trip across the plain to the east with a load of explosives and mines.

Would I care to come along and lend a hand? Thanks for nothing, old chum, thought I. Not only did the whole affair smell a bit dicey but I was supposed to be having a little holiday.

But, two days later, having collected half a ton or so of assorted explosives and material, including petrol for the return trip and an assortment of identity cards and travel permits, all forged and stamped with an impressive variety of swastikas, we donned our civilian clothes. We headed down to a little village. There the mountain road began which led down to the plains, and there Brian kept stabled his pride and joy.

This horrible object was an ex-British army 15 cwt lorry with a tattered canvas cover. It had been abandoned during our retreat of spring 1941, and since then it had been used for black-market purposes until Brian had hired it from its new owner. This machine was splay-footed and with a cracked chassis, sans brakes or lights. It would run miraculously on petrol, kerosene, mazout or even ouzo, depending upon the size of hairpin which Janni, its driver, stuffed into its main fuel jet. Sometimes it ran like a bird for miles. Other times it developed airlocks and bellyaches, which took it farting and banging along in a series of convulsive leaps until the engine gave up and died.

When this happened there was nothing for it but to strip down the carburettor, blow through the fuel system and try again with another size of hairpin. Janni had an inspired genius for dealing with the swine. He really loved it like a brother. I believe he would happily have set off for Salonika, some two hundred miles away, perfectly confident of arriving there. He was also well known to all the enemy checkpoints. The guards would look forward to his passing because he was a fruitful source of wine and tobacco as well as being a cheerful and amusing rogue.

So here I was, dressed in my usual disguise of a black-market spiv: hair long and slicked straight back with a smelly pomade, pointed patent leather town shoes, bright blue trousers with a jazzy stripe and lovely wide bottoms; a white artificial silk shirt fastened at the neck with a brass stud, no tie and my jacket carried slung over the shoulder by my little finger. A cardboard suitcase filled with currency, cigarettes, combs, hair oil and German razors carried my stock-in-trade.

Brian fancied himself as a Greek Orthodox priest, and very splendid he did look too in his greasy black cassock and chimney-pot hat. His filthy fingernails, his beard and his moustache were in character. Only under his hat, where a genuine priest would never have allowed his hair to have been cut, did his disguise fall down.

Into the back of the truck went the explosives. Piled on top were bundles of spring greens and potatoes, two crates of squawking chickens, two small casks of wine, three billy goats and the Reverend Brian Dillon. I had exercised my prerogative as a guest and was travelling up front with Janni. I had with me a few bottles of Mavro Daphne, a strong sweet red dessert wine much liked by the Germans, and several cartons of cigarettes; as an afterthought, I had bought from a villager a basket containing a few salted and dried fish. These I reckoned would do nicely to augment our evening meal at the end of our trip.

Off we clattered just before ten o'clock. It was a fine morning that promised to develop into a scorcher once we were down on the plain. It being all downhill we made good progress until about ten miles on, when Janni warned me that we were approaching the first control point. I shouted back to warn Brian to cease the steady flow of abuse which he had been directing at me, Janni and the truck as into his lap the rough road alternately bounced a goat or a crate of chickens.

We drew up at the first of several checkpoints through which we would have to pass during the next sixty-odd miles. I sat tight. While my Greek was by now fluent enough, perhaps, to fool a German corporal, it would not have deceived a Greek policeman for an instant.

Janni piled out and was greeted cordially. He dispensed cigarettes all round and disappeared into the guardhouse. He had to make out a route report, which would have to be stamped at various control points along our way. The reason for our trip was ostensibly to attend the nuptials of a relation of Janni's, at which the Reverend B. Dillon was going to officiate. I was a cousin of the groom.

Everything went off smoothly and, armed with our route permit, duly stamped, we started on our way. Then Brian had his first bad moment. As we drove off one of the guards swung up his rifle and aimed it at the middle of his stomach.

Poor Brian gave a convulsive start, whereupon the guard, having had his little joke, gave a great guffaw, slapped his thigh and waved us on. For the next few miles Brian maintained a dignified silence while Janni and I giggled weakly in front.

'All right, you bastard,' he shouted finally. 'You come and sit back here with the fucking goats and let the next bloody Kraut point his gun at your guts.'

So we changed places for a spell. I settled in among the livestock and, it by now being extremely hot under the canvas, I dozed off.

I must have slept peacefully through the next two checkpoints and awoke when the truck juddered to a halt again.

'What's up?'

'We need to pee,' said Brian and, realising that I did as well, I pushed a goat off my chest and climbed out.

We had arrived at the beginning of the Copaiis marsh. This was a large, completely flat area of fenland which had been drained and recovered for agriculture. From here on the road ran dead straight across the marsh for about fifteen miles, along a raised embankment with barely room for two cars to pass. Fields and pastures stretched away for miles on either side.

The sun blazed down out of a cloudless sky, and the poor chickens and goats lay panting with their mouths open. After we had stretched our legs and filled our tank with some of the spare petrol, I once more climbed up in front and we set off again.

For about five miles the empty road unrolled in front of us. Then I saw what appeared to be a truck in the distance. As we drew closer I saw to my alarm that we had met a German convoy of about twenty trucks. They were well spaced out and drawn up on the right side of the road, facing the direction from which we had come. Evidently they had halted for a midday break.

The first vehicle was a Volkswagen. An officer leaned nonchalantly against the bonnet, fanning himself with his cap. As we drove very gingerly past I gave him a courteous and friendly salute with my left hand, which was ignored.

It must have been our having to drive so slowly, or something. But, when we had passed all but six of the trucks and I was beginning to breathe again, our truck began to splutter. Janni swore fervently at all his saints and did frantic things with the choke, but to no avail. We came to an explosive halt.

I could tell that Janni was about to spring into frantic action with his adjustable spanner, so I quickly put my hand on his arm and muttered out of the corner of my mouth for him to take it slowly. He got control of himself and slowly climbed down, cursing loudly. He made a pantomime of kicking the radiator and opened the hood. He pulled out of his trouser pocket the adjustable spanner and, with a sigh, began the process of clearing the airlock. I climbed out and had a good scratch.

The trucks were carrying a company of soldiers. They appeared to have finished their meal and were smoking and lying around in whatever shade they could find, waiting for the signal to move on.

As Janni sweated away inside the engine a few of the more curious or energetic soldiers inevitably began to gather around, as soldiers will, to scrounge and take the mickey out of us. They were highly amused at the sight of the Rev. B. Dillon sitting in the back. One wag leaned inside and tweaked his beard, remarking that the reverend brother's goats had better ones. At any other time I too might have thought this funny. The trouble was that I could swear that I could smell the unmistakable odour of gelignite beginning to assert itself over the stench of goats.

The atmosphere remained chummy until a horrible little Feldwebel[2] shouldered his way through the crush and demanded in an aggressive tone to see our papers. These I got from Janni and offered them to him with a carton of cigarettes. This was the accepted manner of doing such things.

'*Nichtraucher* – don't smoke,' he snapped. 'What have you got in the truck?'

'As you see, Sir,' I said, 'just some vegetables and things for the wedding.'

'How do you come to speak German?'

---

2   A rank above sergeant and thus the most junior type of warrant officer. Geoff's Feldwebel doubtless had designs on promotion.

'I was educated at Robert College in Athens, Sir.'

'All Greeks are thieves and liars. Unload the truck! You hear me? Tell that filthy priest to get out and clear everything out of the back.'

'But, Sir,' I quavered, 'please be reasonable. It's so hot and we must be in time for the wedding – perhaps I could offer you a few bottles of Mavro Daphne?'

'I don't drink, you lying swine. Now jump to it!'

My mind was beginning to go numb. I could see Brian's anguished eye though a slit in the canvas. We were unarmed and there was certainly no cover if we tried to make a run for it. I walked slowly around to the back of the truck, playing for time. Surely the damned officer in charge of the convoy would give the signal to start soon. I motioned to Brian, who climbed down, and as slowly as we dared we began to pull out the crate of chickens. A goat came next, then another and then the wine.

'Look, Sir,' I said. 'You can see for yourself there is nothing there except the vegetables and that goat.'

He glared at me, furious now. He was about to order his own men to unload the truck when, at that blessed moment, a whistle sounded from up the column. The commanding officer got back in his car. He waved his arm and started to drive off.

I ran back to the front of the truck and grabbed the basket of fish.

'Here, Sir,' I gabbled. 'Take these nice fish and thank you very much. Yes, thank you very much. The officer's gone. Goodbye!'

He hesitated a moment. Then he took the basket and barked an order to his men. They all got back into their trucks and drove off, leaving us alone.

Brian threw his hat into the back of the truck and mopped his brow. 'I think we need a drink,' he said weakly.

Ten minutes later our truck was running again and Brian reached to put his hat on. A cascade of pellets fell about his ears. That goat seemed to have said it all!

Brian was sitting with me on the veranda of my villa above Galaxhidion enjoying a little pre-lunch ouzo. After our recent trip across the plains with the explosives, life had become rather hectic for him on Mount Helicon.

Exasperated by his impudent mule-stealing raids down on the plains, the Germans had mounted a full-scale sweep of the area in an attempt to clear it of Brian and some ELAS Andartes who were also in the neighbourhood. By a miracle they had failed to find his HQ, but all the same he had been on the run for several days and had generally had an anxious time of it.

Now that all was quiet – for a short time at least – and the Germans had retired, Brian, as was his wont, had come to spend a few days relaxing with me: such interludes in the otherwise grim and relentless business of guerrilla warfare were to be cherished.

The ouzo was disappearing fast and we were gossiping contentedly about this and that and laughing about our recent fright in the truck when I noticed a large motor barge making her way up the Gulf from the direction of Corinth to the east. Rather to our surprise she altered course and made for Galaxhidion. She was flying a German ensign and we wondered what could have brought her our way and what she might be carrying.

I knew that Yotis was down in the town and would be up with news in due course, so we drank up and went in to lunch.

Hardly had we finished when Yotis arrived at the double.

'You've seen the boat, Major?' he panted.

'Yes, we were wondering about her, Yotis,' I replied.

'She is German,' he informed me. 'There are about twenty of those bloody collaborating Greek policeman on board.

They're going to Corfu. Apparently they've called in here for fresh water.'

'How big would you say she was, Yotis, and how long are they staying?'

'I heard she was about a hundred tons . . . would that be right? I don't know how long she'll stay, but certainly overnight. I thought about going down again this evening and picking up some gossip from Athens.'

'Good idea, Yotis,' I said carelessly.

Brian let out a comfortable belch. 'If you were half a man,' he said to me, 'you'd go down there and sink the bloody thing. You never do anything these days but sit up here on your fat arse and booze. Why, it must be months since you struck a blow against the Fatherland.'

'Well I'm damned,' I said. 'Look who's talking. I thought that you spent all last week running around your mountain pissing with fright in case you met a Kraut.'

'Bollocks!' he said easily. 'It wasn't that way at all. I was merely executing certain tactical exercises. Rather brilliantly, I might add.'

'Not quite what I heard,' I said. 'However, as you insist, it just so happens that I've got a couple of limpet mines and, as you're so bloody energetic, you can come along and give me a hand. We'll sink her together.'

'No, no, my dear fellow,' he protested. 'I wouldn't dream of stealing your thunder. I . . .'

'Yotis,' I said firmly, 'Major Dillon would like to see our limpets.'

When Yotis had dug them out from our store of explosives, Brian examined them with distaste.

'Christ!' he complained. 'These must be out of the ark. What about harnesses?'

'Any harnesses, Yotis?' I asked.

'What are harnesses, Major?'

'They're a kind of webbing arrangement with a metal chest plate so the magnets on the limpets will stick to them while you're swimming,' I explained. Yotis went to look but came back to report, 'No harnesses.'

'There you are,' said Brian. 'Typical of bloody Cairo. How the hell are you expected to swim with one of these things in your hand?'

'Teach you to keep your trap shut in future,' I said smugly. 'Think tactically, dear boy, then you won't talk yourself into these situations.'

Perhaps I should explain. A limpet mine is a device for blowing a hole in the side of a ship. It comprises a 2 lb charge of gelignite in a metal container, around the base of which is a row of magnets. You place the mine against the hull of a ship. It is then held in place by the magnets until such time as it is exploded by means of a delay-action fuse, which is inserted into the body of the container.

As evening drew on Brian and I strolled down to Galaxhidion to look the ship over. She was certainly quite large, about 120 foot long and with a twenty-foot beam. The engine, wheelhouse and passenger accommodation were aft, the crew's quarters up forward. She carried W/T and two 20 mm guns. She was deeply laden with something the Germans thought worth transporting, and obviously worth sinking. So far as we could tell the entire ship's company was drinking on shore.

I was thinking that, if we left it late enough, say 4 a.m., it should be no problem to slip into the water by the jetty and place our mines. I reckoned that a six-hour fuse should give her time to get well clear of Galaxhidion before blowing up. To have her sink in the harbour would be acutely embarrassing and would certainly invite severe reprisals on the town – exactly what Cairo was telling us we were meant to be avoiding at this particular phase of the war.

We strolled casually past her up and down the quay several times. We entered a wine shop where I had noticed several German soldiers drinking by themselves. So long as there were none of those Greek policemen with them, I thought I could risk a little chat. So, calling for wine, we went up to where they were sitting.

'Good evening, gentlemen,' I said politely. 'My friend and I ask the privilege of joining you and inviting you to drink with us.'

They seemed rather surprised – probably because my _Hoch Deutsch_[3] accent was unusual in a Greek spiv. Nevertheless, they made room for us quite civilly and we were soon drinking and chatting away about the war. I didn't expect to learn very much from them, nor did I, other than that they did not intend to lie alongside the quay all night. They told us that at 11 p.m. they were going move to the outer harbour and sail on their way at dawn.

This was rather a blow as it meant that we had a swim ahead of us. However, we stayed on, pouring drink into them and each other until just before eleven, and then hiccupped our way back up to the villa to collect the limpets and prepare the fuses.

As we were both half cut we decided to make a night of it. There is nothing worse than having to get up and do something with a woozy head after two or three hours' sleep. We sat and drank steadily until about 3 a.m. We then weaved our way down the hill and through the silent, sleeping little town until we arrived at the end of the breakwater.

In the moonlight I could see the German barge lying peacefully at anchor about 300 yards offshore. Between them and us, in fact, we could count four Greek barges: useful cover.

---

3   The German equivalent of 'Oxford English': in other words as spoken by the governing classes and without any regional dialect. It also happens to be the type of German taught in school in England. Just as, doubtless, English is not taught in Germany with a Geordie, West Country or Cockney accent.

We stripped off and, carrying our limpets, entered the water. It felt glorious. The water was warm and I floated contentedly on my back for a little while with the limpet resting on my tummy.

'Come on,' I said, 'before I drop off to sleep.'

'Hang on,' said Brian. 'I can't swim and pee at the same time.'

I laughed back at him. 'I'll go on ahead,' I said. 'I'll put my one on the far side. You stick yours on this side. Meet you back here and, for Christ's sake, don't splash.'

I paddled off. It was very awkward trying to swim with a heavy piece of metal in one hand and the barge seemed a hell of a long way. Before long I was puffing a bit and starting to sober up.

As I approached the barge I turned over and swam on my back as I found I made less disturbance in the water this way. At about 100 yards I trod water and took stock. There was someone leaning over the rail facing me and smoking. I could see the glow as he drew on his cigarette.

Cursing him under my breath I detoured further out. This way I reckoned I ought to be able to approach the bow from head on, and from there he would be less likely to notice me. Very gently now I floated in, hardly making a ripple, and in a few minutes was supporting myself with the anchor chain. A few feet above my head was an open porthole, through which I could hear the loud snoring of the crew.

I unscrewed the time-pencil from the mine, squeezed it firmly to break the vial of acid and replaced it. I moved quietly down the side of the barge to about midships and, taking a deep breath, dived. As I expected I found a bilge keel about eight feet down and, holding on to this, placed the limpet firmly against the hull. As I removed my hand it dropped straight off . . .!

I made a grab for it, but missed and saw it sink down into the depths.

I ran out of breath and surfaced noisily. What the hell?

Thoroughly disgusted I swam back to shore and waited for Brian. I could not understand what had gone wrong. The magnets had clamped on to everything in sight when we had had an ouzo-fuelled trial run back up at the villa.

I sat in the shallow water and shivered. The dawn was not far off and there was a chilly breeze springing up.

After a short while I heard puffing and a splashing sound approaching out of the darkness. 'How did you get on?' I asked as Brian swam up.

'Wou-would you believe it? The fu-fucking thing dropped off!' he said furiously, teeth chattering.

'So did mine.'

'Bloody hell! Well, come on, let's get dressed. I'm freezing. Sod and damnation take it.'

We dressed and disconsolately toiled back up to the villa. As we arrived, we heard a faint, derisory 'toot' from the barge and, turning to watch, saw her up anchor and chug away.

'Garn, yer bugger!' said Brian. 'I hope you hit a mine.'

We collected a few dead and stunned fish when the limpets went off in the harbour with a 'whoompf' just before noon. But it wasn't until about ten days later, when a similar barge visited Galaxhidion, that I discovered that the damned things were constructed of non-magnetic ferro-concrete.

Oh . . . to answer the question I am occasionally asked: do I hate Germans? Yes and no. No and yes. For me, fear engenders hate. For my German front-line enemies I always had nothing but respect and admiration. Their occupation troops, mostly second-line, their SS and Gestapo, I held in contempt and fear, and I hated their bloody guts.

15

A man betrays his friend

For some time I had had at the back of my mind the idea of using my caique to open up an escape route from Greece to Bari in south-east Italy.

She was a seaworthy and reliable craft, this caique, about thirty-five feet long with good sails and a remarkable old single-cylindered engine. Her absolute maximum speed appeared to be 5.6 knots. This made her a little faster than all the other vessels of a similar type to be found in these waters.

Someone in Cairo had conceived the idea of repatriating to Russia the many Russian ex-PoWs in Greece. These men, having been captured by the Germans during their advances in 1941, had been offered the alternatives of a bullet in the head or service with the Todt[1] organisation as 'Pioneers' in the German army. Having made the latter choice they had taken their first opportunity to desert to the mountains.

I had collected and still had with me two officers and seventeen other ranks. Pleasant fellows though these Russians were, their sustenance was proving a considerable drain on my limited resources. I resolved to put them in the charge of one of my own officers and pack them off to Italy as the first stage in their journey back to Russia. After I had mooted the suggestion to Cairo, several weeks went by while clearance

---

1 The Todt Organisation: named after its founder, Fritz Todt. By 1942 the organisation had been incorporated into the Ministry of Armaments and War Production and used prisoners of war, civilians and concentration camp inmates as slave labour on military engineering projects.

was obtained from our naval people. We spent the time making preparations for the voyage, studying charts and amassing information about those enemy defences and coastal batteries protecting the west coast of Greece which they would have to avoid.

I had been frequently irritated by the sight of large, 120-ton caiques sailing past, flying the German ensign. These vessels had been commandeered and pressed into service to supply the small garrisons on outlying islands. Apart from their crew of Greek collaborators they usually carried half a dozen Germans as guards. It occurred to me that while we were killing time waiting for the 'OK' on the Bari trip, it would be amusing to take a prize on the high seas.

We drew lots for the six lucky ones who were going to come with me. Having armed them with two Bren light machine-guns, Sten guns and long knives – in lieu of cutlasses – we stood awaiting a suitable prey. I let several small caiques pass as unworthy of our attention. Then, one afternoon a few days later, I was delighted to see a likely prospect approaching from the direction of Corinth.

I studied her through my glasses. A good fat boat and a big 'un, deep in the water and making a serene 4.5 knots so far as I could guess. This was it!

I yelled for my pirate crew and we piled aboard and set a course to make an interception. The lads were hidden below decks and only Thalassinos, my skipper, and I were to be seen lolling in the cockpit. Around my neck I was wearing a home-made Union Jack as a kerchief.

We rather misjudged speeds and distance so, by the time we had made the four or five miles out into the Gulf, the big caique was almost past us. We set off in pursuit on a gradually converging course. As a classic naval stern chase it was rather spoiled for me because, for a long time, our quarry failed to realise that they were being chased!

As the distance lessened and it became obvious that we were trying to come up with them, I could see the Germans clustering in the stern of the vessel, looking back at us and obviously puzzled. We closed to about 100 yards and I passed the word to my cut-throats to stand by: they were quivering with excitement. Sixty yards now, and the Germans were looking distinctly uneasy.

'Up, boys!' I yelled, and ran up the full-sized Union Jack that I kept with me for such moments. The look of astonishment on their faces as they saw this was most satisfying.

Two of them made a dive for their machine-gun, which was mounted on a tripod, but they were far too late. My lads were raking their boat with fire. The helmsman fell dead over the wheel, causing their boat to veer towards us, and a few seconds later we boarded her with knives. I'm afraid it wasn't a thrilling ding-dong struggle – in fact I don't suppose the whole business took more than five minutes. There were no survivors, of course, and with triumphant songs we sailed our prize back into our cove where the rest of the lads were waiting to unload her.

It was a splendid haul: 40 tons of grain and fodder, six brand new LMGs still in their boxes, two 80 mm mortars and a ton or two of precious ammunition. There were also four sacks of mail which later made for quite interesting reading.

By morning everything was safely stored away and we set the caique off with the wheel lashed in the general direction westwards, towards the open sea, empty and at full speed.

Clearance for the Bari trip finally came through in March. Up-to-date Admiralty charts were dropped and pored over. A route was plotted by which my caique, flying the German ensign, would make her way past Nafpaktos, then swing NNW hugging the coast for a hundred miles or so before running WNW for Italy, leaving Corfu just to the north. Allied air and naval patrols were alerted.

Ample fuel, basic rations and gold were put aboard and all was set for the departure on the Monday. The ship's complement included one of my best officers, Captain 'Bunny' Warren. An Australian-born and -bred officer, Bunny had volunteered for the Royal Northumberland Fusiliers on the outbreak of war.[2] Then there were the skipper, Thalassinos, engineer Petros, two Russian officers and seventeen other ranks.

Around noon on the Sunday, Yotis informed me that I was expected to appear that evening at the hovel where the Russians were billeted for a farewell party. I got the message and sent down a gallon of ouzo and a cask of wine. Yotis and I arrived just after dark. Let no one deceive you, the ordinary Russian is just as we are: crafty, likeable, horny as hell, but helpless under the yoke of the Communist bastards who add up to at most about 10 per cent of their entire nation.

They produced three not so small glasses which were filled with ouzo; I was handed one and the two officers the others. 'Hooray for Churchill! Hooray for Roosevelt!' we shouted, and down the hatch with a gulp and a shudder went the ouzo. Fair enough, thought I, but soon realised that I was in real trouble when I gathered that I was expected to take a glass with every other Russian in the room.

'Well, dammit,' I thought, 'I'll show these Russians what an Englishman is made of,' and so down went another eight ouzos in short order. We then had a song and a glass of red wine and I felt the ceiling coming down.

'Goodnight and good luck . . . see you in the morning,' I said, noticing a gleam of respect in their eyes. 'Sorry I have to go, but I have work to do.'

Of course, my intention was to nip outside and throw up.

---

2   He was depicted in *Captain Corelli's Mandolin* as an Old Etonian and British upper-class. He was anything but: he was proudly Australian.

No luck: my stomach seemed to be paralysed. I focused one eye on the candle illuminating the window of my own hovel about forty yards away and ran. I made it somehow on rubbery legs and hurled myself face downwards on to my cot. Oh dear!

About eight hours later I awoke to an anxious Yotis shaking me. 'How do you feel, Major?'

'How the hell d'you think I feel? You silly prick, where are those bloody Russians?'

'They left about an hour ago.'

'Well, thank Christ for that. Be a good chap and bring me some of that stuff they call water . . . lots of it.'

A week later, we eventually learned that, having made good progress, they were caught in a severe storm, their engine gave out and they were blown ashore right under the guns of a shore battery on the island of Cephalonia.

Of all those aboard only one Russian escaped by jumping overboard and swimming to safety. The others were all captured and subsequently executed, with the exception of the skipper, Thalassinos, but including Bunny.[3] Thalassinos, pleading coercion, was put into a concentration camp near Lamia and survived the war to tell the tale.

As the months passed and the strength and effectiveness of my organisation for sabotage and collection of intelligence increased, the Germans naturally showed increasing interest in my elimination.

---

3 It transpired after the war that the notes of Bunny's interrogation were subsequently processed by one Captain Kurt Waldheim – thereafter Secretary General of the UN, 1971–81, and president of Austria, 1986–92 – who was working as an intelligence officer in Salonika, where the captured boys were taken. Waldheim's documented categorisation of Bunny as involved in 'sabotage operations' automatically put him under the Hitler Commando Directive. Part of the subsequent controversy over whether Waldheim might have been involved in war crimes is linked to his involvement in the chain of events that led to Bunny's execution.

Their efforts had been rewarded with some success. On one occasion I had been attacked in force and chased out of my HQ. Two of my officers had been captured and eventually executed. I had also lost a W/T set in a night ambush by an enemy patrol while moving headquarters. My dropping grounds were often attacked by fighter bombers and my radio transmissions were monitored.

By and large, life was rather precarious, especially since the Germans had set an extremely high and flattering price on the head of 'Mister Major Geoff', as I was known throughout the two provinces where I operated.

The Greeks always drew a clear distinction between their Italian and their German enemies. The former were held in great contempt. When they were captured or, as was more usually the case, when they surrendered, they were stripped of their weapons and more useful items of equipment and uniform. Then, more often than not, they were used by the Andartes as cooks, barbers, general bottle-washers or even bumboys if they were pretty enough. Many others were left to their own devices to starve or exist on the charity of the civilian population.

The Germans usually either had their throats cut or were shot. Deserters who could talk swiftly enough to prove that they were Poles, Russians, Czechs or even Austrians some-times escaped with their lives and were received into the armed bands to operate against their former comrades.

There was an obvious opportunity here for a brave and resourceful agent to penetrate the resistance movement and relay back accurate information as to the whereabouts, composition and future plans of the various British Military Mission HQs. Following my own recent unfortunate experience with Franz, I was particularly leery of and sensi-tive about the presence of any so-called 'deserters' in my neighbourhood.

With the advent of spring 1944 came the start of 'sabotage season', as the warmer weather again made it possible to live and operate in the mountains.

I had lost no time in moving my entire HQ up on to Mount Giona – north and west of Lidhorikion and the Mornos Bridge, where I had been so active the previous spring. Up here I had several good dropping grounds. I busied myself receiving stores and explosives in preparation for all-out operations against the Germans when they began to withdraw their forces from Greece, as we hoped and expected them to do later in the year.

It so happened that a large band of Communist ELAS Andartes was encamped not too far away on the mountain. The commander of this outfit – we were on cordial terms – was a jolly and colourful extrovert who called himself Orestes. He would pay me a visit after each parachute drop, to collect the ELAS share of the loot and to scrounge from me whatever he could in the way of tea, sugar or tobacco.

As was the custom for a man of his importance he would arrive with his political commissar, his quartermaster and a mounted bodyguard of ten or twelve thugs. After one such visit my Alsatian deserter, Bill the German, who had shown me such good service the previous autumn when I had tried to persuade the Italian garrison to surrender, reported to me that one of Orestes' bodyguards was showing an undue interest in my set-up and was asking too many questions.

'What of it, Bill?' I asked. 'He's on the scrounge like the rest of those buggers.'

'No, Sir,' said Bill. 'You haf not understand; zis man iss a Sherman!'

The following day, when I thought I was likely to find Orestes sober, I collected Bloody Maud and rode over to his camp to tackle him on the subject of this man.

Orestes roared with delight: 'You must mean Helmut?

Don't worry about him. He's one of my best men. He hates Germans and anyway he's an Austrian . . . and a good Communist. Why, when he deserted to us four months ago he brought his rifle with him *and* had a party card. No, no, my friend. We have watched Helmut and tested him and he is still alive.'

I thanked Orestes and eventually got away. Bloody Maud, I am sorry to admit, had become something of an alcoholic during the past winter and, with what sounded like about a gallon of vino sloshing around inside her, was taking her time over the return trip. I had plenty of time to nurse my nagging suspicion, amounting to a certainty, that friend Helmut was more than he would have us believe. Orestes, knowing little or nothing of the world outside Greece, could not be expected to realise that card-carrying Communists would be rarer than hen's teeth in the Nazi army.

I was puzzling over how to expose the fellow when chance provided the opportunity far sooner than I expected.

About a week later there arrived at my HQ three of my old friends from Colonel Psaros's outfit, the EKKA. They brought with them another Austrian 'deserter' and a letter from the Colonel giving the details of the man's surrender, concluding with the request that I arrange for his interrogation as he suspected that he might be a spy.

I had a look at the fellow, one Otto Stahmer. I saw a youngish man of good bearing and obvious intelligence: not, in fact, typical deserter material.

I was about to turn him over to Bill the German for a little bit of light interrogation when I was struck with the thought that here might be my opportunity to test out Helmut. I rode over to Orestes and asked him to bring him to me. I then explained that I had a new deserter who might be an agent and, because we trusted him, I was going to ask Helmut to do the interrogation for me.

Was it my imagination or did I see a flicker in Helmut's eye? Before he could make any reply Orestes gave his enthusiastic approval to the idea and the three of us rode back together.

On the way I spoke to Helmut as man to man. I told him that there were still many who mistrusted him and that here was his chance to establish his bona fides once and for all.

Fortunately for the Allies, the Germans maintained and operated two separate intelligence services, each jealous and mistrustful of the other. One, the Abwehr, was a branch of the German army, while the other, the Sicherheitsdient or SD, was the organ of the Nazi Party. Each service controlled its own secret funds, ran its own agents and played its cards very close to its chest so far as its rival service was concerned.[4] It seemed unlikely to me that both Otto and Helmut would have been sent into the same general area of operations by the same agency – there was too great a chance for confusion. So, if they were what I thought they were, then each probably came from a different and rival intelligence agency and the one would not know who the other was: fertile ground for a trained interrogator like me.

When we arrived back at my camp, I took Helmut to one side. 'Helmut,' I said, 'you will find tied up in that shelter a man who is either Abwehr or SD. Find out as quickly as you can. Go!'

Squeamishly I moved out of earshot after the first few thumps and groans as Helmut went to work with a will.

After a while he broke off and triumphantly reported that Otto had admitted being sent by the Abwehr and that he was ready to talk.

'Good work, Helmut,' I said. 'Now just take down on paper everything he has to say. I must know everything about him:

4   In fact, not at all unlike SOE and SIS (MI6), whose headquarter staffs seem to have spent almost as much energy on occasion trying to foil each other's plans as sabotaging the Germans . . .

which *abteilung* [division or department] of the Abwehr sent him, precisely what was his mission and, above all, how he proposed to get his information back to his own people.'

An hour later I had the lot, an excellent report set out in a most correct professional manner – and that for me was the giveaway! An 'ordinary' German soldier would have had no training in how to produce such a detailed report.

Now for the execution of the unfortunate Otto, who appeared to be in a very bad way. As a nice gesture and mark of my appreciation of his services, I invited Helmut to make one of the firing party.

So far so good.

Although I was more than satisfied in my mind that as Otto was Abwehr, Helmut must be SD or similar, I could not, on the evidence, hope to convince Orestes, who was beaming with happy pride at the performance put up by his protégé. But I figured that the events of the day must have shaken even such a tough nut as Helmut and, if my guess was correct, his next move would be to slip away back to his people with all his information. This would probably result in a devastating attack upon all of us by aircraft and mountain troops.

The nearest Germans were in Amfissa, only about sixteen miles south-east of us across the mountains as the crow flew. So I quickly got together a small force of my men: Poles, Russians and those of my Greek bodyguards whom I felt I could really trust. I sent them off to lay night ambushes right on the outskirts of Amfissa where the mountain tracks led down from Giona.

At about 4 a.m. on the second night they caught Helmut, a bare half mile from safety. He had on him copious notes and a well-marked map showing accurately the positions of my HQ as well as those of the ELAS and the EKKA Andarte HQs.

I was in camp when they dragged him up and flung him at

my feet. He lay battered and gasping and half conscious from the handling he had received from my soldiers, who were impatient to mete out to him the cruellest death they could devise.

As I regarded him with relief and satisfaction I felt a twinge of compassion for the poor bastard and resolved that he would meet his end by a bullet, as befitting the brave man he undoubtedly was.

As if reading my thoughts he raised tortured eyes to mine and croaked out a few words about wanting to leave a message for his wife. I had him dragged to where we had buried Otto, sent away my soldiers and sat myself down beside him.

'Now then, my friend,' I said, 'you can either go by a bullet or over a slow fire . . . so let's have the whole story and quickly.'

I untied his bonds. He sat up with difficulty and seemed to realise that he was sitting on Otto's grave. He gave a deep groan and covered his face with his hands. A tear trickled through his fingers. 'Otto. Otto, my friend,' he choked. 'What have I done? My God, my God.'

He fumbled in his jacket and drew forth a crumpled snapshot, which he handed to me. It showed a wedding group of Helmut and his bride. With his arm about Helmut's shoulders and smiling straight into the camera was the late Otto!

I sat very still with a chill in my heart.

'Tell me,' I said.

In Innsbruck in 1938 two young men, wearing the badges of the Austrian Nazis, hung breathlessly over a small radio. They chuckled at what they heard and, from time to time, punched one another with glee. The Anschluss[5] was a fact at last.

---

5   Anschluss: 12 March 1938, the annexation of Austria into a Greater Germany by the Nazis.

Though strongly contrasting in appearance and character, the two had been close friends since boyhood. Otto, the elder by a few months, was tall and dark, fond of his books, sensitive and idealistic. People liked him for his quiet manner and charming wit. His friend Helmut, on the other hand, was a typical example of the German ideal of those days: a magnificent blond specimen and a ruthless womaniser; selfish and rather cruel in his nature, he took the lead in whatever devilment he and his cronies would get up to.

In due course both had joined the German army and had distinguished themselves during the Polish campaign. Otto, with his knowledge of languages, had transferred to the Abwehr and received training in counter-intelligence, which he put to good use in Russia. He was decorated and promoted to sergeant.

Helmut fought with distinction with the Waffen SS, also in Russia. He was severely wounded and on his recovery had been posted to the SD. He quickly earned a reputation for ruthless efficiency as an interrogator of captured partisans in Yugoslavia.

The pair had met from time to time on leave, and it was on one such occasion in 1942 that Otto had stood as best man when Helmut had married a local Innsbruck girl. Thereafter they had drifted somewhat apart and Otto had found his job increasingly distasteful. The mounting tide of partisan activity in Russia was provoking increasingly stringent and cruel retaliation from the German side. He had wangled a transfer to the Balkan theatre.

As a result of our various sabotage operations, both the Abwehr and the SD were resolved to do something about us. To this end each organisation, independently of the other, began to send reliable agents into the mountains to try to infiltrate the resistance and to discover the extent of the material help being supplied by the Allies, the number of British officers operating in the mountains, the locations of their W/T stations, and so on.

By a fantastic quirk of fate, I was the specific target of both Helmut and Otto.

On the face of it, Helmut was sitting pretty. He was well in with Orestes. He had gleaned all the information he needed and was ready to slip away, his mission accomplished.

It was a devastating shock to be suddenly confronted with Otto, and a worse one when he realised that he was obliged to interrogate him. He had had a moment of blind panic as he caught a look of amazed recognition in Otto's eyes and then his mind raced to an immediate conclusion. If it had to be one or the other then Otto must be sacrificed. His first act had been to break Otto's jaw with a savage kick. He had then proceeded to reduce his friend to a messy pulp so that he was quite incapable of uttering a word. Only his eyes, sick with pain, horror and reproach, bored deeply into whatever soul Helmut still possessed.

From his own professional knowledge it had been easy to concoct Otto's apparent confession, and it was with relief that he had helped to execute his friend before he could recover sufficiently to blurt out something compromising.

The reaction had set in later. Back at Orestes' camp, with his sick heart in a turmoil, he had had to suffer the congratulations of the Andartes and to hear and applaud cruel jibes about the unfortunate Otto. It had been too much for him and he had decided to make good his escape at once.

Helmut had been speaking for almost three hours, at first haltingly and in evident anguish. He was now composed and in control of himself, having got his confession off his chest. He handed me a few letters and papers and begged me to inform the Germans of his fate so that his wife could receive a pension. I promised that I would do so.

He then got to his feet with difficulty, took a deep breath and set his shoulders.

'I am ready, Herr Major.'

At this moment there was a clattering of hoofbeats and Orestes galloped into my camp. He flung himself off his horse and came striding up, his face a mask of demonic fury. He demanded that I should surrender Helmut to him so that he could personally, as he put it, tear out the bastard's liver and eat it in front of him. No idle threat, let me assure you!

I refused and, to save further trouble, immediately assembled a firing party of eight Poles. Helmut was stood up against a tree and I hurriedly ranged the Poles at about fifteen yards and gave the order to fire.

They clean missed!

Then Helmut, alone and surrounded by his executioners, was magnificent. A look of supreme contempt came over his face. 'Call yourselves soldiers?' he spat. 'You Polish crap!' And then he gave a great shout, 'The Führer will care for my wife and children. *Heil Hit*—' His words were cut off as, with animal howls, the firing party hurled themselves upon him and hacked him to death with their knives.

Shaken to my very soul, I thought, 'Dear God. Could I, when my time comes?'

16

Thirty pieces of gold

I have been involved directly and indirectly in the deaths of scores of men. How do or should I feel about this? My answer must be nothing. With perhaps one exception, when I took a potshot at that chicken-thieving Italian and missed, I have avoided the occasion for killing individuals just for the hell of it.

War is morally destructive and it takes a good man, exposed to years of conflict, to withstand the insidious temptations that are presented by a licence to kill, loot and so forth. Of course, duty bound, one is prepared *en principe* to kill the enemy. But if the enemy is misguided enough to try to kill one such as me, then let him beware.

I am a peace-loving and timid man, but once frightened or severely angered I act on a ferocious impulse which is alarming. The adrenalin flows and I can actually feel the hairs on the back of my legs rising up like a dog's.

I was glad when Nikitas cut the throat of that bastard Franz who had betrayed my trust. I was glad to bury my fist with all my force into the solar plexus of someone I had caught trying to steal a bag of sovereigns. I was less glad when he suddenly spewed forth gouts of frothy blood and presently expired. How was I to know that he was tubercular and that my blow had burst all the lesions in his lungs?

See what I mean? In peacetime I am up for manslaughter; in wartime I just tell someone to bury the bugger. I have had considerable training in what are now known as the martial arts and I am terrified of my knowledge. I pride myself on my self-control, but in certain circumstances of surprise and provocation my reflexes might be too fast for my reason. Like the majority of us, I suppose, I fear not death itself but the manner of my death. Pray God mine be sudden.

I remember so well during the desert campaigns being envious of my friends who were killed suddenly. They had made the jump and left me to die my thousand deaths in my imagination and fear. Heroism is beyond my ken. I witnessed it once when I stood with twenty others around a blazing Lockheed Hudson when the heat was so fierce one couldn't be within thirty yards of it. An Australian pilot I knew, the best-looking man I ever saw, ran from among us straight into the flames in an attempt to rescue his friend, who was in the cockpit. Stupid ass, I suppose would be the general verdict. But yet . . . I remember that most of us looked at our feet for a while afterwards.

Cold, cool bravery is also not for me. I recall a horrendous occasion in the desert. My squadron was on detachment to a column of mixed tanks, motorised infantry and artillery commanded by one Brigadier Jock Campbell, VC.

It so happened one day that we were confronted by an even larger column of the enemy and Jock, who was a gunner by training, immediately sent out some unfortunate young man in a wireless truck to act as the observation post for the two troops of 25-pounder guns we had with us. The OP truck halted within about 4000 yards of the enemy and nervously reported an 88 mm gun being unlimbered.

It was my misfortune, being the nearest tank, to catch Jock's attention. As he had no armoured vehicle of his own, he hopped on to the back of my vehicle and, with blood in his eye and hanging on to the turret for grim death, directed me to go at full speed towards his OP. This I did and halted when I got there. Blistering invective ensued and I had no option but to charge on towards that bloody 88 with the OP truck now tucked in behind my tail. At around 1500 yards, virtually point-blank range for an 88, Jock halted and barked a fire order to his guns over my radio.

The 88 fired and missed us by a whisker.

Next moment our guns fired and six 25-pounder shells dropped about fifty yards short of it, raising a lot of dust between it and us, thank God, because that gave us a few more seconds' grace to move – had we failed to do so the next shot would have blown us to pieces.

Jock barked a corrected fire order just as the German 88 fired again. I could see the shell coming by the dust it raised with its low trajectory and colossal velocity. I shut my eyes: this was it. There was an enormous bang and the OP truck behind me was blown to hell. Given our relative positions to the 88, I have never understood how this could possibly have happened. A split second later and six 25-pounder shells did the same for the 88.

What did I do? Almost wet myself.

What did Jock do? Snuffed the wind and proceeded to use his guns and our tanks to tear hell out of that enemy column.

He did give me a nod afterwards and said: 'Thank you m'boy . . . That was fun, wasn't it?'[1]

★   ★   ★

---

1   The flip side of tales of extraordinary bravery and survival is how even the most exceptional hero can be killed in the most random way. Brigadier Campbell, a gunner, won his VC in late November 1941 in a nearby battle to the one 2 RGH fought at El Gubi. Just as described here – and this incident might well have been one of those which led to him being awarded that VC – Campbell commanded his men from the front, either from his open staff car or on foot or from any tank he could jump on to. He even ended up loading and firing field guns at near point-blank range at critical moments in the battle. He displayed ferocious bravery and it is quite incredible he survived. A few months later he was dead, his car having overturned on a stretch of road.

Geoff's great friend from the Asopos raid, Don Stott, died likewise – and Stott had plenty of other tales of derring-do to tell. After all he survived, it seems likely that he drowned in his small folding canoe when paddling ashore on another mission from a submarine in 1945. Hollywood would have us believe that it takes a mass of the enemy to take down men such as these. The reality can be somewhat more mundane.

For some time I had been under some pressure to visit Athens and to try to bring some organisation and purpose to the resistance effort there.

The situation was that, apart from the major Andarte groups, there were also several other small organisations, mainly right-wing or monarchist, existing in Athens. Though they were playing no active part in affairs at the time, it was thought – and I concurred – that supplied with money and with such materials as hand grenades, submachine-guns and explosives, they could be co-ordinated into an effective urban guerrilla force. The idea was that they could be useful in giving the Germans a torrid time when they started to pull out.

In fact, in Foot's history of SOE he concludes that one of the main achievements of SOE in Greece was to keep the anti-Communist groups in existence as a fighting force. This meant that when British troops finally entered Athens on 14 October there were non-Communist parties for the British to ally themselves with, thus preventing an otherwise inevitable Communist takeover.

The key word was co-ordination. The Athenian is a some-what different breed of cat to his country cousins: highly intelligent, highly articulate and highly political. It would hardly be an exaggeration to state that, among any group of 1000 Athenian men, there would be ten parties of differing political opinion and that in each party there would be ten men each convinced in his heart that he should be a member of parliament . . . if not prime minister. We British went into Greece thinking we knew what was going on and what we were meant to achieve. It took the first year of being there just to realise that we did not.

I had been making excuses to myself for not having gone to Athens, mainly because the whole idea of donning civilian clothes and making the dangerous journey through numerous enemy checkpoints scared me stiff.

However, I eventually sent a courier to Athens. He took with him a letter to Don Stott – my friend who had dropped with me and was my number two at the Asopos Viaduct – who was now living in the suburbs. I asked Don to study a draft of a document prepared by my superiors which, it was hoped, would become the basis for what we called a 'National Bands Agreement'. By this, the signatories, representing all the resistance organisations, were to pledge themselves to shelve their political differences and stop fighting one another for the duration of the occupation and to concentrate their efforts, under our broad direction, on the disruption of the Nazi war effort and preventing as many Germans as possible getting back to Germany. Every German killed or captured in Greece would be one less to fight our boys come D-Day. We, the British Military Mission, would ensure supplies of gold and weaponry.

I asked Don to convene a meeting, which I would chair. Needless to add, I implored him to exercise the utmost discretion. He was to use cut-outs, changes of venue and so on: the normal SOE procedures to minimise the chances of betrayal and capture.

My courier was back within a week. He had instructions from Don as to when and where to meet the contact who would eventually lead us to the meeting place.

A day or so later Yotis and I, with bogus travel permits and passes fairly plastered with swastikas, set off from Delphi in a ramshackle bus to negotiate the hundred and fifty or so miles to Athens, along a terrible road which would take us through four or five checkpoints.

I thought it expedient to wad my cheek with cotton wool and tie my jaw up with a bandage. My pallor and appearance of anguished suffering as each checkpoint came up were all too real as I was soon feeling nauseous from riding in the back of the swaying and smelly bus.

We rolled into Athens that evening covered in dust. We had a meal of sorts in a street café and then looked around for modest lodgings within easy walking distance of our rendez-vous in the morning.

We found a squalid hotel of three storeys fronting on to a back street. Concrete stairs ran up to each floor from the cubicle that served as the reception. Our room was on the second floor, bang opposite the stairway – number 203. I will never forget that hotel or that number. There were five other rooms on our floor, a verminous bathroom and a foetid and evil-smelling lavatory which defies description.

We retired to our iron cots at about 11 p.m. and I lay awake for a while, thinking. I was not too worried about our safety as I knew no one in Athens had the faintest idea where we were, and if no one knew we were here we could not be betrayed: that risk would come the moment we showed our faces at the meeting the next day. What was more, I had carried out all my drills and I was certain that we had not been followed. We had done nothing suspicious or anything that might have given cause for someone on the other side to notice us.

At about 5.30 a.m. I came suddenly awake with that old familiar premonition of acute danger. By the end of the war I reckoned I could smell a German.

Yotis was lying flat on his back, snoring his head off. I got out of bed and looked cautiously out of the window. Taking position on the other side of the street and facing our hotel were twenty or so Germans with submachine-guns.

I shook Yotis awake. 'Quick,' I said. 'Grab your clothes and hide in the crapper. Bloody Krauts everywhere. Here, take all the papers and my identity card and flush the bloody things. Quick, for God's sake. MOVE . . . If you get away, tell Cairo what happened . . . don't just sit there, *MOVE!*'

Poor Yotis, his senses scattered and his face ashen, collected his shoes and trousers. He gathered up all the papers I thrust at him and shambled off to that excuse for a lavatory.

I went back to the window and peeped out. As I looked, a sinister black Mercedes glided quietly down the street and stopped outside the front door. Two Gestapo in civilian clothes got out. They looked briefly around. One of them checked the address from his notebook.

For some reason it seemed to be important to be arrested wearing my shoes and trousers. Hurriedly I pulled them on and sat waiting on the end of my bed, my heart thumping. On a sudden thought I quickly made up Yotis's bed to try to give the impression that I was alone. I sat down again and I do believe that I sent up an urgent message to my patron saint, St Anthony. He must have been surprised at hearing from me again after so long!

I sat without daring to breathe, straining my ears. Suddenly I could hear them coming . . . softly, softly up the stairs. Oh God, I thought, here it comes.

There was a loud clanking from Yotis's lavatory down the passage.

I waited, with every nerve screaming. Nothing happened.

Then I could hear them creeping on up the stairs, up to the floor above. There was a short pause, followed by a crash, as the door of number 303, directly above me, was kicked in. There followed a terrified woman's scream, thumps and oaths and, then again, silence for a few minutes.

Loud voices and clattering feet told me that the Gestapo were hauling their prey down the stairs. I peered out of the window to see a man and a woman, half clad and bloody about the face, being bundled roughly into the Mercedes. It drove away rapidly. The soldiers formed up and, at the word of command, stepped smartly off, singing loudly in unison one of their hateful marching songs.

I fell to my knees with my forehead on the window sill and permitted myself a sob of sheer thankfulness and relief.

I was distracted by another dismal clanking noise from Yotis's department. I went out and banged on the door.

'Excuse me, gentlemen, ju-just a minute,' quavered Yotis. 'I can't get this thing to flush properly.'

'It's OK, Yotis,' I said. 'It's me . . . the bastards came for some other poor sod. You can come on out.'

He opened the door: 'Oh Lord, Major,' he said. 'Can't we go home?'

I put my arm around him. 'Yotis, you silly old fart,' I said. 'You were absolutely bloody well . . . splendid!'

Although the hotel was full, not a door had opened throughout the raid and there was not a sound to be heard. I thought of a hundred terrified mice shivering in their holes, temporarily safe from the savage tomcat on the prowl outside.

We made contact with our guide at 9.30 a.m. as arranged.

We walked and bussed around, apparently aimlessly, for an hour and, being thoroughly jittery from the night's events, I was hard pushed not to go along with my head on back to front looking for spooks. Yotis swore that he had aged ten years.

Eventually, and to my considerable surprise, we walked straight up the steps of the town hall and were shown into the mayor's parlour. There, to my delight, was dear old Don, grinning from ear to ear. His ugly freckled face with its bottle nose was much as ever, but he had dyed his ginger hair a murky black and had grown a horrible moustache. How the hell he got away with what he had done to himself defeats me – he looked enormously un-Greek.

I rapidly told him what had happened. It shook him a bit and I could tell that he was having uneasy thoughts about this meeting from a security angle.

When I thought about it, Don having assured me that the

mayor was 100 per cent trustworthy, I agreed that it was the perfect place and I congratulated him upon the venue. It was a hive of activity, with people coming and going about their legitimate business. The delegates, ten or eleven in number, assembled in due course.

Just before we got down to business the representative from the EAM (the Communist, political wing of the ELAS), an ex-professor at Athens University, got our attention. 'I must inform you,' he said with a nasty look that embraced us all, 'that there has been treachery. Early this morning there were a series of raids by the Gestapo. This resulted in the arrest of some twenty of our people, including the EAM delegate to this meeting from the Peloponnesus, who was arrested in his hotel, together with his wife. However, he had not been informed of the venue . . . otherwise,' he added with a wintry smile, 'I assure you that I would not be here myself.'

Yotis caught my eye and we joined with the others in expressing our sympathy and regret.

It took hours. The professor was scornful of the necessity or desirability for armed groups other than the EAM/ELAS. Of course it was the last thing the Communists wanted, but I was determined to get the professor's signature on the agreement. That would give us a legitimate excuse to withhold supplies in the event they broke the agreement – which we all knew they would do the moment it suited them. It was blackmail on our part: undeclared, but plainly inferred. But it was the only language the Communists understood. We knew that well enough by now.

At 5 p.m. the agreement was signed by all parties. Details of the various groups' requirements and plans would be discussed at a future meeting, to be held as soon as possible.

The delegates left and I turned to Don. 'I'm bushed,' I said, 'but buggered if Yotis and I are going back to that poxy hotel.

Christ, wasn't it bad luck having that Communist bastard staying at the same place? I wonder who shopped him? You know, that's just the way one gets caught, through sheer bloody bad luck!'

Don agreed. 'Tell you what,' he said. 'We'll go to a safe café I know for a drink and a bite and then you can spend the night at my place. It's on your way out of town anyway.'

'Fine,' I said, looking forward to a long chat with my friend. '*Allons.*'

We found a table on the pavement outside Don's little restaurant and ordered ouzo, nuts and a bowl of whatever culinary horrors constituted the *plât du jour*.

I must now digress for a moment. In the spy or agent business a most valuable attribute is inconspicuousness. This is what they drilled into us at SOE school: the grey, faceless man in the drab raincoat, at whom no one looks twice, is who one strives to be. To attract curiosity and attention is to invite some smart bastard to demand to see one's papers. Then it is usually all up with you. Englishmen of a certain background, training and education used to have a natural air of authority and command. This may sound pompous and conceited but it was nevertheless true – after all, they and their fathers had ruled the populations of a quarter of the globe and had a natural tendency to deport themselves accordingly.

We in the field were well aware of the fact that when we entered a restaurant, for example, we entered with an unconscious air of owning the place and of expecting immediate attention, if not deference. This stuck out like a sore thumb and was extremely dangerous. So we used to practise what we came to call the 'beaten look'. It was a delicate compromise between arrogance and cringing. Actually it boiled down to being careful never to catch anyone's eye. In this way one avoided empathy or antipathy. The drill was, therefore, eyes down, bury your nose in a newspaper, but keep your antennae waving.

To revert: Don, Yotis and I had almost finished our meal when I became aware of two small and extremely dirty urchins trying to sell me a lottery ticket. I nodded at Yotis and he fished out a million or two inflated drachmae and bought a ticket from one of them. This was unfortunate as it turned out that the successful guttersnipe was poaching on the other one's beat. They started squabbling. The injured party picked up a handful of inedible offal out of the gutter – with typical Greek hygiene standards it must have been chucked there by someone from the restaurant – and hurled it at his little friend. He missed, but landed his load fair and square on the windscreen of a German army truck a few yards away.

Behind the wheel of this truck was sitting a large, meaty Kraut reading a newspaper. The oaf was startled. Moving with surprising speed, he was out of his cab. He grabbed the brat, threw his tray of lottery tickets to the wind and snapped his arm across his knee. Without a backward glance he stumped back to his truck, leaving the child crying in the gutter.

This was too much even for the fear-stricken Greeks and much too much for me. My plate smashing against the side of the truck brought the rest of the customers to their feet. A veritable fusillade of crockery, chairs and knives followed. I felt myself being frogmarched rapidly away through the kitchen and out to the rear.

'Come on, Geoff, for Christ's sake,' hissed Don. 'You're as white as a sheet and the place will be swarming with the swine. Let's get the hell out . . . quickly!'

We hadn't gone far and I was beginning to get control of myself when we heard behind us a shrill cry: 'Engleesh . . . Engleesh! Hooray for Churchill! Hooray for Roosevelt!' We turned in horror to find we had a tail of five ecstatic small boys. One of them turned a cartwheel and landed in a heap at my feet.

I reached down to pick him up: he kissed my hand. 'I love you, Engleesh,' he said.

'Hooray for Greece,' I groaned. 'Yotis . . . give them some scratch and tell them to piss off, for God's sake!'

We fled. For some reason Don thought it all hilarious. I didn't. So much for my 'beaten look', I thought.

We finally got to Don's place, a nice villa in a fashionable suburb. The day had been altogether too much for me and I felt drained. Several hours and many bottles later, I felt strong enough to remark: 'Thank God I can get out of this fucking place. One thing I swear is that the first Kraut I meet I'm going to shoot in the guts, just to see him squirm. Yotis, we'll take the first bus out of here tomorrow.'

'I'm sorry, Major. We won't.'

'Why won't we?'

'I flushed your papers down the loo.'

'Shit! So you did. Well, we'll have to walk.' We did, and it took us damn near ten days.

In these modern time of universal ill will and mistrust, few large pieces of engineering, be they dams, bridges or viaducts, are constructed without provision being made in their construction for their possible future demolition by high explosives. The Marathon Dam, from which Athens draws a large part of its water supply, was no exception.

Towards the end of 1944 the Germans were finally preparing to pull out of Greece. They were leaving happy in the knowledge that the Allies, apart from having to face an imminent Communist revolution, would also have to face a tremendous rehabilitation task if the Greeks were not to suffer yet another winter of appalling hardship and privation. By cutting off the supply of water to Athens the Germans were aware that they would add immeasurably to the Allies' difficulties and cause horrendous hardships for their old enemies the Greeks. This, of course, was exactly what they had in mind when they decided to blow the Marathon Dam before leaving the country.

That remarkable man Don Stott had become aware of this plan through one of his chief informants, the Greek interpreter to the German area commander. Don arrived at my HQ one day to discuss certain measures he had in mind to thwart their plan.

After weeks of cautious negotiations using the mayor of Athens as an intermediary, Don had managed to make contact with the German engineer who would be responsible for the demolition of the dam when the time came. While this man, a major, seemed not unresponsive, Don felt that he ought to now bring me into the negotiations. Not only did I speak reasonable German, I also had at my disposal large sums of money in gold sovereigns. We thrashed the matter out at length, and the upshot was that I accompanied Don back to Athens. We passed an anxious few days before re-establishing contact with our German. Finally, late one night in the mayor's house, we confronted one another across a table.

Having satisfied him as to my identity, I proceeded to argue as follows. By destroying the dam the only result would be to increase the chaos in Athens. The sole beneficiaries would be the Communists, who were Germany's most deadly enemies. It looked as though the war was already lost for Germany so why, through such an act of wanton destruction, add to the bill for reparations? By doing as we suggested he would be serving the true interests of his country, as against the Nazis who seemed resolved upon their own and everyone else's destruction.

Our plan was to supply him with electric detonators for the job: exact replicas of the real things. They would respond to circuit tests, but they would not detonate when the time came. If, as we expected, the demolition was left until the last minute before the final evacuation – the civilian population would have risen up and torn them apart had they still been there to face the consequences – there would be no time to re-excavate down to the demolition chamber deep inside the face of the dam and replace the dud detonators with proper ones.

For his co-operation, I promised him 1000 gold sovereigns in cash once the detonators were in place and another 9000 to be placed in his account in a Swiss bank. I promised British passports for himself and his family and a passage to any part of the world if he survived the war. To show my bona fides, I plumped down on the table in front of him a bag containing 1000 gold sovereigns. He was clearly tempted, but it took two further meetings and much urgent persuasion before he agreed.

Several weeks later the specially prepared detonators arrived from Cairo. They were handed over to Brian Dillon for delivery to the German, Major Weissman, as Don and I were on the point of leaving Greece. Brian handled the whole affair from then on with great skill and at no little risk to himself.

Waiting until the eleventh hour he delivered the money and the detonators. He then returned to his mountain, having made certain dispositions for the future. Through his excellent contacts in the city he knew within the hour when the dam mysteriously failed to explode.

The whys, the hows and the wherefores are not yet for publication and may never be, but suffice it to say that among the many ambush attacks made on the departing Germans, there was one which showed every sign of careful planning. His fellow officers deplored the death of Major-Engineer

Weissman who, they agreed, had been a very decent fellow, if rather reserved of late.

His luggage, however, had yielded to his assassins what they were looking for – a small, remarkably heavy white canvas bag.

When he came to the 'official' count of the gold, Brian reported back to the anxious Cairo bean-counters that, oddly enough, there were exactly thirty pieces missing.[2]

---

2 I've read this on a number of occasions and my only conclusion as to the meaning of this somewhat opaque comment from Geoff is that the British double-crossed Weissman. After all, the British were known as 'perfidious Albion' by those we used to rule, and with some reason. Then again, had he not been offered the money, Weissman would have doubtless blown the dam, with catastrophic consequences, and thought little of it. After all, that is what Germans did during the war.

This also demonstrates that the British were playing to a very different rulebook back in World War II.

17

How about a sexy tango?

Fifteen months is a long time to live as I had been living – clandestinely. Fear is accumulative. Not once during all that time had I been able to settle down to sleep in absolute security. Each dawn had brought fresh anxieties and problems. The atmosphere in Greece was one of increasing bitterness and terror.

By late 1943/early 1944 the Communists were in firm control of the mountains and had recently come out in their true colours by attacking the other resistance organisations and liquidating all liberal influences in the small towns and villages.[1] Colonel Psaros had been murdered by them in April 1944 and I was beginning to suspect that, jealous as they were of my influence among ordinary people, I might be the victim of an unfortunate 'accident' in the near future. I had narrowly escaped assassination by that crazed royalist officer; I had lost two officers and a sergeant to German attacks; I was discouraged, disillusioned and ill again with dysentery; and, let me be honest, my courage was failing.

In early summer 1944 I radioed Cairo and received their

---

1 As Geoff had long feared, and predicted, civil war did break out on the Germans' retreat in October 1944. When the ELAS – the Communists – made an armed bid for power, upwards of two British divisions were committed to stop them: perhaps the first real battle of the Cold War that was to dominate world politics for the next half century. British losses against their former 'allies' in the ELAS – not that Geoff ever thought of them as such – were 237 killed and 2101 wounded. Come early January, the ELAS had been comprehensively defeated, although this was but the prelude to years of warfare and turmoil to come.

immediate permission to evacuate. An officer to replace me was dropped by parachute and a fortnight was spent in handing over and making many emotional farewells. Finally I set off with Bill, Yotis, an American pilot and four members of my Greek bodyguard. Bloody Maud and Pearl carried our gear.

First our route led northwards to a village beyond Karpenision, where I was to collect a party of seventy-four Russian ex-PoWs who were awaiting repatriation. I was then to make my way eastwards across the plains of Thessaly, past the town of Velos, to Pelion and the coast. There I would pick up a caique operated by MI9 – Military Intelligence 9, the wartime military escape organisation – and sail to Turkey.

Our journey of some two hundred and fifty miles, otherwise uneventful, was marred by one sad incident. Rashly crossing the railway line north of Velos in daylight, we were attacked by a patrolling aircraft. It killed one of the Russians and poor Bloody Maud.

I was very upset as I had come to love the old girl. Through thick and thin she had soldiered gamely along. Always in a filthy temper – except when she was plastered – she had never lost her head, never faltered and never played the fool. For my money you can keep your damn horses.

We waited a few days amid idyllic surroundings at Pelion and then embarked in great discomfort on the caique. I took a sad farewell of my bodyguards and my loyal friend Yotis.

Our trip to a secret base in Turkey took three days as the caique broke down en route. It was with huge relief that we finally entered Turkish territorial waters, shortly after we had slipped between the German fortified islands of Chios and Leros.

At the base in Turkey, ostensibly neutral, all was bustle and efficiency. The whole party, including the Russians, was fitted out with hand-me-down civilian clothes and we were given hot showers and a good meal, our first for three days.

With the American pilot I was driven into Ismir, on the north-west coast, and installed very comfortably in a large modern hotel on the seafront. My first act was to subside gratefully into a barber's chair and order 'the works'. My neighbour, I noticed, was a large beefy German who was having a manicure. Emerging from under my hot towels, I gave him a broad wink. He scowled and looked away. Ah well.

A smooth young secretary from the Consulate kindly invited me to dine with him and his girlfriend. From him I learned that train reservations were being made for all of us for the trip east to the capital, Ankara. There we would connect with that most romantic of trains, the *Taurus Express*, which would take us south to Aleppo in Syria.

'Oh, by the way,' the secretary said, 'I hope you don't mind but there's a Polish girl who came out on last week's plane whom I am tacking on to your party. I gather that she is the daughter of some big tit in their government-in-exile and has family in Cairo. We've been especially asked to keep an eye on her and see that she gets down there OK. You'll meet on the train, which incidentally won't be leaving for a day or two.'

A day or two suited me very well. I was very content just to bathe, sleep, eat and revel in the sensation of feeling my nerves unwind.

A couple of days later I was notified that the train would leave that night. We all assembled at the station and I was given a bulk ticket with about eighty names on it. I remember thinking that if some of the Russians chose to bolt there would be nothing I could do about it. In the event it was a pity they didn't.

I looked over the train and saw that two second-class coaches were reserved and in addition, for myself and others unspecified, two two-berth compartments in the wagon-lit, a sleeping car.

I climbed aboard and slid open the door of the first sleeper. There was a pretty grey-eyed girl of about twenty sitting staring out of the window. Of course! I remembered and hastily consulted my list. There she was, a Miss Erben.

I entered. 'Good evening, Miss Erben,' I said. 'It appears that we are to be travelling companions.'

One never knows . . .

She looked up, startled, and blushed.

'But I . . . we, er . . .' she stammered, at a loss and not knowing how to phrase what was on her mind.

'Please don't worry,' I lied cheerfully. 'Later on I'll speak to the attendant to see if I can't possibly get you a compartment to yourself. In the meantime I had better move my stuff in with you as there are seventy hairy Russians with me who will be looking for places to sit.'

She went a little pale and hastily helped me to arrange my few possessions. Later on I did see the attendant and bribed him to ensure that, if asked, there was no alternative accommodation on the train. She and I dined together cheerfully and duly retired for the night. I chivalrously took the top bunk and never stirred off it until the train ran into Ankara the next morning. To tell the truth I was thinking of the next phase of the journey, which would take a day and two nights, and I was anxious to maintain the big brother image until we were safely en route.

I parked Nina, for that was her name, at a hotel in Ankara to rest up for the day until the *Taurus Express* got in from Budapest that night. I then went back to the station for an expensive chat with my friends the wagon-lit people.

Thus: 'Dammit, Nina,' I was able to say with perfect truth at about ten that night, after the great blue train had hissed and clanked to a halt beside the platform. 'They've put us in together again. I'm awfully sorry. Perhaps they think we're married or something.'

She gave me a sharp, quizzical glance but I looked quite guilelessly back and motioned her aboard.

We had a very cosy little trip indeed and by the time we reached Aleppo really felt quite attached to one another.

When we finally crossed over the Syrian border, after endless formalities, I and my party were passed over to our own security people. They were aghast to see the Russians, about whom, typically, they had received no notice! The poor devils were eventually put on a train and shipped off to Basra in Iraq, where they were to be handed over to the Russian Supply Commission. At my Russians' request I had gone to a lot of trouble and had provided each man with a reference or 'chit' to the effect that they had served the Allied cause well by fighting with the Andartes against the Germans in Greece. With the knowledge of hindsight, I suspect it was this evidence of 'contamination' that ended up sealing their fate.

I learned, much later, that on their arrival in Basra the Russian Mission at first refused to acknowledge their existence. The Russians eventually stopped procrastinating and accepted them from our people with ill grace. They were handed over to the Russian Mission one morning. The Russians shot the lot the same afternoon . . .

I took a temporary farewell of Nina, who left by car for Beirut. I would have gone with her but the brigade major from the HQ in Aleppo, Syria, whom I happened to know slightly, had asked me to dine with the brigade staff. I knew that I could spare the time and still catch up with her as the final leg of the journey by train from Beirut to Cairo would not begin until the morrow evening.

I had been surprised to find that there was a brigade staff in Aleppo anyway, as I couldn't for the life of me see the need for a brigade of troops along the Turkish frontier at that late stage of the war. The mystery deepened when I learned that one of the brigade's attached regiments was the 3rd Royal

Gloucestershire Hussars, which I knew had never even existed. I discovered over dinner that it was an elaborate blind, aimed, I suppose, at making the Germans think that we were about to try to force the Turks into the war against them. All very hush-hush and, I thought, pointless to have 150 dummy tanks and guns prominently displayed on a skyline near the Turkish frontier. But I could understand why they were pleased to see me, a genuine Royal Gloucestershire Hussar, wearing the regimental badges, to back up the deception.

Declining their pressing invitation to stay for a few days and be seen around, I hurried on to Beirut, arriving with a promising thirst in the foyer of the Hotel Normandie just before lunch.

I was vaguely aware that just in front of me was a small fragrant bundle of mink with perfect legs, escorted by a tall officer. As I stood for a minute surveying the elegant crowd of pre-lunch drinkers and their partners, trying to decide whether drinks or lunch would have priority, the couple in front turned about.

I heard a little gasp.

'Joff? Joff! Joffie dolling! But ees *un merveil*! Vair you been, *chéri?*' With an excited squeak, the little numero danced up, stood on its toes and flung its arms around me. For a moment I was dazzled and confused by this assault upon my senses. Then I clicked.

'Tonks, darling!' I said, delighted. 'My goodness, you *do* look nice.'

'Umm,' she went, giving me another big kiss. 'You air more loffley zan before! You vill lonch wis us?'

Without waiting for my reply she turned to her escort, an immaculate and extremely handsome brigadier, who had been standing by the while with a look of well-bred indulgence on his face.

"Umphrey dolling, you mus know my fren. Joffie, zis ees Sir 'Umphrey Cutling. E ees vair important.' She beamed up at him and patted his cheek. 'Vee lonch now, eh?' She went on. "Umphrey ees vair beezy; ees making a beeg plan vis ze army in Aleppo to make ze Jermans sink e ees coming!'

The Brigadier shook hands. He was looking a little hunted at these remarks delivered with shrill penetration in the presence of the other diners of divers nationalities and allegiances.

'Howdedo,' he said. 'Perhaps we should go in before she blurts out anything too ghastly.'

As we seated ourselves, 'Er . . .' he said. 'I gather that you and the Countess are old friends?'

'Well, yes,' I replied, cocking an amused and enquiring eye at the 'Countess'. 'Matter of fact we knew each other quite well some time ago.'

I should now explain that the wicked little minx known to me and various others as Tonks was Dutch with a touch of Javanese or Laotian in her. Where she came from, God alone knows, but she was tiny, quite exquisite and remarkably talented in bed. We had enjoyed a brisk little walkout a while ago in Cairo. Now a self-styled countess, she had evidently moved into a higher bracket.

I nearly wet myself through lunch watching the Brigadier's face waiting for her monumental military indiscretions, and the time passed agreeably enough until two thirty, when 'Umphrey rose to leave. 'See you at five, m'dear.' He nodded to me. 'Staying long?' he asked.

'No, Sir. I have to catch the train to Cairo this evening.'

He seemed relieved. 'Well, I'll trot along.' He nodded to me and saluted Tonks politely.

We regarded one another. She took my hand. 'Come, dolling, vee enjoy a leetle matinee ontil fife o'clock.'

We fled, and a short while later we were tumbling

desperately around in the most sumptuous apartment, which I gathered had been set up for her by 'Umphrey.

I like to think that I put up a worthy performance, but some while later, overcome by train-induced fatigue, I was lying back lazily thinking charitable thoughts about 'Umphrey for his kind hospitality when Tonks beside me stirred.

'Dolling,' she said.

'Ummm?'

'Dolling! Wake up.'

'What is it?' I murmured. She tweaked me where it hurt.

'Ow! What d'you want?'

'Joffie dolling, put on some music for us.'

I sighed, rolled over on to my feet and padded across about an acre of carpet to an enormous radiogram that took up half the far wall.

'Well now,' I said. 'What shall we have? How about a sexy tango?' I was bending over looking through a stack of records when I suddenly yelled and jumped about four feet. The sexy tango flew out of my hand and shattered. I seized my rear end and spun around, my face contorted with rage and pain.

There stood Tonks, bright-eyed and with a whip in her hand – she had stalked me across the room and had let me have a fourpenny one!

'Bitch!' I shrieked. 'What the . . .? Christ! You bloody little . . .!'

I leapt at her and seized the whip; she gave an excited little squeak and took off around the flat, with me after her, slashing furiously at her little bottom. Every time I connected, which was not often; she'd have a loud squeal and scuttle all the faster, screaming with excitement. In my fury I walloped over a vase of flowers and 'Umphrey's photograph, which smashed. Eventually I got her pinned down on the bed, where she lay under my hands, writhing and panting with her little pink tongue darting in and out of her mouth.

Undecided whether to rub my backside or just throttle her,

but realising all too well what was now expected of me, I paused to consider my immediate situation.

Eventually I sighed and kissed her gently on the nose.

'Sorry, love,' I confessed. 'I'm afraid you've just flogged a dead horse, as it were.'

She pouted prettily. 'What do you mean?'

'Ask old 'Umphrey,' I replied. 'I suspect the poor bugger will know very well what I meant.'

Time had flown; I dressed in a hurry and in fact passed 'Umphrey in the hall downstairs. He glanced at me in a rather old-fashioned way but said nothing and hurried on up with a gleam in his eye which, in the circumstances, boded rather well for Tonks, I thought.

Once safely outside, I climbed into a taxi and, though my new wound twinged a bit if I moved carelessly or the taxi hit a pothole in the road, I laughed helplessly all the way to the station where my train was waiting. As I wandered down the platform looking for my carriage, I saw something that wiped the smile smartly off my face.

Leaning out of our compartment and anxiously scanning the crowds was dear little Nina. She waved delightedly as she caught sight of me. I sighed; it looked like a long hard night!

Well before our train drew into Cairo, I was up and dressed and had my luggage stacked in the corridor so as not to compromise Nina in front of her family. We sat quietly together and she laid her cheek gently against mine for a long moment. 'You have been very sweet,' she said softly, 'but perhaps you had better not come and see me off – perhaps later, we shall see.'

A short while later I watched rather sadly as she was swept off by a large mob of relieved relatives. I never saw or heard of her again.

I took a cab to Shepheard's and was welcomed by the manager, Charles Muller, who greeted me effusively with a bill for

£40 – being my share of the breakages after a wild party in my rooms some seventeen months past.[2]

After lunch I drifted along to Rustom Buildings, wondering what my reception would be. To my surprise the affable Walker – the very first of the SOE men to interview me when I had first been introduced to the organisation almost two years earlier – was still there, now a major. 'Hello, old fellow,' he said. 'We've been expecting you. My word, you've done pretty well! I know the Colonel is most anxious to have a word with you. How was it over there, by the way?'

'It had its moments. What happened to Blair?' He, if you remember, was the tubby little fellow I had first spotted gyrating wildly at Madame Badia's nightclub: a man who obviously enjoyed his grog.

'He just dropped dead, old boy. Blew up, I expect. Damnedest thing actually, no warning at all.'

'Well, that's the way it goes. What about some leave?'

'Yes, well of course,' he replied. 'We thought that you might take a month.'

'That would be nice,' I mused. 'I think that I'll go back to England.'

'Can't do that, I'm afraid. Not allowed.'

'Kenya, then?'

'No good either, old chap. I'm sorry. They've made some new rules while you were away.'

'Well, where the hell can I go?' I was nettled.

---

2 What is it with the armed forces and war and money? When I was preparing to start my march up with 2 Para, prior to the eventual battle of Wireless Ridge, we were told there had been a helicopter mail drop and there was just time to write a 'last letter' home. I scribbled a note to my then girlfriend, using my helmet as a writing base – very warry and 'Hollywood' it felt, too! The incoming letters arrived literally as we were moving off. Great excitement as my name was called. There was but one for me: a missive from the secretary of my sailing club informing me they had not yet received that year's subscription and asking what I intended doing about it . . .

He hesitated. 'Well, we thought . . . perhaps Cyprus?'

'Bugger you!' I exploded. 'If you think I'm going back to being surrounded by Greeks after what I've just been through . . . you can stuff that idea!'

'Oh,' he said, rather taken aback. 'Well, there are one or two people who are anxious to chat with you before you disappear again. So, if you wouldn't mind sticking around for a few days, we'll try and organise something a bit different with regard to your leave.'

Disgruntled, I went back to Shepheard's. During the next two weeks there were numerous frustrating interviews during which I tried to present an accurate picture of what was really going on in Greece.

I had a long and profitable interview with that most excellent man, King George of the Hellenes, and a short, acrimonious one with a left-wing British MP – a real little horror who did not relish, nor was he prepared to listen to, what I had to tell him about conditions on the ground in Greece.

In the end it was the King's public declaration that he would not return home unless and until there had been a plebiscite and a vote in favour of him so doing, that was to help cut through all the posturing taking place in Athens. The Communists had been telling anyone who would listen that the British were there to restore the monarchy, at the point of a bayonet if necessary. By putting the question of his future return to a popular vote, the King removed some of the sting of the allegation and helped add legitimacy to the British position. When the vote did finally take place in 1946, it was in favour of the return of King George – but also heralded the start of another bout of bloody fighting: this time three years of war.

Wearying of it all, I began to suspect there might be a plot developing to send me off to the Far East to fight the Japs. Not so fanciful as it turned out, as this was the fate that was to befall my friend Don Stott on his return from Greece. So I sat down and sent off a signal to the Belgian section of SOE in London. I informed them that my French was bilingual (not quite, actually), that I knew the Ardennes country like the back of my hand (not quite, actually) and that I was prepared to take the field immediately. Faced with this onslaught of talent, the Belgian section was powerless to resist.[3]

Within forty-eight hours I was on a flying boat, loaded with VIPs, headed for England and a wife from whom I had been parted on my wedding day and whom I had not seen for three years.

I was determined on a nice long leave to be spent getting to know her again before setting off for Belgium, or anywhere else for that matter. And to hell with them!

Settling myself comfortably on a pile of mailbags, I dozed off.

3 Perhaps there is more to this reference to not wanting to fight the Japs than meets the eye. It is now known that many of those who had been fighting for years felt, by this stage of the war, that it was the turn of those back in England to 'do their bit'.

Come D-Day and the terrible slugfest that was the battle for Normandy, General Montgomery had assumed that it was his veteran divisions from North Africa and Italy who would be his key shock troops. Wrong. His veterans had 'been there, done that' and had nothing left to prove. They knew only too well what dying was about and, having survived this long, had little intention of doing anything rash. It was the fresh divisions who tended to show more flair and take the risks that can so often swing battles. His veterans fought all right, but they were often much more careful about it. Geoff might also have thought – not that he has said so – that it was now 'some other bugger's turn' to get themselves killed, and who could blame him?

18

Supernasties, shits and bastards

I returned from the Middle East in about July 1944. What happened upon arrival back in England and London? A happy reunion with Ursula, my wife, – who, if you remember, I had married back in 1941 and not seen for the last three years – and a spot of leave down in Cornwall, where she was living with a Wren friend of hers. It was a modest but nice place on the outskirts of St Mawes, fronting on to the river.

Once a week along would come Mr Pascoe, the gardener/handyman. I discovered by chance that Pascoe drew a small annuity from the Duchy of Cornwall for protecting the royal oyster beds, acres of which lay but a few yards from the end of our garden. I soon formed a cosy understanding with him, and all I had to do was drift along to his favourite watering hole, buy him a drink and indicate with my fingers how many oysters I wanted. He charged 2/6d a dozen, but it was understood that he would open them for us and share the bounty. 'Long live His Majesty' was our loyal toast!

Six months later, when I was back at the war, he came as usual, did his work and then, instead of cycling back home, went down to the river's edge and left his clothes neatly folded with his boots atop the pile. No trace of him was ever discovered.

All too soon my happy reunion was over and it was up to London and Baker Street, where lurked the Belgian section of SOE. Sad to say I found there a coven of idlers, poseurs and poofs, who had done nothing so far and were not about to risk their health by starting anything at this stage of the war. I was totally disgusted and fulminated for about six weeks before quitting to join SHAEF.[1] I attended various courses before being sent off to France and Belgium. I was delighted to get out of London as the V1 buzz bombs were scaring me witless.

I have never made any secret of my mistrust and dislike of the French, even though my maternal great grandmother was from Normandy. From the archives I learn that a distant ancestor, Robert de Bourbel – *le bien dote*, roughly translated as the 'the donkey-hung' – nobbled in marriage the eldest daughter of Robert the Devil, great uncle of none other than William the Conqueror.

Anyhow, one Frenchman who was a splendid exception to his sorry compatriots was Jean, Prince de Chimay: an anglophile and a very parfit, gentil knight – that's from Chaucer for any of you who didn't know. He was head honcho of Veuve Cliquot champagne and resided in a most splendid chateau just outside Rheims.

When the Krauts arrived in 1940, they had decreed that the entire Veuve Cliquot production would be reserved for the Wehrmacht and, to this end, they exempted the vineyard workers and staff from deportation. They commandeered the Prince's chateau, but offered him the west wing to live in with his family.

Dressed in Saville Row tweeds and wearing his MCC tie, Chimay thanked them politely but let them know that he could not possibly agree to spending even one night under the same roof with an enemy. He removed himself and his family to the farthest end of his park, where he built a modest dwelling in which to wait out the war.

1 SHAEF: Supreme Headquarters Allied Expeditionary Force.

The entire 1943 vintage, which was a good one – most Krauts had no idea what they were drinking and went by label alone – he concealed from the Germans by bricking up a corridor in his labyrinthine caves, but not before each bottle had been labelled 'Reserved for the Allied Armies of Liberation'.

Magnifique!

Very shortly after the liberation of Paris at the end of August 1944, I wangled myself a swan[2] through France with a Movement Order signed by Ike,[3] no less. I had a Jeep and an American driver and my assignment was to assess the threat, actual or potential, for mischief by any last-ditch Nazi fanatics. These were 'Werewolves', and other phantoms with suicidal tendencies, dreamed up by geeks and wets intent on hanging on to their nice safe jobs in SHAEF by coming up with threats for the likes of me to investigate and neutralise. I knew it to be a load of bollocks. Once overrun, the Krauts were only too happy to get to the safety of a prisoner-of-war cage and, safely ensconced there, few were showing any inclination to escape and rejoin the fight for Herr Hitler's new world order.

The intelligence blokes at the three army HQs concerned all reacted similarly.

'Why, that's just chicken shit, Major,' exclaimed the American.

'Ain't got time fer that crap,' said the Canadian.

'Never heard such balls, old chap,' the Brit concurred, delighted for once to be able to agree.

I was incoherent with agreement but enjoyed my trip, which shortly took me to Rheims and Cliquot. I sent in my name and Chimay received me. 'In four years,' he observed, 'you are only the second Englishman to call here. The first left only

---

2 Military expression for a 'jolly': a trip of some type involving maximum enjoyment and minimum effort or, in times of war, danger.
3 'Ike': General Eisenhower, Supreme Commander Allied Forces Europe.

about an hour ago – he was an old friend of mine, Ralph Cobbold. I wonder if perhaps you know him?'

Can you believe that? My Uncle Ralph had just left with a 3-ton lorryload of champagne for the Coldstream Guards – getting in smartly before military bureaucracy nabbed the lot.

Well, as you can imagine, the party was on. When I left, Chimay insisted on presenting me with a twenty-five-bottle case and let me buy another.[4] I drank the one with my mates and eventually flogged the other in Brussels for an obscene profit.

In Paris I was expecting to freeload with Great Aunt Rosie. I barely knew the old bag except as the besotted owner of a couple of misanthropic Pekinese who ate only foie gras, slept upon silken cushions and insisted that all the blinds be drawn during their afternoon 'nappynaps'.

I found the enormous *hôtel* behind its imposing gates and hauled on the bell.

After an age a shambling old retainer appeared and regarded me with nervous apprehension. I remembered him. 'Monsieur Pierre,' I said. 'You do not remember me? *C'est le petit Geoffroy.* How is Madame my great aunt?'

The poor old fellow peered at me through rheumy eyes. 'Yes, yes, I do recall. There was a terrible fuss because you kicked Chingching after he bit you. Oh Monsieur, we have had a terrible time, a terrible time and poor Madame . . .' He paused and then, to my embarrassment, began to weep a little.

The sad truth came out in dribs and drabs. Aunt Rosie, it turned out, had been one of the most prominent hostesses in Paris during the Occupation. About three minutes after the last German had left, members of the heroic Resistance had shaved old Rosie's head and painted a swastika on her bum.

---

4   A tradition that I happen to know continued for very many years between the grateful owner of at least one other major champagne house and the lucky cavalry regiment that liberated it.

She had deemed it prudent to leave for her place in the country until things cooled off.

I saw no reason not to move in – and did.

And then it was on to Brussels, which had been liberated just over a week after Paris. There I met Jacky, who was to turn into one of my long-time on/off loves. Ours was one of those 'fatal attraction' scenarios. A reception in one of those huge houses set the scene. Jacky was slim and attractive, a bit toothy – but with the all-important gap in the right place – superbly turned out, and spoke perfect English. In those days I too was slim, superbly turned out and spoke perfect English.

We were in bed well before midnight.

The affair prospered rather too fast for Papa le Baron, a dreary old fart worth millions.

Jacky had her own sumptuous apartments on the second floor of the family mansion and I was happy to pleasure her mornings and afternoons to my utmost and her limit. But women can be funny and enough is never quite enough. Jacky was so besotted that nothing would do but that we spend an entire night together in each other's arms. I had a funny feeling about this but gave in to her. I am nothing if not a survivor and so made damn sure that my clothes were tucked safely out of sight under the bed and close to hand.

We set to. It was well past the hour when gentlemen friends should have said their adieus. Jacky was one of those slow starters but her breathing was getting a bit shorter when, sure enough, Papa tapped on her door demanding entrance. He knew full well that her officer friend was in there with her.

The officer friend, giving his well-known imitation of a rat zipping up a drainpipe, was out of the window in a flash. He found himself standing on a six-inch ledge above the Avenue

Emil Demot and clinging to the outside of the shutters. It was freezing and he was, of course, naked.

Through the shutters I watched Papa scuttle around the apartment like a red-eyed ferret while Jacky, with a sheet up to her chin, was a picture of injured innocence.

The moon was shining on my arse. My 'precious gift to womankind' had shrunk to nothing and a small but enthusiastic crowd was beginning to collect below.

Bloody Papa, having made abject apologies for his unfounded suspicions, felt obliged to have a little father–daughter chat which seemed to last for ages. I was getting desperate out there.

At last he left and I was able to stumble back into bed. Jacky had the helpless giggles and it took her quite a while to get us back to where we should have been.

Come the end of the war, the powers that be must have decided I had been doing a pretty good job tracking down all those imaginary werewolves and what-have-yous, because they made me the counter-intelligence head honcho for all Germany north of the Kiel Canal up to the border of Denmark. In my area were elements of two German army corps. Trying to escape from the Russians and the retribution they were known to be dishing out to their old friends in the Wehrmacht, they had ended up in my bailiwick at the time of the German surrender on 8 May 1945.

In addition there were 90 per cent of what remained of the ruling Nazi hierarchy, some of whom had formed what came to be known as the Flensburg Government: the doomed attempt to form a German government, post-Hitler. To wit: Doenitz, Speer, Rosenberg, von Fritsche, Himmler – the list went on.

There had been compiled a list of about 4000 names split into four categories of arrest priority.

Class 1: Supernasties   24
Class 2: Nasties   about 320
Class 3: Shits   about 1500
Class 4: Bastards   the balance.

Anyone with an SS rank of corporal and above was a man-datory arrest. Members of the Abwehr, Gestapo or SD were, of course, prime targets. Many of these types, masquerading as privates, orderlies or whatever, were trying to hide among the tens of thousands of ordinary German servicemen in Schleswig-Holstein.

A top priority was to capture Himmler, probably the very nastiest of the surviving supernasties, who was said to be advocating continued resistance. We heard that he was holed up in Glucksburg Castle, an imposing late medieval castle set on the edge of a lake.

What happened next was described by Geoff's Swedish friend Carl Aschan in a letter to the *Daily Telegraph* after he had read Geoff's obituary in that newspaper:

Colonel Gordon-Creed was then in charge of 21 Army Group Security in the above area bordering Denmark, where I collabor-ated on behalf of MI6. A top-secret signal reported the presence of Heinrich Himmler at the former Danish Royal Castle of Glucksburg near Flensburg.

Colonel Gordon-Creed promptly raised a troop of fifty Belgian special forces, and we raided Glucksburg, whose owner greeted us in acceptable English:

'Gentlemen, what is the meaning of this intrusion? Do you realise who I am? The Grand Duke of Mecklenburg, cousin of King George VI and grandson of Queen Victoria.'

Colonel Gordon-Creed replied: 'Yes sir, we know, but would have preferred that you did not remind us.'

We did not find Himmler, but we arrested Speer, Hitler's

armaments minister, later sentenced to twenty years' imprisonment.

Geoffrey was a friend I never forgot. The duke later accused us of having stolen his family jewels, and complained to King George. I received a visit by a CID inspector whom I informed that our duties were more important than ducal jewels, of which we knew nothing.

Regrettably we did not benefit from this or other booty, as we might have done in earlier wars.

Geoff too was investigated. The interviewing Scotland Yard inspector carried a letter of authorisation signed by no less a person than the Home Secretary. Geoff was much put out by this allegation, not least because, as far as he was concerned, had he helped himself to the jewels he would have avoided the financial problems that he was to endure later. Aschan was equally indignant. In an unpublished memoir, which he copied to Geoff, he wrote that the only war booty he took home was a pair of German army binoculars taken from a captured general. He felt so guilty about this one bit of opportunism that, had he had the man's name, he said, he would have returned them.

The investigation ended in both men being exonerated and, as far as I can ascertain, the jewels have never been found.

On 23 May 1945, the stage was set for the big Nazi round-up. I had fourteen Field Security sections under my command for the search and arrest operation, together with two infantry battalions and a tank regiment to form the cordon. Were we worried? Not really. But no soldier relishes the idea of surviving five years of war only to get hurt when it is all meant to be over bar the celebrations. Less than a month before, the Kraut die-hards had been fighting to the last man, stringing up from lamp-posts anyone – be they 70 or 10 years old, or anyone in between capable of holding a rifle – who did not share their vision of their 1000-year Reich. So I was going in mob-handed. That, I reckoned, should prevent any resistance. Were there to be any trouble there would be only one result. In the event, and as expected, they gave us no trouble.

I naturally considered that I should be the one to have the personal satisfaction of arresting Gross Admiral Doenitz who, since Hitler's suicide on 30 April, had been the president of the Reich. Doenitz was supposed to be in the VIP quarters in the large naval barracks in Flensburg. As it turned out he wasn't, but he was pulled in anyway by one of my officers about an hour later.

His deputy, Grand Admiral von Friedeburg – newly appointed as commander in chief of the German navy – was there, however, when we arrived, and I rapped on his door. An aide, who I subsequently learned was his son, opened the door.

'I wish to see the Admiral.'

'*Jawohl, Herr Major. Ein moment, bitte.*'

When he appeared I said: 'We are arresting you, Admiral.'

'*Warum?*' He turned very pale and I made no reply. 'May I pack some things?'

'Of course.' The Admiral turned on his heel, took a hand-kerchief from his breast pocket and appeared to blow his nose. Before he had taken five steps he paused, swayed and crashed to the floor unconscious. His heart stopped beating about five minutes later. His son was greatly distressed and I felt sorry for him.

The top-priority targets were collected in a schoolhouse and there I went to count the 'bag'. We had again missed Himmler, and three others. We learned later that Himmler had already been picked up in Bremen. He too took cyanide rather than face trial.

Before putting the rest of them on a plane for Rhine Army HQ, I addressed them: 'I am responsible for delivering you alive to Rhine Army. One among you, Grand Admiral von

Friedeburg, has chosen to take a cyanide pill and so, regret-tably, I am obliged to search each one of you.'

There were angry protests, which I ignored.

'Admiral Doenitz, you will accompany me to the next room.'

In the next room my German-speaking corporal sat at a deal table.

Under his long black raincoat Doenitz was in full naval uni-form and carried his marshal's baton. He made a very imposing figure. At my order he began to strip. The metamor-phosis was remarkable, and whoever coined the phrase 'clothes make the man' was no fool. Eventually there was revealed a spindle-shanked and furious man who, believe it or not, was wearing four sets of underwear!

For me the moment of final victory in Europe came with my corporal's finger firmly rammed up the arse of the head Nazi.

We found poison sewn into the clothes of a couple of the others.

On arrival at Rhine Army they all complained about my treatment of them and my lack of respect for their position and importance. Arrogant bastards! They had not yet accepted the reality of what they were – war criminals.[5]

It was not until some time later that I learned that Admiral Doenitz was a really fine and honourable man. I regretted the humiliation that I had subjected him to. *Enfin*, I was not to know at the time. *Vae victis*, and all that.

I enjoyed a year or so in Flensburg, set right on the German–Danish border, living in a very large house furnished in typically bad taste. Where the prosperous owners had gone to

5   Doenitz was sentenced to ten years in prison at the Nuremberg war crimes trials. He lived the rest of his life in relative obscurity and died of a heart attack in 1980.

ground after the place was requisitioned I had no idea, but they had kindly left behind a cook and a skivvy, presumably to count the spoons from time to time.

Physical manning of the frontier post was done by the military police, but control of who was permitted to come and go came under one of my Field Security sections and, there-fore, under me.

I got on well with the Danes and could appreciate their deadpan sense of humour, which must have driven the Krauts wild. Their war effort never amounted to much more than consuming as much as they could of all the butter, cream and cheese that they produced, thus ensuring that there would be less to export to the Reich.

Co-operation between my office and their police and intel-ligence people was 100 per cent – I made sure of that.

They had their own Quisling,[6] whose name escapes me and who had yet to be found and arrested. Obviously he was not going hang around in Denmark after the surrender, so where might he be? Somewhere on my side of the frontier presumably. The Danes provided me with all the info that they had on him and I circulated it among my sections, put-ting a high priority on his arrest.

It didn't take all that long. About two weeks later one of my officers drove up with this large, blond and perfectly self-composed Dane. 'I'm pretty sure this is your man, Sir. He's not talking.'

'Very good, thanks. I'll get the Danes over this eve-ning . . . they should know immediately.'

We locked him in a secure coal cellar and I sent urgently for

6 After the conquest of Norway by the Nazis in April 1940, Vidkun Quisling led the pro-German collaborationist government. 'Quisling' has been a term of opprobrium ever since. Quisling ended up against a wall in 1945, shot as a traitor and for war crimes. It is possible this Danish Quisling was Nils Svenningsen, who effectively ran the Danish government after it had been dissolved by the Nazis in August 1943.

my two special chums, the local assistant superintendent, CID, and the intelligence bloke. We scratched around and put on a pretty decent dinner with, of course, any amount of akvavit firewater and wine.

'I hope I may have a little surprise for you chaps,' I said over coffee and cognac. 'I'm not entirely sure, but I'm hopeful.'

I had the prisoner brought up from the cellar and I certainly got my effect. Chairs were scraped back and pistols were reached for. 'My God, Major. How did you find him? Where?'

'Is it him beyond doubt?'

'Oh, yes.'

'Good. Right, well I never saw him. Take him back with you and make up your report all about patient police work paying dividends, but do mention that it was with some small help from your friends across the frontier.'

Oh boy! The headlines, the promotions and the medals . . .!

I did pretty well out of it too: the exclusive use of a very fine villa on the fjord, property of ex-Consul-General Best – who had been the head Nazi in Denmark – and the exclusive use of a 100 square foot sloop, also the property of the above, for as long as I remained in Germany. To the victor the (modest) spoils!

I even got to go on leave occasionally. I was on my way back to England for a much needed week off and was humping, as part of my baggage, a case of Hennessy cognac – as rare as hen's teeth in benighted, rationed England. The train was routed through Hanover for some reason, and when we got there I remembered that Bertie, an old mate of mine whom I had bumped into occasionally during the war – a bon viveur, dedicated cocksman and a pretty fair cricketer in his day – was stationed there doing some intelligence job. On the spur of the moment I decided to look him up. A military police Jeep took me to his quarters.

'My dear fellow. What a nice surprise. How long can you stay?'

'Not more than a day or so. I'm expected back on the nest.'

'Well, it's a bit late for today, but tomorrow evening we can take along a bottle of cognac to this place that I know of. There's two gorgeous birds, both about twenty-four or twenty-five. The blonde is the daughter of some defunct Kraut field marshal and the other is dark and a real stunner, but I don't know much about her. Sound good?'

Did it!

'In fact we'll make up a hamper. That should cheer them up.' At that time food meant as much as money to the Germans, some of whom were near starvation. For that matter, their women were out of bounds. We were not meant to be 'fraternising with the enemy', as the killjoys liked to describe it. Not that I gave a hoot about that.

We arrived at the huge apartment they shared, bringing with us incredible riches in the form of two bottles of cognac, coffee, tea, chocolate, sugar, twelve tins of bully beef and a couple of hundred Benson & Hedges: anything they did not use themselves they would be able to barter.

Things trotted along at gratifying speed: blonde for Bertie, brunette for me. It must have been around 11 p.m. and we were humping with great enthusiasm on her enormous bed when suddenly the door was flung open and the light was switched on, to reveal . . .

Hubby!

Could ever a man find himself at a greater disadvantage than I did then? I had no idea there even was a bloody husband.

Hubby stood tall in the doorway for perhaps a quarter of a minute.

'God save ze King,' he declaimed in a loud voice. He switched off the light, backed out and closed the door quietly.

After another very stiff cognac, I concluded that, at least so far as I was concerned, the evening's entertainment was over. For the next fifty years, whenever Bertie and I met, our first greeting was always: 'God save ze King' – it was our little joke.

The big round-up day when we pulled in a few of the nastier 'nasties' had just been the beginning. Over the next fourteen months there were to be something like thirty thousand arrests as we attempted to carry out our masters' de-Nazification plans. Both of the following incidents occurred on the same day.

I was behind my desk after the round-up, writing a report for my boss, when one of my officers came in. 'I've a bloke who has pitched up whom I think you ought to see, Sir.'

'Oh? What sort of bloke?'

'He says he is a rocket expert.'

'Does he, by God? Well, trot him in.'

I had better explain here that it shortly became clear that, while our leaders wanted to stick Nazis in prison and put them on trial for war crimes, when it came to their scientists they took a very different approach. The atomic bombs that were shortly to be dropped on Japan were, in certain respects, already old technology in that rockets were the way forward. Hitler had already demonstrated this with his truly terrifying V2 doomsday machines that had started devastating London in the latter part of the war. Had he had more of them and had he got them into action earlier, things might have turned out a bit differently. Anyway, we wanted their scientists in general and their rocket scientists in particular, as did the Russians. The race was on as to who could get hold of them first. So bringing in a rocket scientist would be a definite feather in my cap.

The man who was ushered in looked tired and drawn. He bowed politely and introduced himself: Ludwig von Hutten.

The name meant nothing. I gestured to a chair. 'Please tell me what this is all about, Herr von Hutten.'

He started off with a great flood of words; I caught *rock-etten*, London, Peenemünde, *Vergaltungswaffen*,[7] Russians.

I held up my hand. 'Please,' I said. I offered him a cigarette and sent for my German-speaking corporal.

'Now then. Perhaps you would begin again. A little more slowly.'

I soon realised that perhaps I had here a real plum. Terrified of falling into Russian hands, von Hutten had left East Prussia with Wernher von Braun,[8] with whom he had been working closely on the top priority rocket programme. They had separated when von Braun wanted to head for the Bavarian Alps, where he had kin and where he thought it more likely to find Americans to whom he could surrender, and to whom he did. Von Hutten had continued westwards alone, preferring the British alternative.

Could I, would I help him?

The wires hummed.

I sent him with my driver to my rather grand house and gave instructions that he be offered a hot bath, a meal, drinks and a bed. A plane from Hamburg would pick him up tomorrow.

I was feeling pretty good about this but was still in my office a bit later than usual, writing up my report about what had happened – always the effing reports – when there was a commotion outside in the corridor. My office door was flung open and a beefy, very nasty-looking Kraut filled the doorway. Behind him was a red-faced MP corporal.

---

7   The German rocket research centre based on the island of Peenemünde, off the north German coast. *Vergaltungswaffen*: literally 'vengeance weapons', the V1 and V2 rockets with which Hitler had hoped to change the war.
8   Wernher von Braun had been in charge of the V2 (Vengeance weapon 2) rocket programme. He became the pre-eminent rocket scientist of the last century and was the man in charge of the Saturn programme – among others – that was to first put man on the moon. The fact that he had joined the Nazi Party and was a major in the SS was of less importance to the Americans than the fact he helped put them ahead of Russia in the space race. He became an American citizen in 1955.

'Sorry, Sir. Couldn't stop 'im, Sir. Says 'e's . . .'

The Kraut interrupted. 'I'm Wilhelm Pieck. Order this fool to take his hands off me. I demand that you . . .'

Of course I knew all about Herr bloody Pieck. A hard-line Communist from way back who had spent most of the war in Moscow and who had just returned with the Red Army. A few years later he was to become president of East Germany.

I barely looked at him. 'Corporal,' I said, 'arrest this man and lock him up somewhere by himself. If he resists you may shoot him. Have him stripped and body searched and bring me every scrap of paper you can find on him.'

I left the bastard in solitary for forty-eight hours, on rye bread and water, and then sent for him. 'I am satisfied that you are who you say you are and not some SS Obersturmbann-führer, as I suspected you might be from your arrogant attitude. You are free to leave.'

'But I demand transport to . . .'

'Demanding again, are we, Pieck? I will go so far as to give you a *laissez-passer*. Now find your own transport and do not pass this way again.'

The sod eventually found his way to SHAEF headquarters in Paris. In response to his yells of outrage, some brown-nosing nerd was actually dispatched to verify his story of a drunken British major in control of affairs in Flensburg who did nothing but booze, play the piano and bellow out the *Horst Wessel Lied*.

He was wrong, of course. The song I always liked to bellow out, and still do, is that wonderfully over-the-top Nazi march-ing song: '*Wir fahren gegen Engeland*' – 'We sail against England'. Somebody must play the piano, as I can't, and I must have a few good blokes to crash in with the 'pom-poms'. Great stuff when you are in the right mood. *Sieg Heil!*

★   ★   ★

After Germany, just as my demob was in sight in mid-1946, they offered me the job of military attaché to the legations in Beirut and Damascus, with the acting rank of lieutenant colonel. It sounded like fun. Having no other plans and like a damn fool, I took the job for two years.

It turned out that I was to be the service attaché, based in the embassy and representing the interests of the army, navy and air force in Syria and the Lebanon. Not to put too fine a point on it, I was back in the spying game, but much more at the drinks and socialising end than the sharp end. What the hell. Lebanon was a sybaritic paradise in those days before the religious maniacs managed to rip it apart. They used to call it the Riviera of the Middle East: sophisticated towns, wonderful beaches and great skiing a few hours back in the mountains.

However, I discovered that the honour of serving my king in those capacities had cost me around four thousand quid of my own money – the tight bastards expected you to carouse and entertain on an epic scale, but had no intention of paying you for so doing. That was a fortune in those days and I couldn't afford to keep it up. So, come the end of February 1948, I decided I had had enough of khaki, resigned and had myself demobbed back to Kenya.

Somewhat bizarrely – and this is the way the army works, especially in wartime when promotion tends to come rather quicker than you might expect and for all the wrong reasons – by 1948 I was still officially only a captain. That said, I had worn a major's rank ever since we had dropped the Asopos Viaduct back in summer 1943. I had remained a major in north Germany, and for my last two years in the Lebanon I wore the rank of lieutenant colonel. But when I retired, it was still only with the rank of captain. However, out of the good-ness of their hearts, the War Office then granted me the rank of 'honorary major' – not that this concession meant the bean-stealers had to pay me a major's pension. To hell with that, I decided, I had been a colonel for the last two years, and a colonel I would remain.

I had been a soldier almost since the day I had left school, back in those far distant days of 1939. I had not made too bad a fist of the military. It was time to see if I could prosper in the civilian world.

EPILOGUE

The answer, sadly, was that Geoff was to discover, and very quickly, that the qualities that had made him such a feared and effective warrior were not necessarily the qualities that made for a successful businessman.

Soldiers the world over dream of getting into the booze trade when they retire – having spent long years in uniform downing the linctus, they make the mistake of thinking they will be brilliant at selling it. Geoff was no exception:

I come from a longish line of alcoholics on the male side. Uncle Raymond lost an eye to the cork coming out of a bottle of Bollinger held between his knees at a coming-out party at Blenheim Palace. Great Uncle Cecil toppled backwards off a balcony and broke his neck. There have been countless others in my family too numerous to count, but oddly enough there has never been any mention of their women tippling.

Anyhow, and perhaps following that primal family urge, he bought a wine business in Kenya. It was the cause of much fun but, and sadly, having fun is no driver of a successful business. He ended up 'losing a bundle', but managed to sell out before it ruined him.

Next up, he decided to profit from a government initiative to use fish as a cheap source of protein by building a sea-fish farm on the coast of south Tanganyika – modern-day Tanzania. Ponds were dug to grow the fish. He failed to anticipate one thing, though. The local hippos appreciated the ponds as much as did

Geoff's fish. By moving to and fro, as hippos tend to do, they smashed down the banks. The fish escaped: another disaster.

Next, and still in Tanganyika, he pegged out a 500-acre farm in the bush. This was altogether more brutal work. He built himself a hut and then had to start clearing the ground. His first task was to shoot a man-eating lion which, to his certain knowledge, had eaten twenty-three locals in the past two years. Come the day, everyone for miles around formed a beating line while he and his .350 Rigby Magnum rifle were placed at the far end, under a tree and with limited visibility.

I sat and waited.

In due course the line of net carriers, drummers, spearmen and musketeers formed up and began beating towards me. From the sound, as I could see nothing, they had got to within a half mile of me when there were was a sudden hullabaloo, a few bangs from some ancient muskets and then a loud hubbub. The lion, I discovered, had broken back through the line, fatally swatting a couple of drummers on its way.

'And that should be that,' I thought, much relieved.

Not so. To my vast surprise the line was re-formed.

Just before dusk, up he trotted. I duly drilled him at about thirty yards. He was a huge beast, well over ten foot and in his prime. It had to be done, of course, but what a shame to kill something so magnificent.

Never in my life had I been anywhere so snake-infested – cobras, mambas and pythons – the damn cobras were the most intrusive and kept coming into my hut at night.

One morning the foreman pitched up to ask where to find one of the boundary marker posts which were under three or more years' growth of grass. I knew where one was and set off on a compass bearing, walking behind my head man swinging his machete at the eight-foot buffalo grass. I was close in behind him and was on my left leg stepping over a small wag-a-bikje thorn bush when up pops Snaky, licks his chops and pins me in the right calf.

I yell and fall on my arse. The head man yells and fucks off left. The snake pisses off right.

What to do?

I took from my breast pocket that part of the Fitzsimmons snake bite kit I always carried with me. I knew I was meant to make an incision across each puncture wound to induce local bleeding and use a tourniquet to inhibit the poison travelling up my leg. I made one brave slash but lacked the guts to much more than scratch across the second hole.[1]

I opened the rusting tin and found two 10 cc phials of murky serum and a hypodermic syringe with a rusty needle. I was not encouraged to note that the serum had an expiry date of some six months back.

Disregarding all this, I stuck myself everywhere: around the site of the bite; in my thigh and in my belly – as per the instructions on the tin. Not nice.

My leg was beginning to swell and hurt like hell. I then read the small print on the inside of the lid of the can. It described in detail the symptoms I could expect:

'Pain.'

'Swelling.'

'Shortness of breath.'

'Acute anxiety.'

'Delirium.'

And then the punchline at the bottom: 'Followed by collapse and death.' Oh boy.

They were spot on with the first five, and for a time it was touch and go with the sixth. I lay half in and out for days, it

---

1 Modern snake bite kits tend to use a vacuum for extracting the venom, doubtless for this very reason: it takes a very desperate person to start hacking at themselves to extract snake poison.

seemed. My workers arranged themselves helpfully in a circle around my hut, keening: 'Woolawoolawoola'.

Eventually I felt capable of staggering to my shotgun and blew off both barrels through the screen door. 'Get back to work, you bastards.'

A doctor told me later that I had been lucky as the bite had been far from my heart and the teeth had missed any large veins. To be safe I should have injected twice the amount of serum. Despite this, I have never had any fear of snakes and never harm them in any way if I can possibly avoid doing so. I was trespassing on his patch and would have done the same in his place, and that is an end of the matter.

Matters got worse. Ursula, his wife, had accompanied him to the Lebanon and then to Africa. At some stage she caught tuberculosis. TB is now entirely preventable by immunisation and treatable if caught. Back then it was a killer. Ursula had to leave Africa and go to a TB clinic back home, while an increasingly desperate Geoff worked the farm and tried to pay for her treatment while keeping his head above water . . . and have some sort of fun out of life in the meantime.

He was also now as good as wifeless once again, always a recipe for trouble.

As a youth of 16 I had pasted up in my locker at school a glossy picture of Ginger Rogers. Oh, how I used to fantasise about kissing those luscious lips. Decades later and back in Kenya, I met and made a friend of the actor John Loder, who had until fairly recently been married to a fabulous beauty, actress Hedy Lamarr. John was a brave soldier – he had fought at Gallipoli in the First War – but a lousy actor. However, thanks to his incredible good looks he had scratched along fairly well, starring in rubbishy Hollywood B movies.

We used to drink quite a bit, John and I, and late one night, well into our cups, I asked him: 'Tell me, John . . . How many pokes do you reckon you've had over the years?'

'Well,' he said, 'I've never really thought about it, but let's see.' He started totting up on his fingers.

'Right,' he said. 'I've been on dozens of films, OK? That means the same number of leading ladies and, of course, their stand-ins. Then there were about thirty years of parties, starlets and bimbo wannabes. So I suppose, give or take about fifty either way, about a thousand would be a fair figure.'

I gaped, almost lost for words in admiration. 'Er . . . What about Ginger Rogers?' I ventured. 'Did you ever . . .?'

'Ginger?' he said. 'God, yes. But she's got hairy tits, you know . . .'

Somehow I survived the crash of my boyhood dreams.

That was about 1952 and Clark Gable, Grace Kelly and Ava Gardner were in Kenya making a film called *Mogambo*. My current love at the time was working on the film so I had occasion to visit her on location once or twice. Everyone on the set adored Ava – in fact the world appeared to be in love with her and some even reckoned her the most beautiful woman on this planet.

Anyhow, once filming was through many of the cast came up to Nairobi for some fun. I happened to be there and met Ava again, and the chemistry was mutual and compelling. She laid it on the line. If I so wished she would be my woman, and only mine, for one week. After that I would never hear from her again, nor would she expect to hear from me. No calls, no whining, no nothing. Finito!

'You want? No?'

'I want.'

She was the perfect lover and courtesan. Not another man even existed in the universe while I was in the saddle. I was privileged. In the end I had eight days.

But it did bother me a bit to think that I was related, 'by

injection' as it were, to that cretin actor Mickey Rooney and that wop Frank Sinatra and certainly scores of others. But enough! She was memorable. Come to think, and looking back over the field, I have barely achieved a fifth of old John's tally and, of them, there have only been about a dozen of my partners who remain in my memory as truly 'memorable', but Ava was certainly one.

At that key moment – with funds running low – there was an eight-month drought: catastrophic on a 500-acre farm in Tanganyika. Nevertheless, the labour had to be paid and the animals fed. It would also have been nice to have been paid myself.

What was the best option? Plough and plant for the third time, and hope? I needed to raise some scratch, and fast.

I wrote to a hunter chum of mine. 'Try shooting crocs' came his reply.

I lost no time. I bought a twenty-foot canoe and attached a bracket to affix an outboard engine. My tented camp on the riverbank housed my cook/servant and two skinners. With me in the canoe would travel three guides of the Makonda tribe.

One would swing a grappling iron on a fifteen-foot rope, the second would wield an axe and the third would carry a back-up flashlight and lengths of strong cord. I had the main flashlight and the 9.3 mm Mauser, a brute of a rifle with one hell of a kick. It was designed to stop just about anything, although I would not have recommended it for elephant. Ever since the Western Desert I have been a firm believer in having more than adequate firepower at my disposal. The Mauser was a perfect croc-killer.

The drill was simple. I would shoot a hippo or two and a few waterbuck. They would be cut open and pegged down as firmly as possible on the sandbanks at the water's edge, each carcass about a mile apart. After a few days, when the baits were stinking to high heaven, we would chug up the river after sundown looking for the red eyes of feeding crocs in the torchlight. We always could, and did, approach to a few feet before I fired at the head. I wanted to kill them as quickly and cleanly as possible.

Then the bloke with the grapple would haul the croc up and across the side of the boat. The croc would be dead at that point, but its nervous system didn't always know that. It was the job of the second chap to whack down with an axe on to the base of the tail, paralysing the brute. This was essential, as the power in a croc's thrashing tail has to be experienced to be believed and none of us wanted to be knocked half senseless into a river full of the said croc's cousins and close family. The third chap's job was to lash the dead beasts alongside for towing to the camp for skinning, salting and sun curing.

It was a horrible three months of stench and fevers – malaria and dengue, potential killers both. It was the usual story of the prime producer getting bugger all for his efforts. The bastards in the Kenya tannery only paid £5 for a skin.

Doing this and that over the next twelve months, alluvial gold-mining for instance, I netted about £3000. That paid a lot of medical bills for my wife in those days.

It was all for nothing, as she died anyway.[2] They invented a cure for TB not long afterwards.

Coronations and funerals are functions for which the Brits display a true talent. A thousand witnessed wartime deaths left me unmoved, except for those of a very few close and loved comrades. Peacetime funerals always induce in me uncontrollable giggles. Back in England, at my first wife's funeral, we all, sisters, brothers, in-laws, were helpless. Under

2   Ursula died in England on 13 July 1954, although the drug that finally took the fight to TB had been introduced in about 1952: it seems as if she, and he, were literally a year or so too late.

stress one's perceptions are so much more acute. Her funeral had it all: the Dickensian caricature of an undertaker, the ghastly platitudes of an ignorant priest, and even the clumsy drunken oaf who only just saved himself from falling into the hole and landing on top of the coffin. All potentially absurd, and given the choice of laughing or crying I have always tended to the former. Why, even at such a desperate funeral? But then, why not?

The widower returned to Africa, but not to abstinence.

I was best man at Johnny T's wedding. During the reception I sniffed up behind his sister Claire and, half in jest, reminded her that in 'the better social circles', to pleasure the chief bridesmaid had traditionally been one of the best man's perks, if not an actual duty! This got her attention.

'Are you sure?' she asked. 'I wonder why nobody ever told me before?'

Anyhow, in no time a plan was formed. Then she dropped her bombshell. 'I'm staying with Granny, but you mustn't come before half past ten and you mustn't drive up the driveway because of the noise of the gravel. I'll put a light in my window so you'll know which is my room.'

Let me tell you about Granny.

A Dame of the British Empire, a Grand Master of the Masons, the arbitrix of morals and a blinding snob, she could fairly be described as a snorter of the old school and a great pain in the ass. One chum who took a wigging from her as a youth said that, given a choice, he would sooner face a cow elephant defending her calf.

On the dot of ten thirty, having homed in on Claire's beacon, I was climbing through her window. 'We mustn't make a sound,' she hissed in a horny whisper, clawing off my jacket and trousers. 'Granny's in the next room.'

There was no time for further disrobing before we arrived, with a loud twang, on the Field of Action, an ancient brass bed, sway-backed and with knobs askew. This being our first encounter I was not to know that Claire was remarkably quick out of the gate and that, once cranked up, there was no stopping her. I could do nothing about the bloody bed, which sounded like a Souza march, but – mindful of the She-Beast next door – did my best to muffle her with a pillow.

I rode a hard finish, but a loud honking from Claire, coupled with a convulsive heave which nearly unseated me, told me that she had beaten me to the wire by a 'twang'!

My final and triumphant thrust a second later coincided with a furious banging on the door and the stentorian voice of the She-Dragon, demanding to know:

'WHAT'S GOING ON?'

Holy shit! What indeed? Quicker than a rat up a drainpipe – a manoeuvre I had been perfecting ever since that episode with Jacky back in Brussels towards the end of the war – I grabbed my clothes and legged it out of the window: ground floor this time, thankfully!

Back in my room and hopefully safe, I cracked up laughing. I wondered whether Claire would break under torture. She didn't. I sometimes wonder whether the modern young get it all handed to them on a plate. No chase – no danger – no fun? Who knows? Who cares? The world wags on.

At some stage in 1954–5 Geoff gave up on his farming efforts in Tanganyika and returned to Kenya, and straight into the Mau Mau rebellion against British rule.[3] And here Geoff's story

3 Kenya Land and Freedom Army (KFLA), more commonly known as the Mau Mau, which, as its name implies, demanded independence from Britain. A state of emergency was first declared by the British on 20 October 1952, when extra troops were flown in to try to suppress the Mau Mau 'Emergency'. There

becomes somewhat vaguer and, to modern sensibilities, a whole lot murkier. He was happy to admit, though, that he was, as he put it: *'the head anti-Mau Mau honcho for the whole of Mount Kenya area'.*

The armed gangs were no longer up to much by the time of which I write; there was just the occasional attack on cattle. But the civilian sympathisers, or what we called the 'passive wing', were still active and needed to be kept firmly suppressed, lest the terror wing was allowed to explode once again. We used to mount 'sting' operations when we had reason to suspect there might be dirty work afoot.

Genuine captured terrorists were 'turned' and, in return for their lives, formed into 'pseudo'-terror gangs whom we would then use to gather yet more information.

Through interrogations and informers, we would get information about active members of the Mau Mau. Then, with a blackened face, wearing a woolly wig and vile-smelling rags – had our clothes not smelt suitably rancid, the locals would have instantly scented the difference – I, or one of the other officers, would set forth at nightfall with five or six of the pseudo-gang to investigate. Usually, and despite our best efforts, they spotted us for what we were and the reaction was panic and yells for help. We would fade back into the night.

Occasionally, we would be accepted as genuine Mau Mau and, as any terrorists worth their salt would do, we would demand their help with food and clothing and, even better,

followed a period of bloody and, it must be said, brutal warfare by both sides, but particularly by the British who did not cover themselves with any glory in their suppression of the uprising. White settlers appear to have been granted near carte blanche to fight an unofficial 'dirty war' alongside British forces. John Nottingham, a district colonial officer at the time, told the BBC in 2002 that what went on in the villages and camps was nothing less than 'brutal, savage torture'. Kenya finally got its independence in 1963.

ammunition or weapons. Then, when they supplied us with the goodies, we had them cold. Sometimes our target group would also be supporting a genuine Mau Mau terror cell and, when that happened, we would arrange to meet them: a meeting which would inevitably end in a kill or a capture.

Perhaps mindful of the consequences of such irregular behaviour, Geoff was appointed a Special Police Officer in March 1955, although it is unclear how long he had been active in anti-Mau Mau operations by then.

Unsurprisingly, while fighting terrorists he was up to some equally nefarious amorous activities of his own. His next move, however, took the biscuit.

He was newly widowed, somewhat down on his luck and certainly short of funds: the simple solution was to remarry someone with the supposed wherewithal to keep him in the manner accustomed. The problem for Geoff was that, while he had a coterie of girlfriends, many of whom adored him and continued to adore him and would do almost anything for him, they tended to realise marrying him would not be such a clever idea. One such wealthy girlfriend recalled him being quite put out when she turned down his proposal: having Geoff as a lover was one thing, having him as a husband something altogether different.

However, deliverance was at hand. One of his unofficial intelligence jobs required him to be at Nairobi Airport checking passengers – obviously looking for any troublemakers, but also checking that they were, literally, well enough to travel. Into Nairobi, one fine day in 1956, flew the young and glamorous Belinda Vaughan.

She was a woman on a mission. Her plane was refuelling at Nairobi before flying on to Rhodesia (modern-day Zimbabwe), where she was going to meet up with her fiancée. She never made it to the departure lounge.

Geoff, seeing his opportunity, declared she looked too ill to continue, and she was persuaded to stay

Back in England, the first the bemused Vaughan family knew of the change in plans was that, instead of being informed as they were expecting that Belinda had arrived safely with the family of her titled fiancé, they learnt instead that she had got no further than Kenya and, in September 1956 had married 'some man called Reed' – as Belinda's father put it in a clearly shocked telegram to one of her brothers. Put bluntly, once the wily hunter had made his mind up, the young and naive English socialite never stood a chance.

A few months after being made a Special Police Officer, in June 1955, Geoff was recommissioned into the British army as a lieutenant in the Intelligence Corps. The next day *The London Gazette* announced his immediate promotion to captain and the fact that he was to drop his honorary war rank of major. Geoff was back in the game again and doubtless grateful for some much needed income.

However, there is another possible reason for Geoff's return to the military intelligence fold. Back in the Cold War, elements of the Intelligence Corps could get up to all sorts of tricks. The following story has its roots in a family legend which the present generation are convinced is true. According to Belinda, Geoff had been re-employed for an altogether more sinister reason.

In Cyprus, at the eastern end of the Mediterranean, the Greeks were causing trouble once again, but this time for the British. Many on the island, a Crown colony,[4] were demanding *enosis* – independence. On 1 April 1955, a resistance movement called EOKA – ring any bells with wartime Greece and those confusing 'E' resistance movements once again? – led by General George Grivas, declared the start of an armed independence struggle. By

---

4 So critical is Cyprus to Britain, and thus NATO, in the eastern Mediterranean that there are still a couple of bases on the island that are deemed Crown colonies. From there, radio antennae monitor the chit-chat of the Middle East, right up to southern Russia. The Russians had their spy trawlers floating off our coasts, monitoring our signals traffic. We had Cyprus, monitoring theirs.

mid-1955 a full-scale insurgency was under way. An ever larger number of British soldiers were being committed and there was a rising death toll on both sides. Being a 'Greek' war, it was up close and vicious.

While Grivas might be the general in charge, Archbishop Makarios, the senior Orthodox churchman on the island, was EOKA's spiritual leader and, many reckoned, a whole lot more besides.

Priests are usually assumed to be unwarlike, but the British knew better. After all, many Orthodox priests had played important roles in the resistance in Greece back in the Second War. British security – as this was a Crown colony anti-terrorism operations were run by MI5, rather than MI6 – knew that priests were among the first to bring guns into Cyprus, and the Greek clergy were administering the loyalty or 'death oath' to those who joined EOKA.

Field Marshal Sir John Harding, DSO, MC, was a tough, uncompromising, infantryman who had fought in some of the same battles as Geoff in the Western Desert. Whether they ever met one another has to be pure conjecture. Then again, why not? Geoff, if you remember, served for a time on the staff of 1st Armoured Division under General Lumsden, when Harding was commanding the nearby 7th Armoured Division.

Come 3 October 1955, Harding had retired from the army – although, to be technical about this, a field marshal never 'retires' – and was appointed the new governor of Cyprus. Harding soon concluded that he had to choose between going one of two ways: either the peaceful, talking route, or getting really nasty and playing EOKA at their own game. Whatever his personal preferences, Harding had no intention of losing the colony and was, in the final analysis, fully prepared to take the less pleasant route if pushed.

The situation was sort of being contained when, on 3 March 1956, EOKA upped the stakes. Their plan was to explode a bomb on board a British Handley Page Hermes passenger plane which was due to be flying sixty-eight passengers – wives and children of service personnel – from Nicosia back to the UK. Set to explode two hours into the flight, the bomb blew prematurely, just as the passengers were about to embark. Nobody was hurt, but the plane was destroyed. The consequences, had it gone off when it was meant to, would have been cataclysmic. And, to add further insult, a terrorist took a potshot at the bus as the shaken passengers were being driven back from the airport. A month later EOKA repeated the trick and destroyed a Douglas Dakota on the ground.

Modern sensibilities have grown semi-accustomed to what can be expected from terrorists. Back then this was deemed as going beyond the pale. The gloves were now off as far as Britain was concerned.

On 9 March 1956 – six days after the failed bombing – Archbishop Makarios was lifted by British troops in a sting operation. Arriving at Nicosia Airport thinking he was to board a plane to Athens for talks with the Greek government, he instead found himself ushered at gunpoint to a different plane, which flew him to the Seychelles and temporary exile.

If the plane bombing was not bad enough, matters then got personal. Almost a fortnight later, on 21 March, EOKA placed another bomb. This time it was under Field Marshal Harding's bed. The fuse again failed to work properly, although this time in reverse. Instead of the bomb going off too early, as it had at Nicosia Airport, it went off too late. The Field Marshal had enjoyed a full night's sleep and was already up and about the next morning when it was found and taken outside, where it exploded in spectacular style. If there was ever a reason to get really nasty, this had to be it. Apparently British intelligence had been warning of a terrorist 'spectacular' against Harding in person for some time. Harding put a price on Grivas's head. But, if the following story is true, he may well have done more besides.

The story – folklore, call it what you will – in the Gordon-Creed household is that Geoff was tasked to be the gunman should Archbishop Makarios, the figurehead of the rebellion, need taking down (although I think that it is not impossible that for Makarios – who, as we have seen, was now exiled in the Seychelles – we might read Grivas). EOKA was killing British soldiers, up close and personal – shooting them in bars, putting bombs under their beds, targeting their wives and children – and someone was needed who was prepared to get equally nasty with the EOKA leadership. The family story is that that somebody was Geoff.

Back in the Lebanon in 1946, Geoff had become good friends with one General Farid Chehab. By the late 1940s, when Geoff had served his last two years in Beirut, Chehab had long been very senior in Lebanese intelligence, and by the time Geoff was leaving Chehab was Director General of the Sûreté Générale, and Director of Interpol for the Middle East.

Family legend has it that, just as Geoff was getting ready to rock and roll, General Chehab – soon to be Deputy Head of Interpol and a man who really did tend to know what was going on – contacted his old mate to warn him that his cover had been blown. Don't forget that Cyprus is but a short hop from Lebanon and there had long been a tradition of the island being a melting pot for spies of many different persuasions. So it would have been logical for a spymaster like Chehab to have known if there was something untoward about to blow.

All this is, of course, but conjecture. There remains, however, one tantalising, supporting footnote.

Twenty or so years later, over drinks in Geoff's study in South Carolina, the question of why his eldest son, Nick, had an extra name in his passport – albeit and confusingly, one which did not appear on his birth certificate – was raised by said interested son. Geoff became unusually cagey and would not answer. In fact, if the extra name had been something 'normal', something broadly

Anglo-Saxon, Nick might never even have thought to raise the matter.

But: 'Why have I got the name Farid in my passport?' That had to be a legitimate question, and there had to be a reason. And there was ...

It was, said Geoff, the name of his old spymaster friend.

And why, Nick persisted, did he carry the name?

It was, said Geoff, because he owed Farid his life.

Fascinated, Nick wanted to know more. But Geoff clammed up, saying, 'You don't need to know.'

Nick has no more to offer on this story except that, according to Belinda, they had been based in the UK during the lead-up to 'the job', and when it went wrong the family – Nick had arrived on the scene in January 1957 – had to leave England in a tearing hurry. This is something that a wife, even a wife being kept in the dark, would have known all about. Come March 1957 they were on a boat bound for Jamaica, where Belinda's father lived. Geoff's commission was terminated at much the same time, April 1957 (it is something of a given that you get a month's termination leave in the army).

Why Geoff? The answer to that may have been that he had a track record second to few when it came to clandestine operations with or against the Greeks. His exploits at the Asopos Viaduct had certainly earned him a certain celebrity status among his fellow warriors back in the day.[5] Moreover, he was still in action and proving himself as effective as ever in counter-terrorism 'black ops' in Kenya.

---

5 Today, the one exploit from Greece we all tend to know is Patrick Leigh Fermor's capture of the German general commanding Crete – a daring coup immortalised in the film *Ill Met by Moonlight*, starring Dirk Bogarde. However, back then, dropping the Asopos Viaduct was seen in similar celebrity terms. Carol Mather, Geoff's old mate from the SAS raid on Benghazi (and the Ski Battalion), who had gone on to work for Field Marshal Montgomery, puts a footnote in his book about Geoff and hearing about this escapade: high praise indeed from a man who had mixed with most of the key adventurers of the last war.

That, in the event, Geoff did nothing in Cyprus, we know. Whether and what he was meant to do the British government certainly isn't telling, and nor was Geoff. Like some of the more unsavoury aspects of Mau Mau, it will doubtless remain buried in a deep hole.

There was one follow-up, though. Having written these last few words, I went to the pub for a much needed drink. Conversation moved to Cyprus, and one of the guys said that his father had worked on the secretariat side of things during the Emergency. Although only of middle rank, he had sat in on many meetings where the military and the intelligence boys had hatched their plans as well as warn what EOKA was up to next. I told him this story and asked, from what he knew from his father, whether it was credible. He said he had no doubt that exactly this sort of thing was being planned in Cyprus at that time. He went further. From what his father had told him of those far off and dangerous days, it would almost have been tantamount to negligence had the British not had a contingency plan that involved the elimination of the troublesome Archbishop, and General Grivas for that matter.

Now Geoff was out of the army for the second time, without a proper job and with a wife and child to support as well as – although he did not yet know it – a second on the way. But women still adored him. That at least had not changed, and nor would it.

'Grandpa' Vaughan, living in style at Brimmer Hall in Jamaica, was less than impressed to have Geoff and family arrive on his doorstep. Rather than have them living in his house, he gave them the use of a one-bedroom cottage at the end of the drive. Geoff may have been boozing it up in style late into the night, telling tales of times past with chums like Ian Fleming, but he had to find work, any work, to support his family. One job was working for Reynolds Aluminium, running their operations at the Bauxite Port in Ochos Rios: not exactly what he had had in mind for himself even a few years earlier. Stuck in a tiny bungalow with two squalling babies, it must have been, as Nick puts it, 'hell'. For Belinda it must have been every bit as uncongenial, because by 1960 she was gone, 'buggered off back to England', as Geoff put it. A divorce was soon to follow.

Geoff's next move was more reasoned. At some time during this period he met Miss Christy Firestone, the highly eligible daughter of the president of the Firestone Tire and Rubber Company. The divorce from Belinda must have been speeded through somehow because by late 1961 he was ready to marry Christy in a huge society wedding back in her native Akron, Ohio. There was only one fly in this particular ointment: Christy was already well pregnant.

Plan B involved a switch of continents and of venues and, even, of 'blushing' brides: Mary Cunningham Reed, one of Geoff's great girlfriends, took the starring role in Geoff's next bit of skulduggery. On 23 January 1962, Geoff and Mary beamed at the waiting news photographers as they made their way to the door of the Chelsea Register Office. Christy was waiting inside and the conspirators were duly married. Back out of the front door went the 'newlyweds', Mary and Geoff – Mary careful to wear gloves! – and out the back door went Christy, now the third Mrs Gordon-Creed. When the press realised they had been duped they were furious, but it was too late: the miscreants had scarpered. Geoff, as can be imagined thought the whole thing hilarious, especially when one of the photographers, running backwards to get the perfect shot, tripped over a kerb and went arse over tit into the gutter. His second son, also called Geoffrey, said to me of this incident: 'Dad always had a great "banana skin" sense of humour, falling around in heaps when anyone had a pratfall.'

And for a time he was happy. Geoff at last had emotional and financial security. With his base secure, as it were, he was free to carry on on his merry way, causing havoc in the bedroom, although no longer on the battlefield – those days were behind him. He went to work for his father-in-law. In time, the couple moved to South Africa, where Geoff had a job with Firestone International for ten years as well as running a smallish farm: he was ever the outdoor, sporting type and remained so to the very end.

But perhaps the luxury of their life in South Africa masked their divisions, because a decade after retiring to the US in 1975 – to Camden, South Carolina, where the climate was amenable for a colonial like Geoff – they were divorced.

Geoff's half-sister Mary recalls visiting him in Camden when his marriage was on the rocks, and being shocked to find the ever-vibrant Geoff sitting in a darkened room, looking chronically depressed. Perhaps, having bought into the luxurious lifestyle, he did not know how, or even lacked the courage, to leave it. It is easy to surmise that he had failed to make a success of his life out of uniform, and, even when he did get a grown-up job with Firestone Tires, he would have been only too aware that he was always the boss's daughter.

Not that he ever learned to conform. He was once 'done' for DUI – driving under the influence – and duly locked up by the Camden police. On losing his driving licence, Geoff, never a respecter of authority, decided to think laterally. No respecter either of the policing skills of the Camden Polizei – as told by him, he was so pissed when they arrested him that he had the driver's door open and was 'feeling' his way home using his left foot to guide him along the central marked lines on the road – he decided on a cunning plan to throw them off the scent. He resprayed his yellow Jeep green. Bizarrely, it worked and the police never thought to check his licence thereafter. He just carried on driving.

The follow-up to this story is that Nick – then stationed in Belize – later went to visit his father with a couple of army chums. Sure enough, and like father like son, Nick and his mates went out for an evening that developed into a monstrous piss-up. The poor sap who was the designated driver was also 'done' by Camden's finest for DUI and ended up behind bars for the night.

Imagine the consternation of this young officer when he was released the next morning and had to return and tell his imposing host, a highly decorated war hero to boot, what had happened and apologise for the huge embarrassment he must have caused.

Geoff, as was his way, already knew full well what had transpired and spoofed his young guest horribly. Having first winked at Nick as the hesitant young man made his way towards him, he listened to his apology in grim-faced silence. Imagine his guest's surprise and delight when Geoff then grinned and asked which cell he had ended up in – in case it was the same as 'his' one – and enquired as to whether he had enjoyed his breakfast of 'grits' (a sort of porridge, very popular in the southern states of the USA): Geoff's idea of the perfect joke.

In later years Nick tried to persuade Geoff to return to Greece with his own son, Charles, and show them his old haunts. The excuses for not going changed, from fear of finding a whole load of little Geoffs to the more considered reason that he was not sure he wanted to see Greece again. He told Nick he had been terrified for nearly every day he had been behind the lines, and he was not sure he wanted to relive the experience. If ever a man deserved to suffer from post-traumatic stress disorder, then Geoff did. Perhaps he realised that by returning he might unleash something that might never be recorked.

The old warrior did, at the last, find peace. In 1996 he married an old friend, Ellen Dvorchak. As both sons tell me, Geoff always said that his first and last marriages were the happiest. Let the final words be Geoff's:

The time of year I most dread is approaching; the time when one makes up one's Christmas card list and has to note the deletions. Worse, of course, is not to have been informed of all the deaths, to have sent cards out to Mr and Mrs, only to get back later a sad little note.

I recently got such a note: the beaten-up envelope had been chasing me around the world for a year. Inside was one of those cards that continentals send out: 'Blah blah – *Entrée dans la paix du Seigneur* (entered into the peace of the Lord) – Blah, blah.'

There, looking about a hundred years old, was my old amour from Brussels: Jacky – the one whose bedroom ledge I had taken refuge on. She had turned out to be a remarkable girl and our affair went on, or should I say 'off', for many years and whenever we happened to find ourselves within reach of one another.

Always alone, she had travelled the trans-Siberian railway and had been the guest of the king of Nepal before that country had opened to foreigners. She had climbed various Andean peaks and had tried for the Belgian two-man Olympic bobsled team. She flew her own plane and sky-dived for fun.

She often used to tell me that she would marry none other than myself. I pooh-poohed this, of course, but when my first wife died Jacky somehow knew and was there in Kenya. When my second wife buggered off, somehow Jacky knew and turned up in Jamaica. When I married my third I got a bitter, scalding and heartbroken letter, which I didn't deserve as I had never, ever talked marriage to her. Marriage could never have been anything but a disaster for a dozen reasons. She never wrote to me again.

Now she has gone on ahead.

Do you think she might be at the end of that bright tunnel that one reads about – waiting to nobble me as I stumble hopefully towards the light?

I have mixed feelings about this possibility although, come to think about it, weightless tumbling on an astral plane could be a whole lot of fun, but it might necessitate the mastering of a whole new technique.

I doubt I would be up to that.

★   ★   ★

Then again, and with Geoff, you never know . . .

Honorary Major, self-styled Lieutenant Colonel Geoffrey Anthony Harrison/Eckstein/Gordon-Creed, DSO, MC, hero and survivor of more bust-ups and battles than most men would ever dread to encounter, died on 26 November 2002 in Camden, South Carolina.

APPENDIX A

Below are the 'verbatim' war diaries, a 'daily' account of what happened to 2 RGH from their deployment in North Africa in November 1941 until their disbandment as an operational armoured regiment just over a year later on 28 December 1942.

As the reader will note, the diaries are, in places, incomplete. No wonder, given what was going on. It is a near miracle that any record was kept.

Geoff had a look at these diaries at some stage after the war and told Nick, his son, that he thought that elements of them were largely 'bunkum', making the point that only someone in the front line would have had any idea what was going on and that, apart from the fact that few in the front line in those dark days survived, anyone in said front line had much more important things to do each day than write up a diary – like fighting the Germans and surviving.

So these diaries were most probably 'written up' sometime after the events they describe, when the regiment had time out from the fighting, and may well be inaccurate in places.

Nevertheless, they give a framework to the regiment's campaign and, in their emotionless language of movements and dead, wounded, men missing or made prisoner – the roll calls at least are probably reasonably accurate, as a daily record of those present and those missing would have been, by necessity, kept – they give a vivid glimpse of the precariousness of existence in the Western Desert in 1941–2.

War diaries for the
2nd Royal Gloucestershire Hussars (edited)
CO: Lt Col N.A. Birley

November 1941

18/11/41
RIDOTTA MADDELENA. **Day 1.**
General Intention. 22 Armd Bde will advance one up, 2 RGH leading, 4 CLY left, 3 CLY right and secure a battle position in the area BIR DUEDAR 432362.0600 – Regiment advanced with 51 tanks, the following officers:

RHQ
Lt Col N.A. Birley, Capt R.E. Maunsell, Lt E.H. Milvain, Lt E.H. Small, 2Lt H.M. Muir

F Sqn
Major J.W. Saleby, Capt G.C.M. Playne, Lt C.L. Clay, Lt S.A. Pitman, Lt E.J.S. Bourne, Lt N.H. King, Lt F.S.G. Wigley

G Sqn
Major W.A.B. Trevor, Capt J. Patterson, Lt R.E. Adlard, Capt M.G. Ling, Lt P.H. Cookson, 2Lt A.E. Mitchell, Lt J.N. Harper, 2Lt G.C. Williams(LO)

H Sqn
Major D.McD. Reinhold, Capt N.D. Hart, Capt W.A. White, Lt T. Elder Jones, 2Lt G. Gordon-Creed, 2Lt G.M. Crossman, 2Lt G.T. Honeysett, 2Lt C.J. Meade (LO)

NCOs and men 582. A1 and B Echelons in rear.

0810 – Crossed wire into Libya south of RIDOTTA MADDELENA with air support.
0950 – Refuelled from petrol dump put down by RASC under direction of Major H.J. Mylne the previous night.

BU SHIHAH 1630 hrs. Completed an advance of 76 miles to map ref 436343 without meeting any sign of opposition. Moved into close leaguer and replenished.

1630 – Made contact with Major A.T. Smail 11th Hussars, who informed us of 10 enemy tanks 5 miles to our front. Failing light prevented any action that night.

19/11/41
Day 2.
Advance continued 0700 hrs with 11th Hussars as screen. H Sqn leading, F Sqn right G Sqn left.

0930 – 4 enemy tanks reported by 11th Hussars (identified as 4 Italian M13s northwest of Pt181 423368). These were dealt with by H Sqn. 11th Hussars reported 18 tanks with artillery to the North – H Sqn knocked out 6.

BIR EL GUBI 1030 hrs. Regiment was ordered to advance towards BIR EL GUBI. Here some 100 MET were encountered by our leading Sqn. There was no opposition and a considerable number of Italians gave themselves up. Shortly after this a force of M13s was encountered on our left flank. These were successfully dealt with by G & H Sqns.

1300 – 3 CLY were ordered to assist 2 RGH on right flank.

1330 – Regt advanced 3 miles north of BIR EL GUBI and two Sqns became engaged with a very large force of enemy tanks estimated between 140 and 160, plus numerous concealed anti-tank positions. H Sqn was held up by strong A/T and artillery positions on the left and did not join until late in the afternoon. Wireless communication with 22 Armd Bde broke down at 1530 hrs and was continued until 1630 hrs. For at least 2½ hours heavy fighting ensued.

1630 – Regiment withdrew to reorganise two miles south of BIR EL GUBI. While withdrawing through GUBI A/T fire was encountered from Italian personnel who had previously surrendered but had remanned A/T guns mounted on lorries and engaged our withdrawing tanks from the rear.

1730 – All runners had been withdrawn. Close leaguer was

ordered at Pt18? – 423368 where A1 under 2Lt T.H. Lawton replenished petrol and ammunition.

Tank strength at start – 46
Tank strength at 1530 – 16

Officers missing at 1900hrs:
Major J.W. Saleby, F Sqn, Capt G.C.M. Playne, F Sqn
Lt G.L. Clay, F Sqn, Capt J. Patterson, G Sqn
2Lt Honeysett, H Sqn (subsequently reported as killed in action)

Officers wounded:
Lt Col N.A. Birley, Capt W.A. White, Lt T. Elder Jones.
NCOs and men:
Missing 17, wounded 16, killed 9.

20/11/41
Day 3 – Pt181423368 – Tank strength 19.
Major J.H. Mylne took command of the Regt in the absence of Lt Col N.A. Birley. One composite Sqn was formed F, G & H Sqns plus RHQ of 3 tanks.

Officers present:
Major H.J. Mylne (HQ), Lt E.H. Milvain (HQ), Major W.A.B. Trevor (G), Capt N.D. Hart (H), Capt R.E. Maunsell (HQ), 2Lt Muir (HQ), Capt M.G. Ling (G), Lt A.H. Snell (HQ), Lt N.H. King (F), Major D.McD. Reinhold (H).

Intention of 22 Armd Bde.
GABR SALEH 454364 1200 hrs. To go to the assistance of 4th Armd Bde in the area of GABR SALEH who had been heavily engaged with a large force of German tanks (170). During the day 22nd Armd Bde advanced east along TRIG EL ABD, 4 CLY leading, 3 CLY left, 2 RGH right and reserve.
1740 – 22 Armd Bde contacted 4 Armd Bde. 3 CLY contacted

the enemy but 2 RGH were not engaged. Action was ineffective owing to dusk.

1830 – 2 RGH withdrew south into close leaguer in conjunction with 4 CLY.

21/11/41

Day 4. An action with the force that was contacted the previous night by 22 Armd Bde nearly developed at first light but the enemy force withdrew NW.

0900 – 22 Armd Bde withdrew NW, centre line: GABR SALEH – BIR BERRANEB – BIR EL REGHEM (440380). Formation of 22 Armd Bde same as on Day 3. 2 RGH were replenished partially by Regtl Air Echelon. 2Lt T.H. Lawton, Capt A.T. Brenchley, Capt A.B. Waters (MO) were present.

1400 – 22 Armd Bde passed through tail of Support Group.

1500 – the 7th Bde was seen on our right flank to be very heavily engaged with an enemy force. Apparently they had been fighting since dawn and 12 fires from burning tanks were seen. 22 Armd Bde worked round to the left flank of this battle. 2 RGH were lightly engaged at dusk without loss. Action was broken off due to a torrential downpour and bad light.

1730 – 2 RGH withdrew about 3 miles into close leaguer.

22/11/41

Day 5.

The right flank of 22 Armd Bde (3 CLY was engaged with the enemy at 0830 hrs (2 RGH although under fire of enemy artillery did not open fire). The enemy after about an hour withdrew northwards in the direction of aerodrome 435405.

1030 – 2 RGH were replenished with petrol

1200 – 22 Armd Bde advanced one up, 2 RGH left, 4 CLY centre, 3 CLY right, northwards towards escarpment 435401 through Support Group artillery who were shelling enemy positions in the SIDI REZEGH Pt167 areas.

1300 – A force of some 70 enemy tanks Mark III and Mark IV were observed moving eastwards along the high ground towards

the aerodrome now reached by 4 CLY, 2 RGH being halted
facing half left (NW) in the depression beyond the escarpment
about 1000 yards in advance of our own artillery on escarpment
with the enemy force about 2000 yards to our front. 4 CLY
became engaged on the aerodrome. SIDI REZEGH 2 RGH
began to move westwards attempting to move round the
enemy's right flank. A long-range tank vs tank duel ensued
during which 2 RGH became considerably involved from
concealed anti-tank positions in the defended SIDI REZEGH
area. 2 RGH held this position for some time to cover the
withdrawal of 4 CLY and 3 CLY and eventually withdrew to
high ground. At this juncture the 4th Armd Bde arrived.

1600 – Engagement was broken off owing to very bad visibility
and general obscurity of position. Infantry of Support Group
were seen to be putting in an attack on SIDI REZEGH on left
flank of 2 RGH.

1700 – 2 RGH withdrew into Support Group lines and as
darkness fell took up a position with 4 CLY right as protection
right to any attempt to engage Support Group at dawn by the
enemy.

Tank losses during Day 5 – 2.
Tank strength at end of Day 5 – 17. Casualties nil.

Col Carr (4 CLY) took command of 22 Armd Bde at 1730 hrs.
Composite Regt of 2 RGH one Sqn, 3 CLY one Sqn (Col Jago),
4 CLY one Sqn (Major Walker).

23/11/41
Day 6 433395

The early part of the morning was spent in reforming a composite
Regt referred to in conclusion of Day 5. The Regt was not in
communication with 22 Armd Bde. 2 RGH Sqn was composed
as follows:

RHQ Major W.A.B. Trevor, Capt R.E. Maunscll, 2Lt H.M.
Muir.

Sqn Tank Commanders: Capt M.G. Ling, Lt N.H. King, Lt E.J.S. Bourne, Lt R.E. Adlard, Lt E.H. Milvain, Lt P.H. Cookson, Sgt Vaughan, Cpl Godwin.

The following officers went into action in a scout car: Major D.McD. Reinhold, Major H.J. Mylne.

Tank Strength 17.

1030 – 22 Armd Bde Composite Regt was formed up in battle position facing south and west with 2 RGH centre, 3 CLY right and 4 CLY left and their left flank the Support Group (South African Camp).

1100 – A considerable force of enemy tanks was seen refuelling to our west at a distance of 3 miles. This column then withdrew further west without being engaged. After midday two large enemy columns advanced on our position from east and west. A very heavy engagement ensued in which our own and enemy artillery were very active. 2 RGH were subjected to some very accurate shelling from enemy gun positions to the north on the escarpment. Control of this battle was difficult and the sequence of events obscure. At 1600 hrs 4 CLY were engaged to the east of 'South African Camp'. This camp was now being attacked by German infantry from area SIDI REZEGH and were withdrawing SE. Many equipment were on fire and RGH tanks withdrew into the centre of SA Camp at dusk. The following officers were present:

Major W.A.B. Trevor, Capt R.E. Maunsell, Capt N.D. Hart, Lt N.H. King, Lt R.E. Adlard, 2 Lt H.M. Muir with 4 tanks. These 4 tanks returned to Bde HQ after dark, some 15 miles SW of our present position. Major Mylne, Major Reinhold, Lt Milvain, Lt Bourne, Lt Cookson, Lt Pitman were already at Bde having extricated themselves from SA camp during the afternoon. Lt Crossman at this stage was unaccounted for. Lts Adlard and Snell were missing at 2000 hrs.

24/11/41

Day 7

The following officers returned to B Echelon:

Major J.H. Mylne, Major D.McD. Reinhold, Capt N.D. Hart, Lt
    E.J.S. Bourne, Lt P.H. Cookson, Lt N.H. King.

0800 – Remnants of 4 CLY and 2 RGH moved 3 miles west BIR
    ES SAUSENNA (445395) as one composite Sqn of which 2
    RGH supplied 4 tanks as follows:-

1 tank

One Troop

Major Trevor, Capt Maunsell, Capt Ling

Two Troop

2Lt Muir, Lt Milvain, Capt D. Hillwood

Three Troop

4 CLY

11th Hussars were patrolling NW of our location.

1630 – The Composite Sqn engaged a column of enemy MET
    that was proceeding SE. A small shoot was had by this force but
    the column of MET outpaced the tanks.

1700 – Composite Sqn leaguered with the following units:

2 Btn RTR 7 Bde (19 tanks)

5 Btn RTR 4 Bde (5 Americans)

3 CLY, 4 CLY, 2 RGH 22 Armd Bde (20 tanks).

2Lt Gordon-Creed arrived with 5 tanks together with 19 A13s
    2nd RTR.

25/11/41

Day 8

22 Armd Bde continued to act protection right to 13th Corps
    New Zealand Div who were in the process of linking up with
    the garrison at TOBRUK. During the day a German Mark IV

was towed into camp and various recovery was carried out by our patrols.

1700 – Composite Sqn of 22 Armd Bde set out westwards to engage a column of enemy MET reported by 11th Hussars at [?] 11th Hussars took 4 prisoners, our tanks not engaged.

1800 – This force advanced 3 miles NW to form close leaguer for the night at 448398.

26/11/41
Day 9

Remained in the same location; some recovery patrols were sent out by us.

27/11/41
Day 10

0830 – 2Lt F.G. Wigley arrived with a tank.

0900 – Moved 4 miles NW to BIR SCIAFSCIUF to investigate reports received from 11th Hussars of enemy movements in the TRIGH CAPUZZO – GAMBUT area. 2 RGH Troops composed as follows:

No 1 Tp
Major Trevor, Capt Maunsell, Capt Ling, Sgt Jeffes

No 2 Tp
Lt Milvain, 2Lt Gordon-Creed, Lt Muir, Lt Williams (brought up tank in afternoon)

2 RGH sent out a patrol in the morning to Pt172 455405 to observe any movement from the east and on GAMBUT aerodrome. Weather was very overcast and rain fell giving generally bad visibility. Patrol of two tanks, Lt Gordon-Creed and Lt Muir.

1130 – TRIGH CAPUZZO. KDG to our east reported enemy column of some 50 tanks and a large quantity of MET including guns moving at high speed westwards along TRIGH CAPUZZO in the direction of TOBRUK. Head of column was reported at Pt212 477935.

1145 – 22 Armd Bde rallied at Pt192 456401 and prepared to take up positions on high ground facing east. 4 Armd Bde had returned from another operation and were on 22 Armd Bde's right flank.

1300 – Head of column was seen by our tanks advancing along TRIGH CAPUZZO.

1400 – Enemy column had halted and put out a screen of tanks, about 50, facing our force on the high ground. Eventually our artillery opened fire on the enemy positions to which the enemy replied with his own artillery causing some casualties to our tanks.

1500 – The enemy had dug himself in astride TRIGH CAPUZZO facing west. Our forces remained on the high ground except that another RGH patrol was sent out north across TRIGH CAPUZZO to observe the MET on the enemy's right flank. Small shoot was had by this patrol on enemy MET (2Lt Gordon-Creed and Lt Muir).

By 1700 hrs the result of the engagement was as follows:

22 Armd Bde had succeeded in holding up enemy movement westwards for that day in his obvious attempt to break through to TOBRUK along TRIGH CAPUZZO. At dusk 2 RGH withdrew westward 5 miles to its previous leaguer area 445399. 2 RGH lost one tank – 2Lt Williams. Lt Milvain succeeded in mending his track during the action.

2 RGH tank strength at 1900 – 4 tanks. 2Lt Wigley was heard on the air at 1800 hrs reporting he was ready to move in one hour and was coming into the leaguer area.

28/11/41
Day 11
2Lt A.E. Mitchell arrived with one close support tank. 2Lt Williams procured another tank from 4 CLY.
Composition of 2 RGH:

No 1 Tp
2Lt Gordon-Creed, Lt Muir, Lt Williams

No 2 Tp
Capt Ling, Sgt Jeffes

HQ
Major Trevor, Capt Maunsell, 2Lt Mitchell

0830 – Moved off eastwards and were engaged on our left flank by anti-tank guns and tanks in large numbers. 2 RGH lost one tank through engine seizure (2Lt Gordon-Creed). This tank was afterwards set on fire by the enemy. 22 Armd Bde withdrew SE and contacted 4 Armd Bde, formed a line of two Bdes facing NW towards an enemy column reported to consist of 70 enemy tanks and MET by 11th Hussars, arca 446401.

1300 – 22 Armd Bde and 4 Armd Bde were ordered to move SW on a bearing of 250 for 6 miles to the area CHARRUBET EZ ZGHEMAT 441388 then turn north and advance two miles to BIR EL REGHEM 442393. 22 Armd Bde Regt moved as follows: 2 RGH leading, 3 CLY left (Major Willis), 4 CLY right (Major Kidson) Col Jago commanding the composite Regt.

1330 – 22 Armd Bde moved on the above bearing.

1430 – Capt Ling's troop on patrol north of our main body observed the column of tanks contacted earlier in the day. This column was moving in a westerly direction. On observing our forces the enemy split his tanks into two main groups of about 35 tanks in each and pushed these out in a SW direction. The MET sheared off a little NW and halted. 22 Armd Bde with 4 Armd Bde on left moved 'tanks left' thus [??????] a very wide arc round the enemy tanks to the south. A long tank vs tank battle ensued (1000–1200 yards) on a wide front as far as our forces were concerned. [????????] 22 Armd Bde and 4 Armd Bde was very active [????????] to have a successful shoot against the enemy. [???????????] anti-tank gunfire was not as active as usual.

1730 – Tank vs tank engagement was broken off and artillery action continued for some time. 2 RGH lost no tanks in this action. However, Lt Milvain towed two tanks out of the battle which were subsequently put on the road again.

Resumé of events on the following days to be amplified at a later date by whom it may concern.

29/11/41

On right flank of 4 Armd Bde opposite SIDI REZEGH. Not engaged seriously.

30/11/41

22 Armd Bde withdrawn to re-equip. Two tanks returned with Major Trevor, Capt Maunsell, Capt Ling, 2Lt Muir, 2Lt Mitchell and 2Lt Williams.

Strength decrease – Officers
Lt J.N. Harper   Killed in action 19/11/41
2Lt G. Honeysett   Killed in action 19/11/41
Lt Col N.A. Birley   Wounded and admitted to hospital 19/11/41
Capt W.A. White   Wounded and admitted to hospital 19/11/41
Lt T. Elder Jones   Wounded and admitted to hospital 19/11/41
Major H.J. Mylne Wounded and admitted to hospital 26/11/41
Major J.W. Saleby   Reported missing 19/11/41
Capt G.C.M. Playne   Reported missing 19/11/41
Capt J. Patterson   Reported missing 19/11/41
Lt C.L. Clay   Reported missing 19/11/41
Lt R.E. Adlard   Reported missing 23/11/41
Lt A.H. Snell   Reported missing 23/11/41
2Lt S.J.G. Skinner   Reported missing 23/11/41
Major J.S. Sinnott   Reported missing 23/11/41
Lt E.J.S. Bourne   Reported missing 26/11/41
2Lt F.G.S. Wigley   Reported missing 27/11/41

Strength decrease – Ors
11 ORs killed in action.

12 ORs sick and admitted to hospital.
27 ORs transferred to LOB Camp MERSA MATRUH.
23 ORs wounded and admitted to hospital.
43 ORs reported missing.

Strength increase
22 ORs rejoined Regiment from hospital.

Strength of Regiment on 30/11/41 27 officers and 490 ORs.

War diaries for the
2nd Royal Gloucestershire Hussars
CO: Lt Col N.A. Birley

December 1941

[?]
Arrived in reforming area.

3/12/41
Lt V.H. Tubbs attached to this Regt from 1st RGH.

5/12/41
Decision to form 'American' Regiment.

7/12/41
Regiment formed. The Regt consisted of 52 American M3 tanks, the following officers and NCOs and 397 men:

RHQ
Major W.A.B. Trevor (acting CO), Capt R.E. Maunsell, 2Lt H.M. Muir, 2Lt G.G. Boyd, 2Lt E.H. Milvain, 2Lt E. Knight Bruce(LO)

F Sqn
Lt N.H. King, Lt S.A. Pitman, Lt V.H. Tubbs, 2Lt E. Ades, 2Lt J.N.E. Slee

G Sqn
Capt M.G. Ling, Lt P.H. Cookson, 2Lt A. Mitchell, 2Lt W.M.J. Jeffery, 2Lt G.C. Williams

H Sqn
Maj D.McD. Reinhold, 2Lt Y. Crossman, 2Lt. Gordon-Creed, 2Lt J. Meade, 2Lt D'Arcy Francis

HQ Sqn
Capt S.L. Lloyd, Capt N.D. Hart, Capt A.T. Brenchley, Lt W.E. Jerden (QM), Capt A.B. Waters (MO), Capt W. Llewellyn (Padre), 2Lt T.H. Lawton, 2Lt S.L. Cowen

9/12/41

Moved NW to Adv 7th Armd Div HQ (G) 56 miles along Div axis with 52 M3s (Honeys) in open formation with complete B Echelon in the rear. Close leaguered in area 395399.

10/12/41

Moved forward a further 15 miles to Adv Div Battle HQ where OC 2 RGH held a conference with General Gott and Brigadier Jock Campbell commanding 7th Armd Div Support Group.

1400 – 14 tanks of H Sqn were put on transporters and ordered to join 'Currie' Column Support Group the next morning.

1620 – 381405, Sgt White G., H Sqn was unfortunately killed by enemy low-flying aircraft who machine-gunned 2 RGH. One petrol lorry was set on fire.

11/12/41

2 RGH less H Sqn moved to HQ Support Group at 'Clapham'.

0630 – H Sqn with Lt Col Currie's mixed column was sent off on a separate mission, NW direction, to GAZALA area to intercept coast road west of GAZALA.

0830 – 2 RGH arrived Support Group HQ and OC of 2 RGH liased with Brig Campbell.

0830 – Moved 12 miles west just north of escarpment to MTEFEL LE CHERIB 355415 where Support Group HQ and 2 RGH halted.

1530 – G Sqn patrol reported 24 M13 tanks in the area GABR EL ABIDI.

1730 – Major Trevor and Lt Muir went out to look at these and were fired on and withdrew.

1800 – 2 RGH close leaguered with HQ Support Group. General Narrative Support Group at this time consisted of 4 columns of all arms operating NW of the above position. Their role was to harass as many enemy positions as possible in the area GAZALA – TMINI while the New Zealand Div and 4th Indian Div came in from the NE. The columns were disposed as follows:

CURRIE Column left (+ H Sqn 2 RGH) directed on road west of GAZALA.

HUGO Column centre directed on GAZALA.

WILSON Column right directed east of GAZALA.

MAYFIELD Column 'holding' column held in reserve.

The role of 2 RGH was never clearly defined, but we were a force that Brig Campbell 'had up his sleeve' should any suitable target for us present itself, and particularly in the case of lurking enemy armoured formations believed to be in this area.

12/12/41
U9261

0630 – Moved west 12 miles to U9261 known from now on as 'Double Blue'. The enemy appeared to be holding fairly strong to the west of our position.

1130 – 2 RGH less H Sqn was ordered to do what amounted to a 'demonstration in force' south of the enemy position in the area MTGATAAT EL ADAM U8562; during this manoeuvre out, two Sqns and RHQ tanks were subjected to sustained and fairly accurate shellfire from unlocated enemy gun positions to our north

1500 – After proceeding about 12 miles west, 2 RGH returned whence they came encountering shellfire as on the outward journey.

NOTE: Although 2 RGH were shelled for the best part of 2½ hours no casualties to personnel or tanks were received bar a few small items such as wireless masts blown away and surface kit such as water cans and bedding damaged. Our guns did not open fire.

CONCLUSIONS FROM OPERATION.

i) 2 RGH discovered that the enemy position was held in considerable depth westwards, roughly along the track running east–west.

ii) Shellfire, even though it may fall within 6 ft of a tank, will cause little or no material damage provided crews keep 'behind their armour'.

1900 – H Sqn rejoined 2 RGH in close leaguer from Currie Column. They had sustained no losses in their exploits NW and had taken some prisoners and Major Reinhold's tank accounted for one M13. Leaguer area same as for last night – Double Blue.

13/12/41

0630 – While static at Double Blue 2 RGH's role was protection left to 5th Indian Div who were advancing westwards to our north.

1100 – 2 RGH was ordered by Brig Campbell to perform same task as yesterday, but with the added intention of cutting the track previously mentioned, thus working our way round into the rear of enemy position while Support Group column and 4th Indian Div pushed in from the east.

METHOD. 2 RGH to proceed due south 5 miles and then turn due west for 10 miles, followed by a turn due north for 6 miles to cut track. This plan was carried out and included a 'top-up' at the end of the second leg.

1530 – At this time 2 RGH had advanced 4 miles north on final leg of the route in the following formation: G centre, F left and H right.

At this time G Sqn contacted rather suddenly a large amount of MET, some anti-tank guns and artillery. G Sqn became considerably engaged with anti-tank guns in rather an unpleasant valley. F Sqn and G Sqn succeeded in making a large mass of transport (60–100 MET) move westward in disorder, but it was difficult to estimate the damage caused. Range of transport about 800 yards. The anti-tank guns to the right flank were only about 200 yards away behind a ridge. H Sqn had a fairly successful shoot as far as disorganisation of the enemy was concerned, but it is difficult to state actual damage done and casualties inflicted. The whole action was 'short', very sharp and rather costly. 2 RGH were heavily shelled.

1620 – DERMERIEM. 2 RGH were dive-bombed by Stukas while reorganising after engagement. Control was difficult for OC 2 RGH owing to many of the American wireless sets breaking down.

9 tanks were lost and left on battlefield.

Killed 5, *Wounded* 8, *Missing* 7

1645 – 2 RGH were ordered to return to Double Blue.
2030 – 2 RGH had withdrawn to close leaguer in this area.

RESULT OF ACTION
The Regt had succeeded in reaching a point 1½ miles south of the track. It is difficult to say exactly what damage was inflicted but it was afterwards said that this action possibly had a bearing of the eventual withdrawal of the enemy from his strong position in this area.

14/12/41
SITREP. H Sqn (14 tanks) once more to be detached from the Regt and join 22 Gds Bde at 'Clapham'. Intention – 'an offensive sweep westwards' at a later date. This Sqn was again put on transporters.

1000 – G & F Sqns + RHQ, – 17 runners
                              – 6 under field repair
                              – 4 under ADW

The Regt less H Sqn moved 8 miles NE to area GABR EL ABIDI U355425 to join 4th Armd Bde (Brig Alex Gatehouse).
1300 – OC 2 RGH liaised with Brig Gatehouse.

1430 – Moved south with 4 Armd Bde in the following order:-
3rd Btn RTR leading, 5th Btn RTR right, 2nd RGH left, 2nd
RHA. Anti-tank Regt (Northumberland Hussars) moving with
4th Armd Bde HQ.

INTENTION 4th Armd BDE

To advance 21 miles south to ZEIDAN (see map) thence 30 miles
west and 30 miles north to HAFGET EL HALEIBA (Boston)
thus coming right round rear of enemy positions which was the
main rearguard of his army. 4th Indian Div and Support Group
to attack again from the east driving enemy on to 4th Armd
Bde at Boston.

15/12/41

ZEIDAN 1700 hrs 4th Armd Bde advanced in same formation as
previous evening on second leg of course.
1630 – 4th Armd Bde reached its objective without encountering
any opposition.
1800 – Odd parties of enemy MET were found.

16/12/41

GENERAL POSITION. 4th Armd Bde B Echelon was unable to
get up to the present position of 4th Armd Bde. The decision
taken to withdraw 18 miles south and meet the Echelon.
0700 – 2 RGH moved SE 18 miles to GARET MERIEM 6460
where regiments were replenished from B Echelon.
1530 – 4th Armd Bde reached GUIERET EL ABD, 5th RTR left,
3rd RTR centre, 2 RGH right.
1600 – 3rd RTR contacted isolated enemy guns and 4 German tanks.
1630 – 4th Armd Bde artillery was employed on scattered enemy
gun positions on track running east–west.
1730 – In this indecisive engagement which had been concerned
Armd cars (Royal Dragoons) and artillery in the main 2 RGH
acted as protection right to 3rd RTR and were not engaged.
1800 – 4th Bde withdrew into close leaguer 3 miles SE.

17/12/41

0700 – 2 RGH dispersed out to the east of leaguer area and remained static till 1300 hrs.

1300 – 4th Bde less F Sqn who were detached on a special mission with 1 Troop A/Tk guns Northumberland Hussars, attached, moved NW for 24 miles to HALEGH EL ELEBA U5790.

GENERAL

On December 17th the enemy was reported to be in full retreat in the direction of TIMIMI. Our mobile columns were following up fast in an attempt to harass his retreat. On this advance numerous enemy stragglers were picked up by 4th Armd Bde.

18/12/41

0700 – F Sqn rejoined the Regt during the march. 4th Armd Bde advanced 5½ miles in the general direction of SW of MECHILL. The going was extremely bad. Speed was reduced to about 8 mph for wheeled equipment – leaguered in area 9267. No enemy movement seen, although 3rd RTR endeavoured to chase up enemy retreating MET towards dusk but were unable to catch up.

19/12/41

Halted in present position all day.

20/12/41

4th Armd Bde withdrawn 0700 hrs. 22nd Armd Bde takes over 0700 hrs. T9560. 2 RGH rejoined 22nd Armd Bde 3 miles SW at T9560.

21/12/41

Made up two full Sqns and 5 tanks in RHQ (36 tanks).

22/12/41

Shortage of petrol compelled 22 Armd Bde to remain in present location.

23/12/41

0745 – 22 Armd Bde moved on a bearing of 215 for 38 miles, then on a bearing of 240 for 37 miles. This march over extremely good going and the total of 75 miles was completed by 1630 hrs.

1630 – 22 Armd Bde moved one up, 2 RGH leading with 30 Honeys (F, G & HQ Sqns), 4 CLY left (30 Mk VI), 3 CLY right (30–40 Mk VI).

The INTENTION OF 22nd Armd BDE

To establish a position at SAUNNU to Dec 24th and to await supplies from coast road communications at this point, which it was hoped would be clear of enemy by this time.

GENERAL SITREP

3rd RTR had engaged remains of ARIETE Div and 21 Armd Div at ANTELAT & BEDA FOMM on 23rd Dec. 22 Gds Bde & Support Group 7th Armd Div were also in this area. BENGHAZI at this date had not been reported as in our hands.

24/12/41

22 Armd Bde remained halted throughout the morning.

GENERAL POSITION 24th DEC SITREP.

Our troops held the following positions:

BARCE, BERNINA, SOLUCH.

Support Group were ordered to contain BANGASI. 3rd RTR had an engagement with a mixed enemy tank force on 23rd Dec at ANTELAT. The enemy force had withdrawn SW in the direction of AGEDABIA. 22 Gds Bde plus H Sqn 2 RGH were in this area (SAUNNU-ANTELAT). 22 Armd Bde was awaiting supplies and FSD to be established at MSUS.1330 – Moved SW 25 miles to area SAUNNU NMS.

25/12/41

Remained in present location. Major W.A.B. Trevor received DSO. Major D. McD. Reinhold reported killed in action on 23/12/41.

26/12/41

0700 – Moved SW towards CHUR ES SUFAN, 48 miles, 2 RGH leading, 3 CLY right, 4 CLY left. Royals patrolling to front. Moved SW 47 miles over bad going directed on CHUR ES SUFAN 290. Towards evening 3 CLY engaged enemy column containing 3 tanks. Leaguered in the area 3802 about 10 miles north of objective.

27/12/41

Moved on down SW to CHUR ES SUFAN and 2 miles SW at CHUER ES SCIAN 3 CLY and 4 CLY were involved with 16 enemy tanks and later were forced to take up a position opposite about 26 enemy tanks on high ground.

2 RGH were watching right flank and were not involved. Our artillery shelled the enemy positions. At dusk 22 Armd Bde withdrew NE to leaguer. The Royals during the day had attempted to find the enemy's right flank. The situation at 1700 hrs as reported by them.

The enemy was holding a line from AGEDABIA south along a track and then east towards 4085, this being the utmost extension of his right flank. 22 Gds Bde was north of AGEDABIA.

28/12/41

0930 – 22 Armd Bde had taken up battle positions with 4 CLY left, 3 CLY centre, 2 RGH right in the same location as previous day. RGH were ordered to guard right flank. The enemy was seen at first light to have 6 tanks along the ridge he had occupied on the previous day. There was very considerable movement over ridge towards our position. At the same time the movement on our right flank developed, a great deal of enemy transport and guns got into position and started shelling our right flank.

1130 – Eventually the enemy succeeded in leapfrogging anti-tank guns round our right flank which was receiving very heavy fire. 2 RGH withdrew to a more suitable ridge about 200 yards NE. 3 CLY conformed to this movement on our left.

1330 – The enemy was stiffening his attack with an increased number of tanks – estimate strength of enemy now reached 50.

1400 – Bde HQ and A1 Echelon had been separated from fighting regiments by a column of enemy who had come down south from the AGEDABIA area.

1530 – Enemy tanks withdrew across our left flank. The three tank regiments with supporting artillery withdrew to the south owing to increasingly heavy pressure from enemy column with A/T guns and artillery on right flank. After going 15 miles south the Bde then turned north-east to contact Bde HQ.

1700 – 2 RGH dive bombed by Stukas. Shortage of petrol became serious and Bde prepared to leaguer as soon as contact with enemy broken. Leaguered a C3574.

Killed
2Lt A.E. Mitchell, Sgt Rumsey, 3 ORs

Missing
1 NCO, 9 ORs

Wounded
2Lt G.C. Williams, 3 ORs

29/12/41
Bde moved NW to CHOR EL CHISMA X2511. 22 Armd Bde acted as left protection to Gde Bde attacking AGEDABIA and remained static all day.

30/12/41
0830 – German tanks attacked from south. Number of enemy tanks estimated to be 60.

0845 – H Sqn rejoined Regt and refuelled. 2 RGH faced south on left of £ & $ CLY. (RGH 36 tanks, 3 CLY 8 tanks, 4 CLY 15 tanks).

Bde held 3 successive positions withdrawing NE to cover B Echelon and supporting artillery.

1100 – At third position X2918 enemy tanks withdrew. 22 Armd Bde leaguered at X3957.

Killed
2Lt D'Arcy Francis, 3 ORs

Missing
Capt M.G. Ling, 2 NCO, 1 OR

Wounded
2Lt E. Ades, 4 ORs

31/12/41
22 Armd Bde withdrew north of ANTELAT X4783.

Strength decrease
Major D.McD. Reinhold   killed in action 23/12/412
Lt A.E. Mitchell   killed in action 28/12/41
2Lt D'Arcy Francis   killed in action 30/12/41
2Lt G.C. Williams   wounded and admitted to hospital 28/12/41
2Lt E. Ades   wounded and admitted to hospital 30/12/41
Capt M.G. Ling   reported missing 30/12/41
14 ORs   killed in action
19 ORs   wounded and admitted to hospital
22 ORs   sick and admitted to hospital
20 ORs   reported missing

Strength increase
2 ORs rejoined Regt from hospital
25 ORs rejoined Regt from LOB Camp.

Strength of Regt at 31/12/41 – 21 officers – 442 ORs

War diaries for the
2nd Royal Gloucestershire Hussars
CO: Lt Col N.A. Birley

Casualties 18/11/41 (Day 1) to 4/2/42

	Killed	*PoW*	*Missing*	*Wounded*
Officers	6	5	5	7
ORs	29	23	22	27

March 1942: Missing

April 1942: Missing

[Transcriber's note: It is probable that 2 RGH spent the period of February to mid-May in resting and training]

War diaries for the
2nd Royal Gloucestershire Hussars
CO: Lt Col N.A. Birley

May 1942

1–25, Not available

26/5/42
Bde moved to cover minefield gaps B.701 380402

27/5/42
2 RGH in reserve faced south while remainder of Bde faced NW. The enemy attacked from the SW with 120 tanks, 60 of which were diverted on to the Regtl box. The box was overrun and the regt lost nearly 30% of its tank strength.

The Regt was ordered to move north at 1000 hrs to pivot on Gds Bde box at Knightsbridge. Regt took up position on ridge east of Knightsbridge and faced south. Unit then replenished and observed 6 pdrs in action for the first time.

In evening at B.653 repelled attack from the west (25 Mark III/IV).

Lt Ades lost in first action with whole troop at 701.

Sqn Leader's tank with rear link was knocked out.

Lt Proctor wounded.

Wounded, 9
Killed, 2
Missing, believed killed, 1
Missing, 14
Missing believed PoW, 10

Awards.
2Lt Summerell, MC
Sgt Yool, DCM
Sgt Poole, MM

28/5/42

Sat all day waiting (BIR BELLIFA).

Lined up at dark from BIR BELLIFA to 653.

Germans expected to break through east along valley north of BIR BELLIFA. 'Thin Red Line'.

Incident when friendly staff car, 2 A/C and 2 15 cwt rushed through the line from Gds Box.

Wounded – 1.

29/5/42

G Sqn went to help 3 CLY B.601 in an attack from the south by the enemy.

H Sqn with RHQ went to intercept enemy column advancing from HARMAT.

In dust storm, one troop got right in among the enemy and lost 1 tank.

4 CLY arrived in the evening and a brief action took place as dust cleared.

Leaguered at midnight.

Lt Meade went back to B1, thence to hospital.

Missing believed PoW – 3.

30/5/42

Reveille 0430.

Went west to help 4th Bde in an attack on HARMAT.

Attack was put in after some delay but ground was not held. Some A/T guns destroyed.

In afternoon lined up to receive counter attack which did not materialise.

2nd Bde on right attacked group of 25 enemy tanks on ridge SW of BIR EL ASLAGH under cover of smoke provided by arty. Leaguered ½ mile east of B.230.

2Lt Summerell wounded.

Wounded – 2

2 troops under 2Lts Jeffrey and Jaques went under comd 9th Lancers for this attack.

31/5/42

Reveille 0430. Everyone now very tired.

LtCol Birley, Majors White, Lloyd, Trevor, Capts Muir, Milvain and 2Lt Wareham went back to A1.

Unit now under comd 3 CLY.

Major King formed composite Sqn with Capt Gordon-Creed and 2Lts Jeffrey and Boyd.

Tank strength 16 Crusaders and 2 Honeys.

In the evening an order was received to stand by for infantry attack. This did not materialise.

Regt Strength 31 officers and 513 ORs.

Missing believed PoW, 3

Wounded, 4

War diaries for the
2nd Royal Gloucestershire Hussars
CO: Lt Col N.A. Birley

June 1942

1/6/42

2 patrols sent forward under Capt Gordon-Creed and 2Lt Jeffrey
to BIR EL ASLAGH to 'test' tanks on ridge.

Tanks found to be derelict but A/T guns dug in on ridge among
tanks. One tank hit.

Crusaders handed over to 4 CLY.

Composite Sqn returned to A1

Capt Gordon-Creed to B1.

Killed, 2
Wounded, 1

Awards, Sgt Ogden MM

2/6/42

Regt moved to rear Bde B.605 to refit with Honeys and Grants
from 4th Hussars. 32 Honeys and 14 Grants collected.

Capt Cookson came from B2 to G Sqn and Capt Maunsell to H Sqn.

Regt temporarily reinforced from Tank Reinforcement Sqn.

3/6/42

Major White went back to B and was subsequently evacuated to
kospital.

Major Taylor took over H Sqn. Capt Tubbs went as 2i/c to B
Echelon.

4/6/42

Capt Pitman came to tanks from B1.

Capt Milvain went back to command Bde B2 Echelon.

Regt moved into position with 4 CLY B.702.

Tank strength:– H Sqn 14, F Sqn 12 (Grants), G Sqn 14, RHQ 4.

2Lt Knight Bruce missing believed PoW since confirmed PoW.

Wounded 1.

5/6/42

After bombardment from 0300 to 0345 (100 guns), composite
  Bde (4 CLY, 2 RGH) attacked west from B.230. Intention,
  to make sweep via BIR EL SCIRAB B.175, and rally B.230.
  Indians with Valentines had attacked before dawn and held
  triangle BIR EL TAMAR, B.202, B.178. Our attack reached
  B.178 where heavy A/T gunfire from guns dug in on ridge
  prevented any further advance. The Bde rallied B.203. 2
  RGH and 4 CLY took up position facing west on ridge one
  mile south of B.203.

2 attacks by Germans, about 20 tanks in each thrust with infantry
  and infantry guns, were held off during the middle of the day
  and afternoon.

F Sqn went to help 3 CLY and Valentines repel attack at B.100 in
  the evening. 4 German Mark IV were destroyed and claimed by
  F Sqn. Regt moved off to leaguer at 167 (BIR BELLIFA) at
  2130 hrs. Reached 167 at 0030 hrs owing to having to pass
  through Indian Bde who were attacked and cut up later that
  night by German tanks.

Lt Peel missing from morning attack now confirmed wounded
  PoW.

Wounded – 4, killed – 1.

6/6/42

Broke leaguer at 0515 to find line of German tanks (25) with
  strong force of guns and A/T guns facing us on ridge T.185 to
  our south.

Regt formed up with 3 CLY on right, Gds Bde to our rear. No
  move was made by the enemy or our tanks but they were shelled

by the Gds arty. The enemy put down some HE among us causing us to lose 2 Grants and 1 Honey.

The German tanks did not advance on to the box and we were ordered to advance east and conform to 3 CLY.

On approaching 167 the column was subjected to very heavy fire from the SE by 88 mm guns and so 3 CLY turned north into valley by BIR BELLIFA. 2 RGH conformed to this movement.

22 Armd Bde formed up facing SW at B.653 to help Box (de Graz) B.180.

Col Birley died of wounds and Capt Muir (Adj) was killed in move east and north round BIR BELLIFA by 88 mm guns.

Leaguered blockhouse B.653.

G Sqn Major Lloyd – 7 Honeys
H Sqn Major Taylor – 7 Honeys

RHQ – 3 Honeys
F Sqn – 2 Grants

Major Trevor in command.
22 Armd Bde Regt:– 4 CLY, – 8 Crusaders, 14 Grants
3 CLY – 5 Crusaders
4 RTR – 15 Valentines
2 RGH – 17 Honeys.
2Lt G. Wareham and 2Lt Jeffrey went to A1. In Regt tank strength, Major Trevor, Major Kink, Major Taylor, Capt Cookson (rear link), 2Lts P. Jaques, J. Eckersley, G. Boyd, P. Crawford.

Killed, 3
Wounded, 5

7/6/42
Regt moved NE to 187 (15 tanks, F fitters).
Mr Jeffrey returned to tanks.
Last 2 Grants handed over to 3 CLY.

8 tanks made a patrol to BIR EL RIGEL, afterwards joined by 22 Armd Bde Regt. No action took place.

Quiet day, leaguered at 2100 at 187 (3842).

Wounded – 4.

8/6/42

2Lt Jaques to B1.

Regt became Patrol Sqn for 22 Armd Bde. Recce SW, west and NW TP.191, B.652.

Major Trevor in command.

HQ, Capt Cookson (rear link), 2Lt G. Boyd (navigator).

H Sqn, 2Lt Eckersley – 3 tanks, Sgt A'Bear – 3 tanks

G Sqn, 2Lt Jeffrey – 3 tanks, Sgt Anderson – 3 tanks

Little activity, quiet day. Trevor Column suggested. Leaguered 0930 hrs 377427.

9/6/42

2 RGH (1 Sqn) again went on patrol to B.154 facing W, SW, NW.

Major Trevor went to see Brig Willison. Talk of forming column with 18 Honeys, 6 Crusader, 4 Grants, one Sqn of A/Cs, one troop of 25 pdrs, one Coy of infantry and six 6 pdrs to go through minefields and harass MET behind German lines. Operation to be known as 'Arduous'. The Echelon of this column would be enormous and the column has quite lost the idea of a quick dash.

10/6/42

At 1000 hrs news came of German attack probably developing towards Knightsbridge in NE direction so column idea off.

2 RGH withdrew to EL ADEM to refit and despatch H Sqn south of BIR HACHEIM to join 7th Armd Div Motor Bde on harassing column.

Casualties to date since Day 1 May 27th:

Killed, 8

Wounded, 31

Missing, 14

Missing blvd PoW, 1

Missing blvd killed, 1

11/6/42

Reveille 0630.

At 1230 H Sqn moved south to join 7th Motor Bde's 'July Column' with complete A1 and B Echelons.

Major Taylor, Capt Maunsell, Lts Eckersley, Crawford, Stuart Jones, G. Wareham (RHQ), navigator, and Sgt A'Bear. 16 Honeys.

2 Lt Kirkby i/c A1.

Capt Tubbs i/c B1.

The remainder of the Regt under Major Trevor moved back to B1 B.894, EL ADEM. Capt Gordon-Creed went to HQ 1st Armd Div Staff (temporarily).

Wounded – 2.

12/6/42

Major Trevor killed at ACROMA by Stukas.

Major Lloyd takes command.

Bde B Echelon moved from 4 miles west of EL ADEM to EL MRASSAS.

11 vehicle loaned to 1st Armd Div HQ RE (CRE) for one week.

Majors Lloyd and King go to see Bde about keeping the Regt together and not allowing it to be dispersed or separated.

Wounded, 3

Killed, 1

13/6/42

Regt remained with Bde B Echelon.

Majors Lloyd and King go to Bde and Div to keep Regt together.

Tank battle between Knightsbridge and EL ADEM.
Germans said to have 80 tanks left.

20/6/42

Ordered to join 8th Hussars (4th Armd Bde), where we were to
provide one Sqn and Echelon to operate with 4 Armd Bde
Support Group in harassing column. Remainder of Regt to go
to MERSA MATRUH.

Wounded, 4
Missing, 2

July 1942

2/7/42

G Sqn were ordered to join 22 Armd Bde whom they reached at
890276 becoming reserve Sqn to Bde under Bde command. The
Sqn consisted largely of G Sqn personnel but was made up to
strength by drawing upon other Sqns. Officers: Major S.L. Lloyd,
Capt P.H. Cookson, Capt E.H. Milvain, Lt G. Boyd, Lt Meade,
2Lt Jeffrey, 2Lt Jaques and Lt E. Taylor (comd Sqn A Echelon).
Bde carried out an attack on German tanks in the afternoon, in
the area 880275.

3/7/42

Sqn still in reserve. 2Lt Jaques was evacuated at 0830 being
wounded in the leg by shellfire directed at Bde HQ.

4/7/42

F & H Sqns and RHQ returned to SIDI BISHR from BAB EL ARAB.
G Sqn came under command 4 CLY (Major H.B. Scott). The
Sqn carried out an afternoon attack against German infantry in
the area 886278.
After advancing a little way they were ordered to withdraw having
taken 6 prisoners.
A direct hit on a tank by HE caused two casualties, 1 fatal.

Killed, 1
Wounded, 2

5/7/42

Regt moved to DAMANHUR as canal guard under command 10 Div. G Sqn handed over Honeys to 5 RTR in exchange for 14 Crusaders, and were made up to strength, 16, by the addition of 2 Crusaders from 3 CLY under 2Lt Sale and augmented by 3 personnel from 22 Armd Bde HQ.

That evening the Sqn passed under command 9th Lancers, commanded by Lt Col R. McDonnell.

The 9th Lancer Regt consisted of one 9L Sqn of Crusaders, one 9L Sqn of Grants and G Sqn 2 RGH.

Lancers remained in position in the area west of ALAM BROSHAZA holding positions alternately on the north ridge and the south ridge. G Sqn took their turn in these operations.

12/7/42

2Lt Jeffrey and his troop captured a Pzkw II almost undamaged, and also captured the crew.

15/7/42

9th Lancers came under command 2nd Armd Bde, 1st Armd Div and advanced with a New Zealand Bde and 22 Armd Bde (on their left), to Pt64 881279. About 4 miles of ground were made.

At about 1700 hrs, in an advance to secure ground 881279, Sgt Gladman and Tpr Wright were killed, their tank being hit by an anti-tank gun. Lt G. Boyd, L/Cpl Eighteen and Tpr Brett had their tank hit by the same gun and were wounded.

Thereafter 9 Lancers patrolled the area 879275 either to the [?] or to the north looking towards EL RUWEISAT.

Killed, 2
Wounded, 5

16/7/42

2Lt C. Kirkby who had come up to the Sqn the day before was killed by machine-gun fire when on patrol.

2Lt Jeffrey was wounded by A/T gun fire.

Killed, 1
Wounded, 1

18/7/42

Regt returned from canal guard.

Postings to the Regt:

Lt Col T.G.G. Cooper

Lts Alltree, D. Gilliat, I.M. Walker, F.N. Norbury, R.I. Turner.

CO: Lt Col T.G.G. Cooper

August 1942

25/8/42

G Sqn arrived at 429899. Capt Milvain stayed behind sick. Sqn ordered to form part of an exploiting force under Major McIntyre 9 Aust Div, to operate in operations at any time after midnight Aug 25th.

The operation known as 'Bulimba' was planned:

a) To pierce the German defences at west Pt23 SW of TEL AL EISA 873299 by means of a barrage by the arty of 5 Australian Bde, followed by an attack by a Btn of infantry (2/15 Btn). They were to be supported by a Sqn of Valentines of 40 RTR.

b) After the breach had been made, the exploiting force was to go through and do as much damage as it could to enemy L of C and workshops as far as the track running south from SIDI ABD EL RAHMEN.

The exploiting force consisted of G Sqn 2 RGH, Sqn HQ of 9 Australian Div, a troop of 25 pdrs, a troop of 6 pdrs, a troop of 2 pdrs, a platoon of infantry, REs and could claim support from a battery of medium artillery, operating from behind. A fighter umbrella had been lain on and bomber support had been promised.

The operation was to take place at first light the day after any attack by German armour in the south.

31/8/42

At 0300 5 RTR moved into battle positions at 43788805 B.79, facing south and SE, left flank Regt. F Sqn left flank Sqn. The order was to stand firm. No withdrawal from that position.

H Sqn (A Sqn 5 RTR) had patrols out at 77 ridge.

G Sqn remained at 429899 till 2300 hrs, when they moved up to 875298 to take part in operation Bulimba at first light.

As the attacking force was unable to hold open the hole which it had pierced in the enemy defences, the exploiting force was not called upon.

H Sqn moved at 0300 and were ordered to take up battle position.

At 1400 they were ordered to contact approaching enemy and their role was to draw the enemy on to our main battle position. 3 tanks were lost, 2 men being wounded. Several enemy tanks were hit, one being definitely destroyed. The Sqn were engaged until 2300 as contact patrol.

CO: Lt Col T.G.G. Cooper

September 1942

1/9/42

At 0230 exchange of shots between enemy tanks and F Sqn. One enemy Mark II destroyed after which the enemy retired (range 500 yards). The enemy advanced from the south and during the day a battle was fought from first light until 1130 and again from 1700 until one hour after dark.

F Sqn (C Sqn 5 RTR) Casualties:

Lt Anderson

Sgt Conner (US Army)

Tpr Benton F Sqn.

10 of our tanks were partially disabled but continued to fight and were recovered later. 9 enemy tanks destroyed.

The Sqn in spite of all tanks being hit continued to fight all tanks and only one man was seriously wounded.

H Sqn patrol assisted by a troop of 6 pdrs had a successful action at first light.

2 enemy tanks destroyed and remainder were forced to retire rapidly from behind our main battle position which they had approached during the night.

The enemy then launched a second attack on our main battle positions and succeeded in working round the left flank. H Sqn were ordered to ward off enemy tanks which were attacking from left rear of our main battle position.

H Sqn tank strength:– 7 Crusaders (3 close support).

The Sqn succeeded in getting a good hull-down position and held off the enemy.

A Sqn of Grants was sent to assist, but in trying to engage with their low 75 mm guns were forced to show themselves and lost 1 tank. The rest retired.

The main enemy attack appeared to be diverted from this front at 1000 hrs.

H Sqn was relieved by Grants from 3 CLY and were then held in reserve.

While the Sqn was in reserve position they came under heavy shellfire and Lt Turner was killed.

Constant activity of our bombers during the night caused large fires in the enemy lines.

H Sqn tank strength: 6
Killed, 1

2/9/42

Major Taylor went out on patrol with a troop and brought in a 150 mm gun mounted on an unidentified tank chassis.

3/9/42

Capt Maunsell, Lt Stuart Jones and Sgt A'Bear on patrol at first light knocked out 2 enemy tanks.

Patrol remained in contact until 2000 hrs. Unable to advance owing to anti-tank gun positions.

Capt Brenchley arrived.

4/9/42

G Sqn ordered to come under command 10 Armd Div and joined 10 Hussars as Div reserve at 434844.

H Sqn little activity. Tank strength 8.

5/9/42

2Lt D. Sault joins the Regt.

Three 6 pdr Crusaders arrived for H Sqn.

Enemy gradually withdrawing.

CO: Lt Col T.G.G. Cooper

November 1942

28/11/42

Motor cycle trial held in the morning. At midday the instructions to move to KHATATBA were cancelled. News was received that the Regiment was to be disbanded. Major M.H. Taylor, in the absence of the Commanding Officer and the 2i/c, made this momentous announcement on a Regimental Parade. He informed the parade that the Regiment would cease to exist and that personnel would eventually join other units. Injunctions were given to dispel the many rumours then current and it appeared that nothing could be done, only wait for the disbanding of the Regiment. Major Taylor went on to say that originally 3 CLY were to have suffered the fate but as they were a first line unit and 2nd RGH a second line unit the blow would fall on the 2nd RGH despite the Regiment's impressive battle record and its seniority in the 22nd Armoured Brigade.

In the evening Major General Norman, AFV, GHQ, informed the officers and SNCOs that owing to the discontinuance of armoured reinforcements from UK to Middle East this Regiment would be used for drafting to units in the field.

30/11/42
Strength as at 30/11/42

Officers, 30
Attch officers, 3

ORs, 518
Attch ORs, 24

CO: Lt Col T.G.G. Cooper

December 1942

25/12/42
Christmas Day.
Holy Communion at 0730 in stable Chapel.
Morning Service at 0915 in stable Chapel.
Inter-Squadron football competitions.
A Regimental Christmas Dinner was held for the men in the NAAFI at SIDI BISHR Camp at which the men were served by the officers and sergeants. In his speech, Lt Col Cooper said that this was the first time in the history of the unit that it was possible to hold the Christmas Dinner Regimentally.
No information could be given about the future but the prospects were not very cheering; still this cloud was not to interfere with our Christmas festivities.
Cpl D.E. Green HQ Sqn replied to the Commanding Officer's Toast.

26/12/42

Boxing Day.

Regimental sports competitions. Officers Mess dinner. Definite news about the disbanding of the Regiment. About 20 Naval personnel visited the Regiment as a result of Lt Commander Thornton's visit on the 22nd of December.

28/12/42

Final Regimental Parade. Inspection by the Commanding Officer.

In his address the Commanding Officer announced that despite the combined efforts of many notable people to keep this famous Regiment intact, word had now been received that we were to disband.

F Sqn would go mostly to the 4th Hussars, G Sqn to the Wiltshire Yeomanry and H Sqn to the 8th Hussars. He reminded the Regiment of their fine battle record and asked them to give of their best wherever they went.

Continuing, the Commanding Officer said that it was intended that a reunion be held after the war and that it would be announced in the Press. Concluding, he wished all ranks good luck, happiness and victory in 1943.

A photograph was taken of the Regiment on this its last parade.

31/12/42

Strength as at 31/12/42.

Officers, 27

Attch officers, 3

ORs, 536

Attch ORs, 21

Geoff's DSO (Distinguished Service Order) for leading the raid on the Asopos Viaduct was an 'immediate' – the best kind and one down from the Victoria Cross.

MOST SECRET

Army Form W.3121

Date recommendation passed forward

	Received	Passed
Brigade		
Division		
Corps		263
Army		

Division _____ Corps _____

Schedule No. _____ Unit. 2 R.G.H.
(To be left blank)

Rank and Army or Personal No. WS/Lieut. (T/Capt.) 16001.

Name GORDON-CREED, Geoffrey Anthony. M.C.
(Christian names must be stated)

MOST SECRET

Action for which commended (Date and place of action must be stated)	Recommended by	Honour or Reward	(To be left blank)
In March, 43, Brig. MYERS reported that sabotage of the important ASOPOS Viaduct on the main railway line between SALONIKA and ATHENS, and approximately 12 miles South of LAMIA, presented a "chancey" likelihood of success. This viaduct is an example of one of the triumphs of railway bridging engineering and is some 200 metres long. It spans a precipitous gorge whose bottom lies 320 ft. below. The railway issues on to the viaduct at either end from a tunnel. Furthermore, the viaduct is on a slight curve, thus making repair extraordinarily difficult. The viaduct is of steel. Brig. MYERS was advised by G.H.Q., M.E.F. that destruction of the viaduct was much to be desired, but the later it could take place the better. Early in May, Brig. MYERS reported that he considered destruction of the viaduct with	M.O.4.	D.S.O. (Immediate).	

General,
Commander-in-Chief,
Middle East Forces.

Awarded D.S.O
L.G. 14.9.43

SECRET 14170

P.T.O.

MOST SECRET

264

the least loss of time was necessary, as, not only was the guard being strengthened, but Italians had been replaced by Germans. Furthermore, workmen had started reinforcing the whole structure at its base with concrete. G.H.Q., M.E.F. replied that they agreed early destruction was not only desirable, but would have important strategic results in the near future.

After the first reconnaissance of the top of the gorge by Lieut. STOTT on 19 May, Capt. GORDON-CREED, M.C., commanding a party of eight, including Lieut. STOTT as guide, left MAVROLITHARION on 21 May to reconnoitre the viaduct. They carried 56 fathoms of rope and improvised ropes plaited from parachute rigging lines. Owing to the weight of the stores being carried, they did not reach the beginning of the gorge until 22 May, and established a Headquarters at its head. Straight away STOTT led six of the party down to the first waterfall where a dump was made, and they returned the same day to Gorge H.Q. On 23 May Capt. GORDON-CREED and STOTT made a reconnaissance from the Northern cliff top, which enabled the whole party to reach the second waterfall with all their stores and explosives. On 24 May the whole party managed to reach a point midway between the second and third waterfall. Here they were stuck and further reconnaissance from the Northern cliff top was made on the 25th, with the result that STOTT and one other managed to reach the third waterfall on the 26th, but could get no further with the amount of rope then available. Capt. GORDON-CREED decided to give up the attempt until further rope and packs suitable for carrying on the head, so as to keep explosives, etc., dry when walking through deep water, could be sent to them. It was feared also that it would be impossible to proceed further than the third waterfall without much more reconnaissance from both the North and South cliff tops. So far the party had not got within sight of the viaduct, although they had reached to within

/ Page 2.

Page 2.

00
Brigade............ Division............ Corps

Schedule No. .... Unit............
(To be left blank)

Rank and Army or Personal No. ....

Name ....
(Christian names must be stated)

Date recommendation
passed forward

	Received	Passed
Brigade		
Division		265
Corps		
Army		

MOST SECRET

Action for which commended (Date and place of action must be stated)	Recommended by	Honour or Reward	(To be left blank)

two miles of it. They returned to
MAVROLITHARION on 28 May and a few nights later
the requisite stores were dropped to them from
an aircraft.

On 12 Jun. a party, again under command of
Capt. GORDON-CREED, with STOTT as guide and
four others, set out once more for the gorge.
They reached Gorge H.Q. on 15 Jun., when STOTT
set out alone to carry out a complete reconnaissance right to the viaduct. He returned
after a most hazardous, but successful, reconnaissance.

On 20 Jun. the whole party moved off, two
hours before dusk, carrying all their mountain-
eering tackle, explosives and coshes. Other
weapons were deliberately left behind to save
weight and to facilitate climbing. The party
was guided by STOTT. He led them unerringly
down the cliff through water and up the cliff

P.T.O.

MOST SECRET

266

to scaffolding belonging to the workmen near the base of the viaduct.
This was all accomplished without a sound being audible to the enemy,
and most of it in the dark. At the foot of the scaffolding they
met a German sentry, but Capt. GORDON-CREED "coshed" him and
tipped him silently full pitch into the bottom of the gorge, some
300 ft. below.

The charges were soon laid by the two Sapper members of the
party, who reported to Capt. GORDON-CREED that they had worked out
that exactly 200 lbs. was necessary; whereupon he replied: "Are
you sure that is exactly what is required?". On receiving the af-
firmative, he ordered them to double the amount. The result was
the complete destruction of the viaduct, which fell to the bottom
of the gorge, 300 ft. below, as has since been proved by air photographs.

Capt. GORDON-CREED's leadership, determination and example of
cheerfulness under the prolonged, most exhausting conditions, both
during the reconnaissance and during the actual operation, was most
marked. His example proved an inspiration to the rest of the party
when they were wet and cold after battling through the gorge through
the evening of 20 Jun., and his coolness in disposing of the German
soldier at the viaduct saved certain alarm which would have rendered
the operation abortive.

With the aid of STOTT he eventually got his whole party back
to MAVROLITHARION. They arrived completely exhausted, with their
knees and arms torn to ribbons, but jubilant at their success.

Capt. GORDON-CREED is strongly recommended for an immediate
award of the D.S.O.

C. R. Kellh

Brig.

30 Jul. 43. SHOULD THIS AWARD BE APPROVED, IT IS RE-
QUESTED THAT NO DETAILS SHOULD BE MADE
PUBLIC OR COMMUNICATED TO THE PRESS.

Geoff won his MC (Military Cross) on his first day in battle; the first of an eleven day battle that saw his regiment all but destroyed.

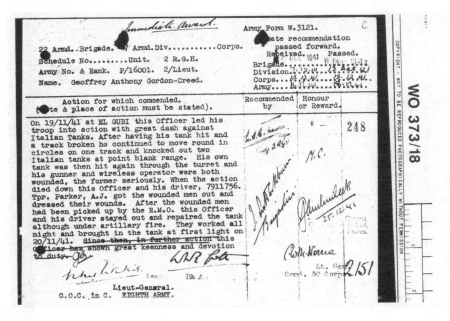

SELECTED BIBLIOGRAPHY

A useful start point for understanding the war in the desert is *Pendulum of War: The Three Battles of El Alamein* by Niall Barr (Jonathan Cape, 2004). While the book is concerned more with the later battles it gives an excellent introduction to the problems and horrors faced by armoured regiments like 2 RGH in the build-up to the break-out battles of El Alamein.

For 2 RGH itself, *Second Royal Gloucestershire Hussars, Libya–Egypt 1941–1942* by Stuart Pitman (St Catherine Press, 1950) is a collation of the Regiment's war diaries, personal diaries, letters and contemporaneous personal testimonies of the survivors: Major Stuart Pitman himself fought through the desert campaign and is an excellent narrator.

Also, *The Royal Gloucestershire Hussars* by Rollo Clifford (Alan Sutton Publishing, 1991), another, although more recent, Gloucestershire Hussar, is a fascinating pictorial history of the Regiment from earliest times till 1990. Rollo Clifford also got me permission for the use of the map on p119 from Stuart Pitman's book and ensured there were no objections to me quoting verbatim from the 2 RGH War Diaries.

For the Desert War/SAS period, I found one particular book of great interest: *Killing Rommel* by Steven Pressfield (Doubleday, 2008). This is a beautifully researched and exciting, albeit fictional, account of a yeomanry officer who fights in the early tank battles of the Western Desert before going on to join the Long Range Desert Group – almost mirroring some of the scenarios Geoff got himself caught up in. What makes recommending this book even more pleasurable is that I was asked to give it a British military 'once-over' for Steven who, being American, was the first to admit that he could not know some of the many nuances and eccentricities of military lore. The fact that I had first served as a regular officer in The Blues and Royals helped, and the fact that having resigned from the regular army I then transferred to a sister regiment of the Royal Gloucestershire Hussars, the Royal Wiltshire Yeomanry, made it something of a slam-dunk, to use American military parlance. Steven kindly thanked me for my help in his book; I am delighted to be able to recommend his book in return.

For Geoff's SAS raid and his time in the abortive 5th Battalion Scots Guards, formed as a ski battalion to fight the Russians in Finland, there was another bit of serendipity: anyone who has ever served in the armed forces of any nation will know that this is the way things can so often work. A great friend, who was at Sandhurst with me, lent me *When the Grass Stops Growing* by Carol Mather (Leo Cooper, 1997). Carol, he explained, was his brother's father-in-law and he had had an extraordinary war. The book gathered dust for a couple of years in my huge pile of 'to reads' as against my 'must reads'.

Then, when reading Geoff's own memoir, I came across Carol Mather's name as one of his travelling companions on the SAS raid on Benghazi. I reached for Carol's book and there Geoff was, viewed from the other side, as it were. The unexpected bonus was a description of the antics of the Ski Battalion which both men had joined in 1940, although they do not appear to have known each other at the time.

Lastly, for Special Forces, *The Imperial War Museum Book of War Behind Enemy Lines* by Julian Thompson (Sidgwick & Jackson, 1998) is a superb resource. As well as being a concise and accurate history of operations behind enemy lines, it is also a treasure trove of memoirs in that Thompson, himself a commando, has accessed the oral and documentary archives of the Imperial War Museum. The voices of those now dead warriors speak across the decades in this book.

SOE: The Special Operations Executive, 1940–1946 by M.R.D. Foot (Pimlico, 1999) is the 'must read' resource for those interested in the fundamentals of how SOE operated, as well as giving a brief overview of some of its many operations during its short existence – established in 1940, it was disbanded at the end of the war. Foot, himself SAS, was the official SOE historian postwar, therefore this book is factual in as far as it is able to go: some operations, it would seem, still remain 'secret'. So, when Foot writes that SOE deeply disapproved of its operatives having affairs with local girls, we can take it that this really was the official line. Not that this was to stop Geoff and his philandering . . .

Finally, for the SOE war in Greece – the heart of Geoff's book – *Greek Entanglement* by Brigadier E.C.W. Myers, CBE, DSO (Alan Sutton Publishing, 1985) is a key source for Geoff and his adventures. Brigadier Eddie commanded the British Military Mission to Greece from September 1942, just before Geoff joined SOE, until late July 1943 – by which time Geoff was in full sabotage mode in the Greek mountains. Although the Brigadier was not there for the last ten months of Geoff's time, his book is brilliant at explaining the political turmoil and motivations of those involved in the guerrilla war. Talk about confusing: the names of the competing guerrilla groups are enough in themselves to make the mind boggle. But, if I have managed to convey a sense of who was doing what and why, then I have Brigadier Eddie to thank.

A final and general point worth making is about accuracy. I have taken Geoff's memoir at face value and have let him tell his tale, including timings, except where I discovered he got something wrong. For example, his account of dropping the

Asopos Viaduct has his attack team making a single assault over very many days, whereas it is clear from the various other accounts – including, for that matter, his own citation for the award of the DSO – that there was an initial attempt which was defeated by lack of climbing rope followed, almost a month later, by the successful assault. Why the concertinaing of time? I have no idea. Apart from the fact that he penned his account some fifty years later and may have genuinely forgotten, it may well be that he was more interested in telling a good tale than detailing the minutiae.

Similarly, when he won his MC, his citation is slightly different from the way he told the story in his memoir, which is again slightly different from the way it is described in the official regimental history. While I know he got the Asopos timings wrong, I am not so sure that he did get his MC details wrong, or that others got them right – not necessarily the same thing. After all, he won his medal on day one of an eleven-day battle, in which his regiment was all but destroyed. I wonder how any of them, Geoff included, remembered anything with any great degree of accuracy. What matters is the tale he has to tell, and what a story it is . . .

INDEX